D0152088

Understanding Educational Reform

A REFERENCE HANDBOOK

CONTEMPORARY EDUCATION ISSUES

Understanding Educational Reform

❧ A REFERENCE HANDBOOK

Raymond A. Horn, Jr.

A B C ☰ C L I O

Santa Barbara, California • Denver, Colorado • Oxford, England

Library of Congress Cataloging-in-Publication Data

Horn, Raymond A., 1947–
    Understanding educational reform : a reference handbook / Raymond A. Horn, Jr.
        p. cm. — (Contemporary education issues)
    Includes bibliographical references (p.   ) and index.
    ISBN 1-57607-808-6 (hardcover : alk. paper) — ebook 1-57607-809-4
    1. Educational change—United States. 2. Educational change—United States—History. I. Title. II. Series.
    LA209.2.H58   2002
    370'.973—dc21

                                                                    2002011732

This book is also available on the World Wide Web as an e-book.
Visit www.abc-clio.com for details.

07 06 05 04 03 02   10 9 8 7 6 5 4 3 2 1

ABC-CLIO, Inc.
130 Cremona Drive, P.O. Box 1911
Santa Barbara, California 93116-1911

This book is printed on acid-free paper ∞.
Manufactured in the United States of America

This book is dedicated to the multitude of teachers who have struggled to provide authentic, caring, effective, and equitable education for their students.

Contents

☙ Series Editor's Preface

The Contemporary Education Issues series is dedicated to providing readers with an up-to-date exploration of the central issues in education today. Books in the series will examine such controversial topics as home schooling, charter schools, privatization of public schools, Native American education, African American education, literacy, curriculum development, and many others. The series is national in scope and is intended to encourage research by anyone interested in the field.

Because education is undergoing radical if not revolutionary change, the series is particularly concerned with how contemporary controversies in education affect both the organization of schools and the content and delivery of curriculum. Authors will endeavor to provide a balanced understanding of the issues and their effects on teachers, students, parents, administrators, and policymakers. The aim of the Contemporary Education Issues series is to publish excellent research on today's educational concerns by some of the finest scholars/practitioners in the field while pointing to new directions. The series promises to offer important analyses of some of the most controversial issues facing society today.

Danny Weil
Series Editor

⚫⟶ Preface

Many who are not educators think that they understand education because they themselves and perhaps their children have been students. When they become directly involved through parent-teacher organizations, as teacher aids, as members of advisory boards, or as school board members, they quickly gain an appreciation of the complex nature of American schooling.

The same holds true for educational reform: On the surface, the problems of education and the appropriate solutions appear to be easy to identify. The more one knows about the problems and the proposed solutions, the more one realizes how complex educational reform actually is. Information inevitably complicates understanding, but at the same time it makes possible the discovery of deep and hidden patterns that can lead to making sense of the complexity that is inherent in all human systems.

The purpose of this book is to help the reader gain a much more thorough understanding of the problems involved in educational reform through an examination of the origins, context, and patterns of reform. Through the information provided by this source, individuals will understand the context of various reform issues and initiatives. The book is designed to provide detailed information about selected topics, or to be used as a reference that allows quick access to information about educational reform.

A real understanding of educational reform is made more difficult by the tendency of reformers (whether educators, business leaders, or politicians) to provide the public with simple explanations, which often reinforce the kind of superficial understanding based only on experience as a student or parent. This oversimplification occurs for at least two reasons. First, even experts find it easier to reduce a complex situation to a few code words and sound bites than to help the public learn about the complexity. Second, most reformers want to promote their own reform agenda. Complicating their message with information that might work against that agenda would decrease the chances of winning public support. In addition, the public is complicit in this superficial representation of reform; people in general have been apt to desire quick solutions to complex problems.

Chapter 1 poses fundamental questions about educational reform, questions that serve as a framework for the rest of the book. Chapter 2 presents the history of reform in American education in narrative form, and Chapter 3 covers the same period in the form of a chronology, making it a quick reference for the more notable and important events and individuals in the history of American educational reform. Those who are using Chapter 3 as a reference will often find it useful to consult Chapter 2 for a fuller account of a person or topic. Chapters 4, 5, 6, 7, 8, and 9 provide detailed information on the various aspects of educational reform: the politics involved in deciding what to reform, the nature of the process by which reform is carried out, the problem of establishing a solid basis in research for deciding what and how to reform, the relationship of reform to what actually goes on in the classroom, the role of the public in reform, and the nature of resistance to reform. Chapter 10 provides print and nonprint resources that will facilitate additional research by the reader. The glossary covers the technical terminology of educational reform. Thus the book can be read in the order it is presented, or Chapters 3, 10, and the glossary can be utilized for quick reference to selected topics and individuals.

Raymond A. Horn, Jr.

Chapter One

◆◆ The Essential Questions about Educational Reform

To many Americans, change in education is a reoccurring event, one that indicates either that educators just can't get it right, or that education must continuously change to meet the changes in society. However, paradoxically, when most adult Americans go back to their schools, they encounter more similarities than differences in basic structure and operation. Despite the ongoing imperative to change education, significant parts of education appear to have remained the same. Is this due to the failure of change, the recycling of past reforms, or to an entrenched status quo? Only an understanding of the complexity of educational reform, an understanding this book attempts to provide, makes it possible to grapple with the paradox and to find answers to the question.

A beginning point in an understanding of educational reform and its effectiveness is to examine four basic questions, questions that will provide a framework for the details of American educational reform. These framing questions are:

- ◆◆ How is educational reform defined?
- ◆◆ Is there a need for educational reform?
- ◆◆ What is the purpose of education?
- ◆◆ Can educational reform be sustained, and when should it be?

DEFINING EDUCATIONAL REFORM

Educational Reform, Change, and Progress

The challenge involved in understanding educational reform begins with the challenge of terminology. The terms "educational reform," "educational change," and "educational progress" are often used interchangeably, but they have distinctly different meanings and implications. For example, the news media may refer to the recent standardized testing initiative as an educational reform, an educational change, or as educational progress toward the goal of more efficient and effective education. However, the terms "reform," "change," and "progress" represent different purposes and outcomes. For instance, "reform" implies that something is wrong or at least could be better. "Change," on the other hand, simply implies that something will be different, altered, or transformed after the implementation. However, neither reform nor change guarantees that the outcome will constitute progress. Thomas S. Popkewitz describes a belief that many share: "The 'common sense' of reform is to assume that intervention is progress. A better world is to evolve as the result of new programs, new technologies, and new organizations that increase efficiency, economy, and effectiveness" (1991, 1). The reality is that one person's reform or change may be another person's reason to initiate new change and that progress is a relative term.

For the purposes of this discussion, the term "educational reform" implies that the reform initiative is attempting to correct a deficiency in the current educational system without changing the essential elements of the system. "Educational change" will connote a transformative change that leaves the educational system significantly different than before the change initiative. Such transformative changes could include changes in what is considered "correct" or "true" knowledge, in the ways schools are organized or structured, in the way power is distributed among the individuals within the school, and in the way knowledge, institutional organization, and power arrangements work together to create a new educational system.

Educational reforms have the greater potential to gain widespread public support, since the more narrowly focused reform can be more simply explained to the general public. In reform, most aspects of the educational system remain the same, therefore creating less anxiety in the general public. Educational changes, on the other hand, have a twofold problem. Whereas educational reform only requires a public relations effort to gain public support, transformative change is very complex and requires a reeducation of the public. Educational reform leaves much that is familiar to the public untouched; educational change affects all major aspects of an educational system. Reform requires no investment from the public except their agreement. Change requires public understanding of something that is new and outside of their personal experience with education. For example, the general public understands and easily accepts reforms such as back-to-basics and standardized testing because they feel they have some familiarity with both "basics" and tests, and because only one or two changes in the educational system will be necessary to implement the change. The real changes involved in open space schools, using portfolios for assessment, open campuses, and continuous progress assessment require a learning curve for the public and create the natural anxiety associated with the unknown. In addition, more than curriculum and assessment is affected. School routines, schedules, and physical changes in the facility may be needed to implement this kind of change. Because of the public relations and political risks involved in change, reforms are more frequently attempted, and educational change tends to remain in the realm of university theorizing.

In addition, any discussion of educational reform requires an understanding that, for a reform to succeed, public support for the reform is an essential requirement. Thus educational reform is inherently a political process. On the other hand, educational change as here defined is a more clinical and less political process, in the sense that those who propose change are not as concerned about the political action required for successful implementation, but rather focus on the substantial and significant change needed in the very structure and organization of the current system. Political considerations are secondary to the theoretical and experiential foundations of the intended change. Because politics is de-emphasized in the construction of the change, change is inherently a challenge to the educational, social, and cultural practices that are in place and targeted for change.

The idea that there is no consensus about the definition of educational reform is supported by the myriad of answers to the question of what would constitute real educational reform. On the surface, the answers to that question initially deal with specific reforms, such as incorporating effective teaching strategies or instituting accountability measures. However, below such superficial answers lie clear definitional philosophies and agendas that are directly linked to the purposes and agendas of the reformers. Interest groups, whether political, social, economic, or cultural in nature, have clear and comprehensive definitions of what would constitute educational reform. In most cases, the educational reforms promoted by special interests are linked to the changes in society that the interests wish to promote, or the status quo that they wish to maintain. One purpose and organizing theme of this book is to disclose what is behind the various definitions of reform given by those who initiate it. In order to understand reform debates and initiatives on any level, one must be aware of the hidden agendas and motives of the reformers. Educational reform is not solely about education. Theories about what constitutes the common good, on the national, state, and local level, and about what will promote the common good are a significant part of all conversations about education. Even though the concepts and objects of reform have been different over time, one constant throughout the history of reform is the link between the efforts of the reformers and their social and cultural agendas.

The Political Context of Defining Reform

An understanding of the multiple definitions of educational reform is directly linked to identifying the object or target of the reform effort and who is doing the reforming. On the surface, the issue of what is being reformed can relate to curriculum, instruction, and assessment; however, on a deeper level this question also relates to broader considerations:

- ➤ Who politically controls the United States, an individual state, or a local community
- ➤ What cultural beliefs, values, and knowledge will be the standard in a specific place
- ➤ What economic philosophy will become or continue to be the norm
- ➤ How social relations will be defined in a specific place

Interest groups who seek to achieve their goals through educational reform may target educational policy, school organization, school culture, funding, or even the necessity of free public schools. These hidden political agendas add to the difficulty of understanding reform because, to paraphrase Michael Fullan and Suzanne Stiegelbauer, the political rhetoric of an interest group may differ from the reality the interest group desires to create (Fullan and Stiegelbauer 1991, 28). For instance, a politician may espouse educator and parent empowerment but through the implementation of rigid state mandates actually reduce the opportunity for educator and parent decision making and problem solving. To further complicate the understanding of educational reform, a call for innovation may be more symbolic than real, depending on the political or personal intent of the reformer.

In the context of hidden political agendas, the target of any reform effort is clearly to have an effect on the larger society. The control of school boards, administration, teachers, students, and parents is the means to this end. Whether the agenda is reactionary or radical, self-serving or altruistic, achieving it necessitates the control of the stakeholders of the education system through the control of curriculum, instruction, and assessment. As an example, the question is often asked, how do we measure the effectiveness of education? On the surface this question appears to be rather clinical and depoliticized. However, there are political implications attached to any type of assessment that may be used. Different individuals and groups not only within the educational system but also within the larger society will be affected in different ways depending on the type of assessment and how the assessment is implemented, a subject covered at length in Chapter 7. In this political context, "school reforms are allocations or reallocations of scarce educational resources. Whoever controls the educational change process has the power to benefit some students or community constituencies more than others" (Scheurich 1997, 24). The effects of the politics of allocation are made poignantly clear in Jonathan Kozol's *Death at an Early Age* (1967) and *Savage Inequalities* (1991).

An attempt to identify who is doing the reforming can be aided by using the following categories of reformers proposed by John Martin Rich (1988). Rich theorizes that there are two types of reformers: establishment educators and reformers. Establishment educators are either conventional or innovative in their view of educational change. Both the conventional and the innovative agree that the current system needs to be maintained but improved. The difference between them is that the conventional educator places a greater emphasis on maintaining the status quo than the innovator. The other main type, the reformer, believes that drastic changes are needed. Again there are subtypes. The system reformer believes that the current system is salvageable with extensive and drastic changes. The options reformer believes that change requires providing options to the traditional public school system, such as free schools and private schools. Finally, the deschooler argues that compulsory schooling must be abolished and control of schooling should pass to the individual and the community (Rich 1988, 10–11).

The foundational premise of this book is that all educational reform is inherently political, and that an understanding of this political reform activity requires a concomitant understanding of the exercise of power by those who hold power, and of attempts to appropriate power by those who have no power or have an insufficient amount to realize their agenda. Therefore, an understanding of any educational reform requires a critical awareness of the motives of the reformers, the power that they wield, the power that they wish to attain, and the consequences of their actions for all those affected. The political agendas of educational reformers are often hidden by a focus on the specific (for example, English immersion, brain-based learning, mastery of basic skills) and on the individual (that is, teachers, students, and administrators), but they are actually part of a historical pattern of attempting to maintain or change the economic, political, social, or cultural status quo. To develop a critical awareness of this level of complexity in educational reform requires the use of what is called post-formal research.

Using a Post-Formal Method to Understand Educational Reform

To disclose the hidden nature of education reform, the following chapters will utilize a post-formal methodology (see Glossary): The origins of educational reform will be explored, a detailed context will be provided, and patterns of reform will be identified and critically analyzed. The purpose of each chapter will be to provide the reader with a basic understanding of the origins, context, and patterns of American educational reform.

A brief inquiry into this quotation, chosen by Ernest L. Boyer from the report on secondary education in America by the Carnegie Foundation, provides an example of how the political nature of educational reform becomes apparent through post-formal questioning. "America believes in *education*. Increasingly, however, it has come to distrust its *schools*" (Boyer 1983, 282). How is America defined? How is education defined? Who distrusts our schools? How do we know that this distrust is a pervasive opinion? What schools are to be distrusted? Where are these schools located? Whose vision of America is being promoted by the reform proposed as the panacea to this assumed distrust? If the reform is implemented, what are the critical implications for all of education's stakeholders? Is there a problem? If so, what is the nature of the problem, and how serious is it? What are the origins of this alleged distrust?

THE NEED FOR EDUCATIONAL REFORM

One thing that almost everyone appears to agree on is that, to some degree, education does need to be reformed or changed. From the jockeying of politicians to become the education president or education governor to the reports of educational commissions, there appears to be a consensus that at least some things need to change in education. This persistent and widespread call for reform comes from diverse political, economic, social, and cultural groups, and it is directed at all aspects of our educational system. At the same time, however, some individuals question the need for this pervasive call for educational reform.

Arguments Supporting the Need for Reform—and Some Caveats

American schools are in trouble. In fact, the problems of schooling are of such crippling proportions that many schools may not survive. It is possible that our entire public education system is nearing collapse. We

will continue to have schools, no doubt, but the basis of their support
and their relationships to families, communities, and states could be
quite different from what we have known. (Goodlad 1984, 1)

John Goodlad's urgent call for reform came at the beginning of
the report of a major study of American education. That he perceived
that a serious crisis was facing American education in 1984 is clearly evident in Goodlad's comment. As will be seen later in this chapter and
throughout the book, others have echoed his sense of urgency at many
different times in American history. And certainly there are current in-
dications that dissatisfaction with American education is pervasive. An
article in the *Houston Chronicle* of August 3, 2001, told of a report by the
Education Department that approximately 850,000 children, or 1.7 percent of all school age children, were being home-schooled. Why are so
many individuals critical of education? Undoubtedly they see a continuation of problems with education or society, or they see changes in society that provide new challenges for education.

One kind of criticism comes from those individuals who see societal problems manifested in American education. David Berliner and
Bruce Biddle summarize this critical position by identifying these problems and the difficulties that they generate for schools. They include income and wealth inequity among groups of people as well as among
schools; growth and stagnation of the economy; racial, ethnic, religious,
and linguistic diversity; prejudice and discrimination; the economic
and cultural implications of settlement patterns that have created sub-
urbs, ghettos, and declining city centers; violence and drugs; the aging
population; competition from other institutions for money to fund education; and the restructuring of work (Berliner and Biddle 1995). In
light of the effects of these societal problems on schools, schools need
to be reformed to better deal with and possibly ameliorate these problems. Individuals who argue for this point of view indicate that current
educational knowledge, practice, and organization reflect assumptions
and views that are incompatible with what needs to be done to remedy
society's problems and their effect on education.

Another way of looking at why education reform is needed focuses on the extraordinary changes that have been taking place in society. The recent millennial change provided an opportunity to assess
these changes. Of course, education must keep pace with these changes.
The most visible area of continuing change is in technology. As we continue our transition from an industrial age to an information age, technology is contributing to a change in the organizational structure of the
workplace, which will require a similar change in the educational learn-

ing environment. In business and industry, the workplace is increasingly characterized by trends toward decentralization, worker empowerment, technological literacy, creative and critical thinking, and a reorganization of the roles of management and labor. Successful businesses are those that can adapt to the changing business environment. Likewise, schools must move in the direction of a flatter organizational structure with empowered and technically literate workers, not only to become relevant institutions in the information age, but also to effectively prepare students for their future citizenship and occupational roles.

This way of looking at the need for reform influences one answer to the question of whether our schools need to be reformed because they have failed. Tony Wagner cautions us that "our schools have not somehow suddenly 'failed.' They have simply become obsolete" (1994, 249). This obsolescence is exacerbated by a "crisis of perception" (Carlson 1996, 304), in which people perceive our information society and its concomitant problems as if it were still an industrial society. Dealing with obsolescence will require educators and reformers to recognize the growing difference in the organizational structure of society and the need to emulate this difference in education. The change in the organization of society is not limited to business and industry. Problems once handled at home and in religious organizations, or by coalitions involving the home, religious groups, and the schools, are, more and more, becoming solely the responsibility of the schools. The change in society resulting from instability in the families and communities requires a redesign of the organization and function of schools, and the development of new coalitions with agencies and institutions sensitive to these changing circumstances (Goodlad 1984; Sizer 1992).

Some individuals have viewed educational reform as necessary solely in response to the perceived erosion of the economic competitiveness of the United States in the world markets (Carnegie Forum 1986). Educational reforms related to this view tend to be regressive, in that they maintain industrial age organizational structures and knowledge bases. Power continues to be arranged in a hierarchical structure with differentiated stakeholder roles and traditional curriculum and instruction. This view is also often accompanied by a belief that the business and educational communities will benefit from the privatization of public schools and the minimization of government involvement. Reforms that move education in the direction of market competition are seen as the most viable response to the needs of society. However, some critics of this view see schools being used as "the new scapegoat for the increasing failure of the American economy to compete in the new global marketplace" (Giroux 1996, 126), or as a straw man, set up to conceal the real reasons certain institutions and political interests have for wanting to reform education. For example, some see the emphasis on school reform as a political maneuver to divert America's attention away from federal failures to deal with domestic problems (Berliner and Biddle 1995).

One response to demographic changes in society involves the promotion of educational reform with the purpose of establishing cultural homogeneity. As the demographic diversity of America increases and society moves closer to the recognition that it is a multicultural society, a "new nationalism" (Popkewitz 1991, 144) will seek educational reform that will promote the traditionally dominant culture, which is white, patriarchal, and Eurocentric. This direction of educational reform requires a coherence and standardization of school programs based on a core curriculum.

Another response to the changes in society involves the need to use education to promote democracy. However, depending on the viewpoint of the reformer, reform could take a radical bent that seeks to promote a participatory democracy of informed, critical, and activist citizens; or a conservative view that would create democratic citizens through the transmission of values and knowledge deemed appropriate by those who control society. The former view would promote reforms that would require students to consider social issues, moral dilemmas, and social action as a way of moving toward a just and caring society (Popkewitz 1991). The latter view would promote reforms that would require students to apply common values, beliefs, and knowledge in the consideration of social issues, moral dilemmas, and social action (Bennett, Finn, and Cribb, 1999; Hirsch 1988; Wynne and Ryan, 1993).

In conclusion, how do we know that there is a need for educational reform? Every study by commissions, committees, and individual researchers provides statistical and anecdotal evidence to support the deficiencies of education as they are identified in that report. Even though some of the data conflict, one thing is common to all the studies—all justifications are highly contextually specific, in the sense that they provide a simplified snapshot of a complex and fluid situation. One source that directly critiques the fundamental arguments and justifications behind the attacks on American public schools is *The Manufactured Crisis* by Berliner and Biddle, cited above. This source provides a detailed critique of the attacks on the conduct and achievements of America's public schools, even suggesting that Americans have been misled about the alleged educational crisis. Therefore, there appears to be no agreement or consensus on the reasons why reform is needed and even to what extent it is needed. Nevertheless, there is a yet more extreme position, one that proposes the end of free public schools as the only viable solution.

Going Beyond Reform—School Choice and Deschooling

The proposal to dismantle the current system of free public schools takes many forms. Most remarkably, those individuals and groups who see little or no benefit in reforming the current public school system include a group of radical thinkers from the 1960s and 1970s and conservative educators and politicians who promote school choice.

In the 1960s and 1970s a group of radicals critiqued the very foundation of American education—the free public school system. In their analysis, deschooling was the only option. John Holt pointed out that "to make it [education] more effective and efficient will only be to make it worse, and to help it do even more harm. It cannot be reformed, cannot be carried out wisely or humanely, because its purpose is neither wise nor humane" (1976, 4). Paul Goodman had earlier succinctly stated a similar conclusion: "I doubt that, at present or with any reforms that are conceivable under present school administration, going to school is the best use for the time of life of the majority of youth" (1964, 16). Ivan Illich (1971) eschewed reform because in his estimation the schools could not be saved no matter what measures were taken. He maintained that even innovation and experimentation in educational practice would result in only superficial changes, because he saw not only the actual schools as bad but *schooling* as bad.

According to these theorists, the problem is that schools are an outmoded institution that "has become almost the only allowable way of growing up" (Goodman 1964, 17). Organized and structured to solve the problems of the centralized industrialism of the modern period, schools in their current form constrain the freedom and individualism of those whom they serve. Conformity rather than independent thought fosters the development of the view that life "is inevitably routine, depersonalized, venally graded; that it is best to toe the mark and shut up; that there is no place for spontaneity, open sexuality, free spirit. Trained in the schools, they go on to the same quality of jobs, culture, politics. This *is* education, mis-education, socializing to the national norms and regimenting to the national 'trends'" (Goodman 1964, 23).

The central problem of this conformity is the hidden curriculum that preserves privilege and power for the schooled. Sumner Rosen summarizes Ivan Illich: "For him schools will always be instruments for socialization into the existing social system, for the perpetuation of a hierarchy based on certified knowledge, for the preservation of monopoly privileges for the schooled minority at the expense of the less-schooled majority, and for domination of social life by institutions built in the image of the school controlled by the schooled" (1973, 101). In opposition to the emancipatory power of truly free schools, as described by Kozol (1972) and A. S. Neill (1960), public schools are restrictive because they are "legally compulsory, not voluntary; age bound, not lifelong; subject centered, not person centered; book oriented, not experience oriented; teacher centered, not learner centered; competitive, not collaborative; bureaucratically fixated on grades, credits, and diplomas, not mastery oriented; controlling of behavior, not responsive to needs; invidious and advantageous, not equalizing and compassionate" (Gross 1973, 153–154).

In addition, these thinkers dismiss all reforms of education "as simply serving to adapt and thus preserve the existing structure of power and privilege" (Rosen 1973, 102). In fact, Goodman claimed that "schools less and less represent any human values, but simply adjustment to a mechanical system" (1964, 21). "Illich questioned the fundamental justifications for the existence of modern school. While radical and liberal educators were simply critiquing the practices of modern school systems, Illich was taking the next step by arguing that the institution should not be reformed but abolished" (Spring 1993, i). Those, such as Neil Postman, who preferred not to abandon the idea of public schooling but were sympathetic to Illich's position, formulated questions based on Illich's proposals to determine whether an innovation is indeed moving in the right direction: "Will the innovation make resources more widely available? Will it tend to de-emphasize the importance of teaching as against learning? Will it tend to make students freer, and their learning less confined?" (Postman 1973, 146).

This seemingly unrealistic and impractical view of educational reform has been presented because deschooling and the school choice initiative of the Right are threats to the American ideal of "a free public school, available to all, commonly educating—the common school" (Goodlad 1984, 34). This theoretical position of disenchanted radicals is far less of a threat than the school choice initiative of the Right. However, it is ironic to hear the same rhetoric coming from two very divergent theoretical positions. In 1970, John Holt, a radical proponent of deschooling, had this to say about school choice: "Only when all parents, not just rich ones, have a truly free choice in education, when they can take their children out of a school they don't like, and have a choice of many others to send them to, of the possibility of starting their own, or of educating their children outside of school altogether—only then will we teachers begin to stop being what most of us still are and if we are honest know we are, which is jailers and babysitters, cops without uniforms, and begin to be professionals, freely exercising an important, valued, and honored skill and art" (265).

As will be discussed in a later chapter, school choice is increasingly viewed as a promising educational reform. Holt's comment was foreshadowing the numerous manifestations of choice, ranging from magnet and charter schools to cyber schools and home schooling. As a reform, the school choice movement has significant implications for the survival of free public schools and for the purpose of education.

REFORM AND THE PURPOSE OF EDUCATION

How is educational reform related to the purposes of education and schooling? Of course, to answer this question, one must first consider the purposes of education. In 1970, Charles Silberman asked these questions: "What is education for? What kind of human beings and what kind of society do we want to produce?" (182). Except for those who engage in change merely for the sake of change, reformers are guided and motivated by their answers to these questions. Educational reform is initiated when education is not achieving the goals of education, as those goals are understood by those individuals or groups who have the power to initiate reform efforts. To understand educational reform requires an understanding of the various positions regarding the purposes of education, and an understanding that there are both philosophical and functional purposes.

Functional Purposes

Schools are asked to serve many different purposes that have to do with preparing students for society. A list (not intended to be complete) of the kinds of education intended to meet these functional purposes might includes sex education; gender equity education; education for racial integration; human relations education; international education; citizen education; environmental education; energy education; drug abuse, health, and safety education; consumerism and basic education; marriage and family education; education in basic skills; marketable skills, and job search skills; music, art, and gifted education; and education for the handicapped (Carlson 1996, 2). In addition, since the late 1800s, a service sector has developed in response to the social and personal needs of immigrants and later other students. In this service sector, schools are expected to provide noninstructional services such as medical inspection, health and nutritional services, rehabilitation of the handicapped, and school lunches. At the same time, public schools must strive to achieve their purposes for all students. In addition to "regular" students, throughout the years the list of at-risk students has grown to include the economically disadvantaged, those with limited English proficiency, and the handicapped. Because of the changing demographics of the United States, the at-risk label may now also include children whose parents are divorced, latchkey children, substance abuse children, children who were born prematurely, children in poverty, children with teenage parents, children with a single parent, neglected children, children with incarcerated parents, and children with incarcerated siblings (Brown 1992).

The many different purposes that our schools are asked to achieve within the changing demographics of our society are further complicated by society's demand that these purposes should be achieved within the context of free and compulsory elementary and secondary schools. In addition, schools are asked to accomplish this task regardless of all the individual differences of their students that result from economic, racial, ethnic, and gender diversity. In the face of this challenging diversity, schools are asked to foster social equality, promote the full creative potential of their students, and integrate these diverse individuals into the social order.

Philosophical Purposes

Because functional purposes are tied more directly and obviously to life experience, reform is apt to be seen as improving the ability of the school system to serve these functional purposes. However, besides these very specific functional purposes, there are broader and deeper purposes of education, and the understanding of these purposes is driven by philosophical positions. Decisions about curriculum, instruction, and assessment, as well as about how schools are organized and function, are mediated by philosophical decisions about the purpose of schooling. Attempts to enact these philosophies are what constitute reform.

Ann Lieberman writes that "the central task of the current reform movement in education is to build and transform schools that endeavor to achieve democratic ideals" (1994, ix). Lieberman's use of the phrase "democratic ideals" brings up what John Dewey referred to as the question of democracy. In the United States, the overall philosophical purpose of education always has to do with democracy. In fact, how we define democracy significantly informs how we define the philosophical and functional purposes of schooling and, in turn, the reform of schools. In fact, one could say that any definition of democracy is actually a definition of what American society should be. It's possible to see definitions of democracy as falling into two broad categories, usually referred to as liberal and conservative. Of course there are in fact many definitions that don't fall neatly into one category or the other, but it does make sense to see all the actual definitions as falling somewhere on a continuum between reactionary and radical. Then for the sake of simplicity we can refer to those on the right of the spectrum as conservative, those on the left as liberal or, for the sake of the greatest contrast, radical.

Essentially, the conservative perspective sees a democratic society as a melting pot, where people of difference (that is, individuals different from the individuals who represent the dominant culture) are socialized into one common culture with one common purpose, as determined by the controlling culture. Societal and cultural stability is to be ensured through the social and cultural reproduction of historically common values, beliefs, and knowledge. Within this context, the purpose of education is to transmit the dominant culture to all individuals within the society. The purpose of educational reform is to correct any pedagogical deviation from this mission, or to introduce pedagogical techniques and procedures that will enhance attainment of this purpose of commonality and stability.

The radical perspective sees a democratic society as a pluralist society, in which people of difference (and in this case, all individuals would be recognized as contributors of difference) contribute to a culture of diversity, with common purpose being continuously critiqued and redefined. Societal and cultural stability is to be ensured through continuous dialogue, mediated by public participation and social struggle. Commonality would be a negotiated and fluid entity shaped through a continuous public dialogue. Within this context, the purpose of education would be to create informed, critical, and active citizens. The purpose of educational reform would be to correct any pedagogical deviation from this mission, or to introduce pedagogical techniques and procedures that would enhance attainment of this purpose.

Ira Shor brings this perspective to bear on education with these questions: "Can education develop students as critical thinkers, skilled workers, and active citizens? Can it promote democracy and serve all students equitably?" (1992, 11). With the goal of education and reform defined as empowering individuals to facilitate their transformation of self and society, "a curriculum designed to empower students must be transformative in nature and help students to develop the knowledge, skills, and values needed to become social critics who can make reflective decisions and implement their decisions in effective personal, social, political, and economic action" (Banks 1991, 131). Shor describes the values that need to be included in curriculum and educational reform appropriate to this perspective on democracy: participatory, affective, problem-posing, situated, multicultural, dialogic, desocializing, democratic, researching, interdisciplinary, and activist (17). Shor promotes the value of a curriculum that

- allows students to participate in their learning, rather than defining students as passive recipients of teacher-transmitted knowledge
- promotes the integration of positive emotions and cognition in the learning experience
- creates an educational experience in which students actively pose and solve problems, rather than sit passively and receive information
- utilizes themes and words from the students' daily lives, so that all subjects gain authenticity for the students from its relevance to their lives
- fosters an awareness and understanding of the multicultural nature of the society in which students live
- utilizes a dialogical rather than adversarial type of conversation that allows the students to participate together in critically reflective thought and action
- desocializes the students, in the sense that it encourages them to question the social behaviors and experiences that surround them and to examine their own learned behavior critically
- facilitates the development of democratic ideals
- develops in the students an appreciation for and skill in utilizing research in decision making
- reviews the holistic nature of reality through interdisciplinary curriculum and instruction
- creates in the students a willingness to take action in the promotion of democratic ideals

The Importance of a Critical Approach

The nature of the continuum that stretches between the conservative and the radical way of seeing democracy, the purpose of education, and the need for educational reform will be clearer if one focuses on the presence or absence of a critical perspective, of a willingness to look closely at society and question it. The definition of democracy that involves seeing the purpose of education as the maintenance of a common core culture has been well characterized as the functional theory (Bennett and LeCompte 1990). "Functionalists believe that schooling serves to reinforce the existing social and political order" (7). As in any other theory of education, the goals of functional schooling include student acquisition of cognitive skills, intellectual skills, and knowledge. However, the purposes are to educate future citizens for appropriate participation in the given political order, to promote patriotism, to promote assimilation of immigrants, and to assure order, public civility, and conformity to law (8). In an economic context, students are to be prepared for later work roles. In functional theory, schools serve a social purpose in promoting a sense of social and moral responsibility, ameliorating social problems, and supplementing other institutions, such as the family and the church (11).

This reinforcing interaction with other societal institutions promotes the "cohesion of the social body" (Gabbard 1993, 27). In an analysis influenced by the thought of Michel Foucault, an influential French philosopher, David A. Gabbard proposes that what has just been described as functional theory is governed by "the messianic principle of discursive inclusion," which creates a pastoral image of the functional school as an inherently beneficent institution (1). This pastoral power is similar to that of the pastoral power once associated with the Catholic Church, in "that it functions to promise the individual and/or society some form of salvation in this world" (26). Here salvation takes on meanings such as health, well-being (as measured by standard of living), security, and protection against accidents. A natural outcome of this power is "the production of a certain type of individual and homogenization of individuals who will voluntarily gravitate toward institutions, disciplining them into dependency" (27).

The implication for reform is that pedagogical methods and theoretical treatments of education are only guaranteed inclusion within accepted reform initiatives (that is, reform initiatives established by those who have the power to attempt significant and widespread change) if they do not deviate from this messianic principle of pastoral power. Gabbard further argues that through this pastoral power the institution of education now serves the needs of its own processes, not authentic human needs related to education—such as the human need to learn. He proposes that the human need to learn is quite different from the institutionalized processes of instruction specific to many schools. Furthermore, schools function to maintain and reproduce their own processes, which serve the institutionalized value of education instead of the human value of education. Reform efforts then tend to serve the purpose of reproduction as well, instead of creating significant or fundamental changes.

Functional theory will be further described in a later chapter dealing with the elements of scientific efficiency and social control in the social efficiency movement.

The work of Michael Fullan falls more toward the middle of the continuum. For the most part, his ideas of the goals of education are similar to those of the functionalists, but he adds one overriding purpose that makes a crucial difference—he believes that education should promote equality of opportunity and achievement, helping students escape from the limitations of their social group (1991, 14). He is influenced here by the work of John Dewey, an influential reformer of the first half of the twentieth century whose contribution will be explained in Chapters 2 and 3. In one crucial way, then, Fullan has introduced a critical perspective; that is, he sees educational reform as ideally reflecting at least some intelligent criticism of society and designed to encourage some degree of transformation, not simply as leading to more effective perpetuation of the status quo.

A radical view would be at the other end of the continuum from the functionalist approach and would be in complete opposition to it; it would also find elements of Fullan's view problematic. In a radical definition of education and reform, not only are issues of social justice, caring, and democratic participation paramount, but all elements of education would have to be continuously scrutinized for oppressive tendencies. In this case, the mission of educational reform would be to promote a critical pedagogy that creates informed, critically reflective students who actively participate in an inclusive democratic society.

In the following list, the difference between an uncritical and a critical perspective is highlighted by following each uncritical statement of the purpose of education with a critical statement of purpose:

- ➥ Uncritical: Society uses education to contribute to the maintenance and stability of the social, economic, and political order. Critical: Society uses education to contribute to the improvement, growth, and transformation of the social order (Astuto et al. 1994, 24).
- ➥ Uncritical: Schooling supports and promotes a common cultural heritage. Critical: Schooling supports and promotes an understanding and appreciation of the diverse cultural traditions in American society (Astuto, 26).
- ➥ Uncritical: The test of the efficacy of an education system is its instrumental contribution to the goals of society. Critical:

> The test of the efficacy of an education system is the extent to which it meets the entitlement of all children to access the benefits of their society (Astuto, 10).

Each of the critical statements promotes a focus on the students' development as critical participants in an increasingly multicultural society. Even though many at every point on the continuum would agree that schools do exist for students, the critical position takes the strongest position, explicitly making children more important than the instrumental purposes of those who wish to promote the dominant culture. The dominant culture in the United States is foundationally a market-oriented culture; however, as will be detailed in later chapters, during the early 1900s a progressive movement occurred in education. This movement attempted to move the purpose of education away from the social reproduction of the dominant culture and the concomitant purpose of guaranteeing an adequate supply of human resources for the market-oriented society to purposes related to the individual welfare of the students and to the promotion of a democratic society. As will be seen, in the 1960s and early 1970s this progressive view was adopted and promoted by the liberal establishment. From the 1980s to the present, however, the conservative perspective on the purpose of education has shaped educational reforms designed to reinforce the dominant culture and to focus on meeting the needs of our business and industrial sectors.

Henry Giroux sums up these reforms as "an attempt to reformulate the purpose of public education around a set of interests and social relations that define academic success almost exclusively in terms of the accumulation of capital and the logic of the marketplace" (1988, 178). Giroux sees those who accept the dominant culture uncritically as promoting what he calls a "technicist" form of education, one that "embodies an idealized tradition that glorifies hard work, industrial discipline, domesticated desire, and cheerful obedience" (178). Giroux further describes a shift in educational and reform purposes: "Educational reform has fallen upon hard times. The traditional assumption that schooling is fundamentally tied to the imperatives of citizenship designed to educate students to exercise civic leadership and public service has been eroded. The schools are now the key institution for producing professional, technically trained, credentialized workers for whom the demands of citizenship are subordinated to the vicissitudes of the marketplace and the commercial public sphere" (ix). In relation to the purposes and definitions of democracy, education, and reform, Giroux's comments contextualize the previous choices as choices between personal betterment and reproduction of a market-oriented culture.

Thomas Popkewitz has described the purpose of education in America, and although his statement relates to the nineteenth century, scholars such as Giroux and Gabbard would argue that it is remarkably accurate in describing the close of the twentieth century: "By the close of the century, schooling was an institution to mediate the relations among the family, culture, economy, and state. Schooling was to promote political conformity by providing social stability, intelligent but acquiescent citizens, obedient children for anxious parents, and productive workers for an emerging capitalist economy. Schools also promised to confer opportunity and status through literacy and the development of character" (1991, 54).

The range of critical and uncritical functional and philosophical purposes can be seen in the following categories of reform rationales presented by John Martin Rich (1988). A reform can be justified through an appeal for quantity, in that larger appropriations of money, facilities, or personnel are needed due to some change in political, cultural, economic, or social conditions. Also, appeals to equity may relate to inequitable resource, financial, or legal distribution. A reform can be justified through an appeal that certain fundamental rights of some individuals have been violated. An appeal to decision making would argue that certain stakeholders or the general community are not participating in educational decision making and that their participation is a critical component in the solution of the targeted problem. Finally, an appeal can be made to restore standards, programs, or conditions from the past. This rationale promotes the idea that past practice is better than current practice (Rich 1988, 11–12).

What is now apparent is that there is a relationship between convictions about how democracy should function and beliefs about the purpose of education and educational reform. Each set of beliefs about the purpose of educational reform serves some individual's or interest group's agenda for the country as a whole. Whatever the purpose of educational reform, however, another essential question is whether any specific reform can be sustained.

THE SUSTAINABILITY OF EDUCATIONAL REFORM

The Persistent Failure of Educational Reform

Questions involving the sustainability of reform involve issues of stakeholder resistance and accommodation. These issues will be explored more thoroughly in Chapter 9; however, a few introductory comments concerning the importance of sustainability will help to provide context for this book's discussion of educational reform. Sustainability is an important issue; as Michael Fullan and Andy Hargreaves make clear, most attempts at educational reform fail (Fullan and Hargreaves, 1996). They cite many reasons for this failure:

» The problems themselves are complex, and not easily amenable to solutions given the resources at hand.
» Time lines are unrealistic because policy makers want immediate results.
» There are tendencies toward faddism and quick-fix solutions.
» Structural solutions (such as redefining the curriculum, or increasing assessment and testing) are often preferred, but they do not get at the underlying issues of instruction and teacher development.
» Follow-through support systems for implementing policy initiatives are not provided.
» Many strategies not only fail to motivate teachers to implement improvements but also alienate them further from participating in reform (13).

Messy Problems and Educational Dilemmas

Another reason that educational reform is difficult to sustain is that most problems educational reform addresses are what system designers refer to as messy, or wicked. In such problems, "the initial conditions, the goals, and the allowable operations cannot be specified or extrapolated from the problem" (Banathy 1996, 30). Problems dealt with by engineers and scientists are well structured, and scientific processes can derive their solutions. Social problems, however, are inevitably wicked, due to the complexity inherent in human relationships, a complexity that wreaks havoc with the best-planned scientific processes. Larry Cuban (1993) refers to these as dilemmas or situations that have no clear criteria for assessment and no universal or permanent solutions. Joseph Murphy (1992) points out that such dilemmas tend to get dealt with rather than solved, and therefore reappear on a regular but unpredictable basis.

The issues involved in resistance to, accommodation of, and failure of reform will be explored further in Chapter 9. However, there is another important question that needs to be addressed. Should all reforms be sustained? This question infers that some reforms should not be sustained. Before engaging this inference, however, it is important to consider why reforms must be sustained over time if they are to succeed.

The Need for Time to Fully Implement Reforms

Put simply, educational reform needs to be sustained because to see any results a reform initiative may need to continue for three to five years. This length of time is problematic for educational reform because of the public's desire for immediate gratification. Many individuals in the general public assume that change can occur fairly quickly in education. One outcome of this unrealistic expectation is that educators frequently view change or reform that is externally imposed simply as faddism. This attitude is especially prevalent among educators who work in states or school districts in which each year brings a new reform and sees the the previous year's reform de-emphasized or discarded.

Time for appropriate design, implementation, and evaluation is critical for any reform. Whether a change is systemic, systematic, or piecemeal (see Chapter 5), time is a critical factor in determining the success of the initiative. Fundamental changes in an educational system cannot be implemented in a short period of time. Three examples of the kind of change that alters something fundamental in a school or school district will serve to make obvious the importance of time in educational reform and change.

First, much has been written about the role that community plays in educational change. The term "community" may refer to the larger community in relation to the school, or to community within a school or school district. Developing new relationships with the larger community in which a school is nested is a complex task and requires a significant time investment. Creating new relationships and displacing the old undesirable ones simply take time. The same is true for community building within a school. All communities, to some degree, require trust, and establishing trust requires time.

To take another example, the use of conversation to promote a vision and facilitate an incremental implementation of the vision takes time. A detailed explanation of making educational changes through the use of conversation will be provided in Chapter 5. Basically, this process supports educational change by promoting an awareness of different conversational types and skill in using them. Some of these types of conversation are generative, in the sense that the purpose of these types is to create new, more systemic, and more critical understandings about all aspects of the school environment, as well as deepening a participant's personal understanding of self. Dialogic, design, and post-formal conversation (see Chapter 5 for an explanation of these types of conversation) are integral components of community building and facilitate the development of trust. These conversational types also can lead to interpersonal relationships with a spiritual dimension, reflecting the I-Thou relationship discussed by Martin Buber (1988, 1992), in which individuals connect with each other in caring, equitable, and emotionally intimate relationships. Since conversation takes time and trust is a factor in certain types of conversation, changes and reforms that rely upon conversation as a change medium clearly need time.

A final example of a reform process in which time is a critical factor in success involves a leadership reform process, in which school improvement is facilitated by moral leadership. This process will also be considered in detail in Chapter 5; the point here is that time is critical in this process because of the moral dimension inherent in it. This type of leadership involves the modeling of moral principles by the educational leader, whether as administrator or teacher. The leader works on facilitating the development of collegial community. Obviously, building trust, developing an understanding of others and self, and developing collegial interpersonal relationships will require time, time each day over a period of years.

Reasons That Some Reforms Should Not Be Sustained

Obviously, the question of whether any specific reform is worth sustaining over a period of time will be answered differently by different individuals or groups, depending on their concept of the purpose of education. This would be assessed differently by individuals whose definitions of the purpose of education differ. For instance, an individual with a critical agenda in relation to democracy, education, and reform, would welcome reforms involving community building, conversation, and moral leadership and would consider them worth sustaining over a long period of time. An individual whose purpose was to maintain a common culture and an established hierarchical social order might be threatened by reforms involving these ideas and consider them not worth sustaining. There are, however, other reasons that some reforms should not be sustained that do not simply reflect their relationship to the purpose of education.

In 1984, John Goodlad argued that most reforms to improve schools fail because they are ignorant of the way schools function in general and ignorant of the inner workings of specific schools in particular. The recognition of the interrelatedness of all components of a school's environment and the connection of the school to the larger systems in which the school is embedded creates the need to critically examine the consequences of all reforms, especially those that reflect ignorance of the way schools function. The consequences of an ill-conceived reform will have systemic effects—effects that reach beyond the intended target of the reform. As Cleo Cherryholmes has argued, it is essential that the examination of the reform and its consequences not be limited to the pragmatic question of whether the reform is likely to achieve its goals; a critically pragmatic examination looks at the effects of the reform on the power arrangements within the human system affected by the reform and the implications of the reform for social justice, caring, and democracy (1999). Reforms should not be sustained that have consequences that are deleterious to those individuals involved in the reform or to others within the environmental periphery.

Should a reform be sustained if its effectiveness will be offset or negated by its incompatibility with the postmodern (see Glossary) condition of the place in which the reform is being implemented? In this condition, modernists (see Glossary) may want to retain their own organizational structures and beliefs and resist postmodern innovations, or postmodernists may actively resist the imposition of modernistic reforms. "Decentralizers are opposed by centralizers. Advocates of process-based learning which acknowledges the uncertainty of knowledge are overruled by imposers of facts-based mandated curricula. Locally based or school-based teacher development is superseded by system-wide training" (Hargreaves 1994, 42). If this kind of philosophical incompatibility is apparent, a continuation of the reform effort only can result in negative outcomes, or at least in more adversarial relationships within the system being reformed.

As detailed in Chapter 9, teacher culture and the conditions of teachers' work can lead to accommodation of or resistance to educational reform. If a teacher culture in a school is balkanized or individualized, a reform based on collaborative and collegial processes will be difficult to achieve (Hargreaves 1994). If the reform requires an expenditure of teacher time that is unrealistic and inordinate in relation to the reality of the time available, the reform will be difficult to achieve. In both cases, not only will the reform be resisted and fail, but undesirable pedagogical practice and human relationships will be reinforced. If a reform will not only fail but even reinforce the practice meant to be changed by the reform, why should the reform be sustained?

Intensive and cumulative attention to the change process may lead to goal displacement (Merton 1957), a situation in which the original goals become neglected and forgotten, displaced by the intense focus on the change process. The reasons that the reform was originally initiated fade into the background (Hargreaves 1994). The result is stakeholder confusion, which can lead to motivational problems as well as behavior that works against the original purpose of the reform. When goal displacement becomes apparent, should the reform effort continue?

When Do You Give Up on a Reform?

Finally, at what point do you give up on a reform? If a reform is initiated and proves to be ineffective or harmful due to any of the previous reasons, how long should it continue? The open school and open classroom initiative of the 1960s and 1970s failed as a reform. Problems concerning the philosophical, pedagogical, and cultural changes that were required to make the reform effective doomed the reform. Within a few years, it quickly became apparent to schools that were attempting to implement this reform that the concomitant changes that were needed to allow open schools to work were not going to happen. Some schools quickly reverted to the traditional pedagogy and organization, but others resisted, causing frustration, strained interpersonal relationships, and an enervating sense of failure. At what point should the implementation have been ended?

Currently, Texas is continuing its implementation of a standards and accountability system started in the late 1970s. This long-term initiative has been the object of a continuous criticism based on dropout data, the effects on certain minorities, teacher shortages, and many other areas of concern (Horn and Kincheloe 2001; McNeil 2000; Meier 2000). This state-sponsored reform is continuously changed or tweaked by the Texas Education Agency, a regulatory agency in charge of Texas education. Each year tens of thousands of children are lost through attrition, the teacher shortage increases, and minorities are disenfranchised. In this case the question is how long a reform ought to continue when the human cost required to achieve the goal of the reform is high.

In conclusion, the questions raised about sustaining reform relate to our definitions of democracy, education, and reform. Of course, if a reform is in opposition to what one believes, one will desire to see it end. The following list represents a growing consensus within the scholarly community as to what is required to create sustainable reform. In this view reform attempts must move

- from individual to institutional responsibility for achievement
- from instrumentality to entitlement
- from control to empowerment
- from bureaucracy to democracy
- from commonality to diversity
- from competition to collaboration
- from intervention to facilitation (Astuto et al. 1994, 87)

In opposition to this view found within the scholarly community is the recently emergent view promoted by those supporting the current standards and accountability initiative. This initiative views the characteristics of sustainable reform as individual responsibility, instrumentality, control, bureaucracy, commonality, competition, and intervention. These divergent views are based on quite different definitions of democracy, education, and reform. Those who hold each of these views feel that only their kind of educational reform will be sustainable.

HISTORICAL RESPONSES TO THESE QUESTIONS

A later chapter will provide detailed information about how these essential questions have been answered over time. However, it is possible to point out some common threads. First, the question of whether there is a need for reform has always been answered in the affirmative; schools are always perceived to be in a state of failure or deficiency. Another common thread shows up in responses to the question of what the purpose of education is; rarely have those who have significant say in how society should be defined "affirmed education as intrinsically valuable. Typically, we have thought of schools as means to other ends" (Murphy 1990, 76). This instrumental and pragmatic view of education will surface again and again in the analysis of the history of educational reform in Chapter 2.

A third common thread that shows up in answers to the question of the purpose of education is a continuing devotion to both academic excellence and social equity (Murphy 1990). The ability to achieve both at the same time has eluded educational reformers. Therefore, one pattern in educational reform has been an emphasis on the one purpose over the other, followed by a perception that the neglected goal is suffering and a subsequent call for reform by moving back to a focus on the other goal. The most recent example of this pattern is the back-to-basics and standards movement, which began in the 1980s as a response to the 1960s emphasis on equity (Murphy 1990).

One important practical consideration has always played a role in the way the central questions have been answered, and that is the cost of reform and who pays that price.

All reform has a price. Smaller classes, adequate facilities in all American school districts, better-trained educators, a general public that is more knowledgeable and more involved in the schools and the determination of educational policy, longer school days and years, equitable and effective remediation for all students who need it, and a national consensus on the purpose of education—all these goals will all cost someone something. Providing the type of education that occurs in the well-funded schools, in the well-funded programs within schools, and in high-achieving private schools would come with a significant cost.

Inevitably, the high cost of real reform raises the question of who will bear that cost. In a discussion of the reforms of the 1980s, Murphy points out that "the costs of the most significant changes were to a remarkable extent imposed on politically powerless groups, including high school students and prospective teachers, which made these reforms palatable to more influential constituencies" (1990, 136). More influential constituencies would include individuals and groups who can contribute to political campaigns and segments of the public who vote in blocks. Students in general and certain demographic groups of students in particular (such as inner city and rural minorities, poverty-level students of all types) have no power because they have no capital resources and cannot vote.

Historically, the answer to the dilemma of how to pay for reform has often been to alter the reform so that less influential individuals and groups will have to absorb the cost of the reform. To avoid large expenditures that would come out of the pocketbooks of influential constituencies, reforms have been altered to take the form of requiring educators to do more in the same amount of time and students to take more responsibility and to be more accountable for the implementation of the reform. In that case, the cost no longer involves money, but it is still a real cost in the effects on the quality of the educational experience, and how that experience affects the personal and professional lives of the educators and the students. It seems then that another essential question concerning educational reform always has to be—who pays for the reform?

REFERENCES

Astuto, Terry A., David L. Clark, Anne-Marie Read, Kathleen McGree, and L. deKoven Pelton Fernandez. 1994. *Roots of reform: Challenging the assumptions that control change in education.* Bloomington, IN: Phi Delta Kappa Education Foundation.

Banathy, Bela H. 1996. *Designing social systems in a changing world.* New York: Plenum Press.

Banks, James. 1991. A curriculum for empowerment, action, and change. In *Empowerment through multicultural education,* edited by Christine E. Sleeter. Albany, NY: State University of New York Press.

Bennett, Kathleen P., and Margaret D. LeCompte. 1990. *The way schools work: A sociological analysis of education.* New York: Longman.

Bennett, William J., Chester E. Finn, Jr., and John T. E. Cribb, Jr. 1999. *The educated child: A parent's guide from preschool through eighth grade.* New York: The Free Press.

Berliner, David C., and Bruce J. Biddle. 1995. *The manufactured crisis: Myths, fraud, and the attack on America's public schools.* Cambridge, MA: Perseus Books.

Bowles, Samuel, and Herbert Gintis. 1976. *Schooling in capitalist America: Educational reform and the contradictions of economic life.* New York: Basic Books.

Boyer, Ernest L. 1983. *High school: A report on secondary education in America.* New York: Carnegie Foundation for the Advancement of Teaching, Harper and Row.

Brown, Frank. 1992. *The reform of elementary school education: A report on elementary schools in America and how they can change to improve teaching and learning.* Malabar, FL: Krieger Publishing Co.

Buber, Martin. 1988. *Eclipse of God.* Edited and translated by Maurice Friedman. 1946. Reprint, Atlantic Highlands, NJ: Humanities Press International.

———. 1992. *On intersubjectivity and cultural creativity.* Edited and with an introduction by Shmuel N. Eisenstadt. Chicago: The University of Chicago Press.

Carlson, Robert V. 1996. *Reframing and reforming: Perspectives on organization, leadership, and school change.* White Plains, NY: Longman Publishers.

Carnegie Forum on Education and the Economy. 1986. *A nation prepared: Teachers for the twenty-first century.* Washington, DC: Author.

Cherryholmes, Cleo. 1999. *Reading pragmatism.* New York: Teachers College Press.

Cuban, Larry. 1993. *How teachers taught: Constancy and change in American classrooms, 1880–1990.* 2d ed. New York: Teachers College Press.

Fullan, Michael, and Andy Hargreaves. 1996. *What's worth fighting for in your school.* New York: Teachers College Press.

Fullan, Michael G., and Suzanne Stiegelbauer. 1991. *The new meaning of educational change.* New York: Teachers College Press.

Gabbard, David A. 1993. *Silencing Ivan Illich: A Foucauldian analysis of intellectual exclusion.* San Francisco: Austin and Winfield.

Giroux, Henry A. 1988. *Teachers as intellectuals: Toward a critical pedagogy of learning.* Westport, CT: Bergin and Garvey.

Giroux, Henry A., ed. 1996. *Living dangerously: Multiculturalism and the politics of difference.* New York: Peter Lang.

Goodlad, John I. 1984. *A place called school: Prospects for the future.* New York: McGraw-Hill Book Company.

Goodman, Paul. 1964. *Compulsory mis-education and the community of scholars.* New York: Vintage Books.

Gross, Ronald. 1973. After deschooling, free learning. In *After deschooling, what?* edited by Alan Gartner, Colin Greer, and Frank Riessman. New York: Harper and Row.

Hargreaves, Andy. 1994. *Changing teachers, changing times: Teachers' work and culture in the postmodern age.* New York: Teachers College Press.

Hirsch, E. D., Jr. 1988. *Cultural literacy: What every American needs to know.* New York: Vintage Books.

Holt, John. 1976. *Instead of education.* New York: Delta Books.

Horn, Raymond A., Jr., and Joe L. Kincheloe, eds. 2001. *American standards: Quality education in a complex world—The Texas case.* New York: Peter Lang.

Illich, Ivan. 1971. *Deschooling society.* New York: Harper and Row.

Kozol, Jonathan. 1967. *Death at an early age: The destruction of the hearts and minds of Negro children in the Boston public schools.* Boston: Houghton Mifflin.

———. 1972. *Free schools.* Boston: Houghton Mifflin.

———. 1991. *Savage inequalities: Children in America's schools.* New York: Crown Publishers.

Lieberman, Ann. 1994. Series editor's introduction to *Changing teachers, changing times: Teachers' work and culture in the postmodern age,* by Andy Hargreaves. New York: Teachers College Press.

McNeil, Linda M. 2000. *Contradictions of school reform: Educational costs of standardized testing.* New York: Routledge.

Meier, Deborah. 2000. *Will standards save public education?* Boston: Beacon Press.

Merton, Robert. 1957. *Social theory and social structure.* New York: The Free Press.

Murphy, Joseph. 1992. *The landscape of leadership preparation: Reframing the education of school administrators.* Newbury Park, CA: Corwin Press, Inc.

Murphy, Joseph, ed. 1990. *The educational reform movement of the 1980s: Perspectives and cases.* Berkeley, CA: McCutchan.

Neill, A. S. 1960. *Summerhill: A radical approach to child rearing.* New York: Hart Publishing.

Popkewitz, Thomas S. 1991. *A political sociology of educational reform: Power/knowledge in teaching, teacher education, and research.* New York: Teachers College Press.

Postman, Neil. 1973. My Ivan Illich problem. In *After deschooling, what?* edited by Alan Gartner, Colin Greer, and Frank Riessman. New York: Harper and Row.

Rich, John M. 1988. *Innovations in education: Reformers and their critics.* 5th ed. Boston: Allyn and Bacon.

Rosen, Sumner M. 1973. Taking Illich seriously. In *After deschooling, what?*

edited by Alan Gartner, Colin Greer, and Frank Riessman. New York: Harper and Row.

Scheurich, James J. 1997. *Research method in the postmodern.* Washington, DC: Falmer Press.

Shor, Ira. 1992. *Empowering education: Critical teaching for social change.* Chicago: University of Chicago Press.

Silberman, Charles E. 1970. *Crisis in the classroom: The remaking of American education.* New York: Random House.

Sizer, Theodore R. 1992. *Horace's school: Redesigning the American high school.* New York: Houghton Mifflin.

Spring, Joel. 1993. Foreword to *Silencing Ivan Illich: A Foucauldian analysis of intellectual exclusion,* by David A. Gabbard. San Francisco: Austin and Winfield.

Wagner, Tony. 1994. *How schools change: Lessons from three communities.* Boston: Beacon Press.

Wynne, Edward A., and Ken Ryan. 1993. *Reclaiming our schools: A handbook on teaching character, academics, and discipline.* New York: Merrill.

Chapter Two

●◆ The History of Reform in American Education

Chapter 2 will present a historical narrative describing the significant events in American educational reform. The chapter will conclude with a summative discussion of the changing nature of the purpose of reform and of the patterns that have emerged over the years. Also included in the summary will be an identification of the origins of current educational reform initiatives.

The events described in this narrative are interesting for the simple reason that the continuous and intense need to reform education over the last hundred years indicates a lack of consensus on an ideological and pedagogical foundation for our public education system. One may agree with David Paris when he says, "It is hard to believe that a country that produced Horace Mann and John Dewey could feel itself lacking a foundation for educational policy" (Paris 1995, 13). As presented in Chapter 1, special interests and political ideology contribute to this lack of a consensual foundation. In another view, Neil Postman wrote that "public education does not serve a public, but creates a public" (1995, 18). An examination of the following events suggests that, in actuality, part of the reason there is no foundational consensus is because education does serve the public in many ways, one of those ways being that education is a valuable, if not the most significant, tool in the creation of a public. Because of its enculturating potential, education is a continuous battleground on which personal and collective interests compete to mold society into their ideal vision.

THE MID-1800s TO 1900

During this time period educational reform was focused on the efforts of Horace Mann to establish a common school system that would create citizens with a common culture, help students develop morally and socially, and ensure the assimilation of immigrants into American society.

Building on the vision of the role of education in America, as proposed by individuals in postrevolutionary America such as Thomas Jefferson and Benjamin Rush, Mann worked to establish a mandatory school system that would ensure social stability by promoting common values and beliefs. Mann believed that public support and public control of the common school could achieve this goal. Beginning in the 1830s, the middle and upper classes envisioned education as the means to forestall social unrest and to create a literate society that would ensure a productive labor force. By providing free education for the children of the poor and disadvantaged, this system could promote common values, beliefs, and knowledge. Generally, as a social control mechanism, the free common school proved to be very effective and enduring.

Publicly funded and locally controlled schools as the way to meet the needs of the children, improve society, and ensure social order has been a foundational concept in American education, one that was not seriously threatened until the last decade of the twentieth century. Aspects of this nineteenth-century reform have recently been challenged, as state and national government has become more involved in influencing and even controlling local schools and as some have promoted the privatization of education. As we begin the twenty-first century, the common school of Horace Mann as the foundation of American education is assailed by school choice initiatives, government takeover of low-performing schools, and the home-schooling movement.

Another enduring characteristic of American education started during the second half of the nineteenth century. During this time period, women were encouraged to be the teachers of the young children. Americans such as Horace Mann, influenced by major European thinkers, thought that women, with their motherly instincts, would be good and caring influences on the children. It was thought that with their less violent nature, women would be better able to guide the children into young adulthood. At this time the pattern of elementary teachers being predominantly female became entrenched in American education.

THE LATE 1800s

In the late 1800s America was changing. Cities were growing, transportation and the print media were connecting Americans on a more frequent basis, and all aspects of society were in a state of flux. During this time of change debates arose concerning the nature and purpose of education.

The Committee of Ten and the Humanist View of Curriculum

In 1893, the Committee of Ten, chaired by Charles W. Eliot of Harvard University and sponsored by the National Education Association, published a report suggesting a traditional liberal education for all students. The essence of the report was that there would be no difference in the curriculum taken by those who would go to college and those students who would enter the workforce. Eliot reasoned that the development of all students would be enhanced by the study of classic and modern languages, mathematics, literature, science, and history. In essence, the committee was proposing a national high school curriculum. This curriculum was devoid of any vocational preparation because the committee thought that all occupational decisions should be postponed until after graduation. Herbert M. Kliebard identifies the efforts of the Committee of Ten as the beginning of the humanists, one of the four major interest groups who have vied for control of the curriculum in American schools (1995).

The humanist position was severely attacked by those who thought that there was so much diversity in the student population that a common curriculum for all was unworkable. Also, those who represented the interests of business and industry contested this common curriculum in favor of a differentiated curriculum, in which students would be tracked into different curriculums depending on their social and occupational destination. Eliot responded to this criticism by expressing his refusal "to believe that the American public intends to have its children sorted before their teens into clerks, watchmakers, lithographers, telegraph operators, masons, teamsters, farm laborers, and so forth, and treated differently in their schools according to these prophecies of their appropriate careers. Who are to make these prophecies?" (1905, 330–331).

Another significant humanist of the late 1800s was William Torrey Harris. Like Eliot, Harris was a proponent of a core curriculum, which he promoted as the "five windows of the soul"—arithmetic and mathematics, geography, history, grammar, literature, and art. Harris differed from Eliot in that he agreed that considerations of child growth and development had a place in the schools; however, he steadfastly maintained that any education would be incomplete without the guiding direction of a core curriculum.

The same humanist viewpoint that proposed a common core curriculum of basic subjects resurfaced in 1982 with Mortimer J. Adler's *Paideia Proposal,* and in the late 1980s with William Bennett's *James Madison High School: A Curriculum for American Students* and E. D. Hirsch's *Cultural Literacy,*

The Child Study and Child Development Movement

An opposing view to the humanist movement was the child study movement. Individuals such as Charles Francis Adams and Colonel Francis Parker promoted a learning environment that allowed more freedom for the students and that better accommodated their developmental level. G. Stanley Hall was a prominent psychologist and philosopher who applied scientific principles to the study of children. Seeing children in a developmental context was different from seeing children in a humanist perspective as passive receptacles of knowledge. Another major difference between the two movements was the developmentalist belief that children needed to be active learners, as opposed to the humanist belief that the development of the intellect should be the central purpose of the school and that that purpose could best be served by the transmission of knowledge from the expert teacher to the passive student. During the 1900s, these two views of curriculum and the purpose of education competed not only with each other but with two other views that quickly emerged in the beginning of the century.

1900 TO 1950

As the 1900s began, social and educational reforms swept America. Prompted by the political activities of the Progressives, the success of the industrialists, and the continuation of large-scale immigration, education was shaped by new reforms. As waves of immigration continued, the schools were expected to "Americanize" these individuals. Each of the different views regarding education and curriculum had equally different views on how to Americanize the students in the schools. This time period saw great change in government processes and economic conditions, and, in all cases, education was seen as the crucial area in which change could take place that would resolve the problems of the time. The key component in effective societal change was the student. How the student would be Americanized would define American society.

The Cardinal Principles of Secondary Education

In 1913, as a response to the humanism of the Committee of Ten and the social realities of large-scale immigration, the National Education Association appointed a committee to examine the purpose of the American high school. The problem with how high schools were conducted involved the fact that all students were being prepared to go to college, an outcome that few would actually realize. In addition, economic necessity drove many students out of high school before graduation. Questions were raised concerning how to create a more relevant curriculum for the students who were not college bound.

In a thirty-two-page document that became known as the Seven Cardinal Principles, this committee presented a platform of principles that shaped the American high school for decades. In opposition to the emphasis on academic subjects of the humanists, the Cardinal Principles included seven aims to guide the curriculum: health, command of fundamental processes, worthy home membership, vocation, citizenship, worthy use of leisure, and the development of ethical character. The Cardinal Principles were significant reforms for two reasons. First, they directly facilitated the assimilation of all students into a common culture, and second, this was the first time that school curriculum became the means through which nonacademic goals were to be attained.

Vocational Education

The continuing immigration of great numbers of individuals to the United States and the accelerating industrialization of America resulted in support of vocational training in the public schools by the federal government. Because this kind of education was deemed to be in the national interest and was strongly supported by industry and agriculture, the Smith-Hughes Act of 1917 provided funding for vocational education, home economics, and agricultural education in the public schools. The nature and implementation of this industrial training initiative was primarily guided by governmental and industrial interests, with educators serving limited roles in the decision-making process. The National Society for the Promotion of Industrial Education was a powerful interest group that successfully lobbied for the federal support of job training in public schools. The vocational education movement was highly compatible with the more functional and less academic purposes of the Cardinal Principles.

Two differing concepts of vocational training emerged. One concept, related to the German model and implemented in Wisconsin, envisioned vocational education as a separate system of technical schools that would serve the employment needs of business and industry. John Dewey, the great proponent of educational reform, whose work is further discussed below and in the Chronology that follows this chapter, opposed this concept because it "would result in a typically 'bookish' education for one group and narrow trade training for the other" (Kliebard 1995, 126). In contrast to the common model, Dewey did not believe in separating intellectual training and vocational training. In his holistic view of educating children, he envisioned all children as receiving the necessary intellectual education to become effective and responsible citizens, never merely the training to fulfill a specific social and occupational role. To Dewey, this was the key to preparing all students for effective citizenship. Dewey even used the term "industrial training" instead of "vocational training" to emphasize the broader purpose of education rather than a narrow purpose of job training. Despite Dewey's criticism, certain students became separated into industrial training tracks in the urban schools and into vocational agriculture programs in the rural schools. Even though all students shared the same school, they were separated into different curriculums designed for different social roles and educational purposes.

Vocational education became one of the most successful reform initiatives in the twentieth century, as the Smith-Hughes Act was extended through additional legislation between 1929 and 1984. In 1984 the Perkins Vocational Education Act extended funding for this initiative to people with handicaps, single parents, and homemakers. In 1963, $235 million was appropriated for vocational education, rising to $950 million by 1986.

The Social Efficiency Movement

In 1911, Frederick Winslow Taylor published his *Principles of Scientific Management,* which promoted a major reform of education that continues to affect education. At the turn of the twentieth century, the American sociologist Edward A. Ross promoted the function of schooling as social control. In response to the perceived problems of society, Ross maintained that the purpose of schooling was to control and direct the actions of individuals who did not adhere to the accepted values of mainstream society. Taylor's scientific management was the perfect organizational strategy to promote order and efficiency in education and subsequently society. A third individual, John Franklin Bobbitt, also contributed to the social efficiency movement with numerous publications on how to eliminate waste in education. Together, these three men facilitated the development of an educational structure that has endured to this day.

One significant change was the introduction of an extensive management level in education. The social efficiency movement resulted in a hierarchical and hegemonic educational structure that at best mimicked and in some cases replicated the routinization, specialization, and bureaucratization of the business community (Bennett and LeCompte 1990). The application of scientific business practice and organization became evident in the need for control of every aspect of the educational process, the standardization of every task, planning and control by management departments instead of individuals, detailed record keeping, specialized roles in and precise execution of curriculum and instruction, and assessment procedures that guaranteed performance and accountability to the curricular and instructional decisions of the planners.

This combination of scientific efficiency and business influence is still evident with the continuation of the platoon system, or Gary Plan, which divided students into groups by age, divided the school day into class blocks (usually around fifty minutes or, with today's block scheduling, ninety minutes), and rotated students from room to room to provide for a more efficient use of space. Also, business accounting procedures are still evident in the continued use of the Carnegie unit, or the use of credit hours to define a course. Besides promoting the platoon system, Bobbitt also utilized business terminology that continues to this day (for example, referring to the school as the "plant"). Our current differentiated curriculum (that is, college preparation, general education, vocational education, and business education) is a result of Bobbitt's opinion that people should not be taught what they will not use. Of course, differentiated curriculum meant predicting the future social and occupational role of children and tracking them into a specific curriculum area. Other outcomes of the social efficiency movement were the deskilling (see Glossary) of teachers through their forced specialization in one subject area and through the development of teacherproof materials to promote the standardization of teaching and teacher accountability.

Progressives, Social Reformers, Social Meliorists

As a counterpoint to Eliot's humanism, to a narrowly focused vocationalism, and to scientific management, a concurrent movement attempted to improve society and create a better educational experience for the child. "Progressives," "social reformers," and "social meliorists" are labels used to describe individuals who criticized what they saw the other positions presenting as the purpose of education and promoted the general view that the society would be best served by an educational curriculum and system that was more child-centered. A progressive view of education also differed from the view of the early proponents of the common school, in that the purpose of progressive education was as much to liberate as to stabilize the public. However, despite this overall similarity in progressive thinking, there were differences among those who were considered progressives.

Some progressives could be described as romantics, in that their beliefs were in line with those of the romantic movement that had begun in Europe. Influenced by the eighteenth-century preromantic Jean-Jacques Rousseau, educational romantics were child-centered, in that they believed that education should provide a freer environment for children to learn through their interaction with their environment. Some of these types of progressives advocated a permissive and laissez-faire educational environment, in opposition to the traditional environment, which was more authoritarian.

John Dewey represented a different progressive philosophy, which can be described as pragmatically child-centered. He agreed that children as active learners were essential elements in the learning process; however, he also believed that a child's interaction with the environment must be mediated by reflective thinking and problem solving. Dewey maintained that educational growth involved a constant reflective interaction with the experience that a student encounters. Dewey differed with efficiency considerations of standardization and precise measurement of standards, and in general with any pedagogy that ignored the social consequences of a child's education. Dewey also differed with the position of the more romantic progressives that children should experience little adult control over their curriculum. Essentially, Dewey was promoting a balance between the involvement of the individual student in the determination of curriculum and the complete determination of the curriculum by the adult teacher. Dewey was also promoting a pragmatic balance between the consequences of education for the student and for society.

In 1919, progressive thinking coalesced in the Progressive Education Association. This association of progressive thinkers rapidly grew through the 1920s and 1930s. The association promoted the seven principles of progressive education: freedom to develop naturally; interest, the motive of all work; the teacher as a guide, not a taskmaster; scientific study of pupil development; greater attention to all that affects the child's physical development; cooperation between school and home to meet the needs of the child's life; the progressive school, a leader in educational movements (Kliebard 1995). The influence of the association was seen in more small-group activities, more interesting curriculum materials, and in the use of playgrounds and gymnasiums. However, the influence of the progressive movement was greatly lessened by the 1940s, leading to the disbanding of the association in 1955.

Essentialist Education Movement

In the early 1920s a backlash occurred against the progressives. Individuals known as essentialists heavily criticized child-centered progressives. The essentialists believed that the purpose of education was to develop the academic capabilities of the students, as well as to prepare them for American citizenship. Essentialism was teacher-centered, with the teacher as the creator of the curriculum, as the objective evaluator of student progress, and as the authoritarian manager of the classroom. In 1938, the Essentialist Committee for the Advancement of American Education declared that it was time to return schools to the "mental disciplines" previously promoted by the humanists.

William Chandler Bagley, a leading essentialist, put out the call for more discipline, more effort on the part of the students, more work required of the students, and more socialization into the workforce and society. Bagley declared that the result of progressive education was that American students were falling behind students from other countries in their educational achievement. Essentialists stressed that the activity- and child-centered curriculum of the progressives actually weakened the students and, in turn, weakened America. In addition, they claimed that developing a common national culture through a child's educational experience was essential.

The Eight-Year Study and the Tyler Rationale

In the 1930s, in response to the slow rate of change in the high schools, the Progressive Education Association initiated the "eight-year study." Under the leadership of Ralph Tyler, this study generated ideas that have significantly impacted educational curriculum to the present.

Based on the study, in 1949 Ralph Tyler presented what has become known as the Tyler Rationale, which was a four-step approach to curriculum development that still affects the organization of curriculum. Tyler proposed that objectives first need to be developed, then followed by the creation of learning experiences that will attain the objectives. These activities need to be ordered in an effective way, and finally the students who engage in these activities need to be evaluated to determine whether the objectives have been successfully learned. In addition to these four steps, Tyler recommended that the content of curriculum be drawn from three sources: studies of students, contemporary life, and subject matter determined by specialists in various disciplines. The significance of Tyler's rationale is his suggestion that knowledge can be efficiently transmitted from one person to another through this process. This rationale has been criticized by numerous individuals and appropriated by others. The back-to-basics movement that continues to resurface is philosophically and functionally related to Tyler's work.

Tyler saw curriculum as a rational process, which facilitated the perception of curriculum as integrated from grade to grade and from activity to activity. Tyler's rationale encouraged the reorganization of curriculum into knowledge, skills, and values. Another significant outcome of the Tyler Rationale was that it increased the influence of behaviorism on education.

Life Adjustment Education

As the United States entered World War II, education was once again perceived to be in need of reform. Consumer education, home management, and vocational training moved to the forefront of the curriculum. The thinking now was that it was necessary for only a small segment of the population to take academic courses. Functionality once again reigned in education. Charles A. Prosser proposed that the ideal objective for a school would be to prepare 20 percent of its students for college, 20 percent for a specific vocation, and give the remaining 60 percent life adjustment training. Life adjustment education included information on dating, marriage, childrearing, work experience, and all other aspects of life. The National Association of Secondary School Principals wholeheartedly supported life adjustment. The effects of the social efficiency movement had created a business attitude in high school administrators that was more receptive to the management of this real-life curriculum than to the academic curriculum of the humanists or the child-centered curriculum of the progressives. In addition, life adjustment was perceived to be a way of handling the school dropout problem.

As the 1950s began, other educational movements mounted a substantial criticism of the life adjustment movement. Generally, this reform was perceived to have softened American education. One example of this softness, a practice that has continued to be criticized, was social promotion, the practice of passing students to the next grade based upon their age and attendance instead of academic achievement.

THE 1950s

Diverse critics of the educational system passionately drove educational reform in the 1950s. McCarthyism's focus on fighting communism saw the schools as targets of communist subversion. Those in the university feared an enervating anti-intellectualism propagated by the professional educators or practitioners in the schools. Most Americans, specifically the military, the science community, and the business community, feared the Soviet Union. In addition to the ferment of change created by the Cold War, the recognition of the inequity of segregation by the federal government started the drive to bring equity to American education. Finally, a back-to-basics movement sharply criticized the life adjustment movement. The 1950s were marked by a concern for both excellence and equity in the public schools.

Sputnik and a Return to Humanism

Concerns over our ability to achieve our foreign policy goals quickly came to a head in 1957 when the first Soviet satellite (in Russian, sputnik) flew over the American sky. This event was perceived as incontrovertible proof of Soviet technical superiority and the failure of American public schools. Prior to this event, Vice Admiral Hyman G. Rickover, the father of the atomic submarine, was extremely vocal in his assessment of the effectiveness of American schools. Rickover maintained that we were not only behind the Soviets but also behind other European countries in academic achievement. Rickover proposed that this was the reason why the United States was losing the military and technology race with the Soviet Union. Rickover claimed that American education had gone soft, and that the gifted and talented students had been ignored. He maintained that the sole purpose of education should be the development of the intellect. Complementing Rickover's concern was Arthur Bestor's attack on anti-intellectualism in education. In 1952 Bestor charged that American intellectual life was in serious danger from the anti-intellectualism of school administrators and educational theorists. Like Rickover, Bestor also maintained that development of the intellect should be the primary concern of the public schools and that the enemies of America and of an efficient educational system were the professional educators, who staunchly supported life adjustment policies. Mortimer Smith and others supported this humanistic position, which attacked not only life adjustment but also the child-centered curriculum of the progressives.

James Conant and the Reform of the American High School

Another vocal critic of American education during the 1950s was James Conant, the president of Harvard University. Conant's criticisms are best expressed in his 1959 book, *The American High School Today.* Conant echoed the essentialist positions of Rickover, Bestor, and Smith on anti-intellectualism and the disregard for the gifted and talented students of America. Conant differed from the extreme essentialist position in that he maintained that an American public high school must not only meet the needs of the gifted and talented but also provide a general education for those who will enter the workforce after high school. Conant also suggested that smaller school districts be consolidated into larger ones in order to ensure an efficient school system. This suggestion resulted in the consolidation movement of the 1960s, in which many smaller school districts were absorbed by larger ones, or became consolidated with other small districts.

The National Defense Education Act and the National Science Foundation

Within a year after sputnik, the federal government created the National Defense Education Act (NDEA). The act immediately provided money for science, math, and foreign language instruction. This act was the legislative validation of the concerns voiced by the critics such as Conant and Bestor. The money allocated to achieve this purpose was funneled through a government agency, the National Science Foundation (NSF), that had been started in 1950. In later years, the NSF has supported and promoted research in other disciplines besides math and science.

One effective implementation strategy was to provide teachers with a stipend to attend summer workshops that promoted the curriculum and instruction developed by the NSF. At these workshops, teachers were to learn how to utilize the new learning strategies and the supposedly teacherproof materials prepared by NSF-sponsored professors. Another strategy was to fund conferences to determine curriculum and teaching strategies that would achieve the government's objectives. One such conference occurred at Woods Hole and was funded by the NSF, the Office of Education, the U.S. Air Force, and the RAND Corporation. Professor Jerome S. Bruner, a psychologist and the director of the program, reported that students learn best by working with examples until they discover the structure of the subject through inductive reasoning. Bruner's cognitive model of teaching became known as discovery learning and became one of the antecedents of the current constructivist learning initiative.

Workshops and conferences ensured that control over this initiative would not be in the hands of local professional educators but in those of scientists and other academics. The Woods Hole Conference also supported the idea that experts should determine curriculum and educational policy and that the role of the professional educator is to implement that policy. The purpose of education had become the need to achieve the policy goals of the national government, the academics, and the Cold War warriors.

Reform Outcomes and Patterns of the 1950s

The educational reforms of the 1950s reinforced some past reform ideas, reintroduced others, and created some patterns of curriculum and instruction that have continued to the present day. The ferment of change created by the Cold War and the private interests who used the Cold War as an opportunity to promote their vision of education spawned an academic back-to-basics movement as a backlash to life adjustment and progressivism. There were many immediate and long-term outcomes resulting from this reform, outcomes that ranged from changes in curriculum and instruction to changes in who controlled education.

One outcome of the focus on the development of the best and the brightest was the development of the advanced placement program. Through this program students could take college-level courses while in high school that would count toward college credit. This was one example of the effective incursion of the university into the curriculum and instruction of the public schools. Also, research on cooperative learning, critical thinking, problem solving, and discovery learning eventually led to the establishment of formal methods for the use of these learning strategies that were given to classroom teachers through workshops and in-services conducted by academic experts in these techniques. Reforms like these, especially the advanced placement courses, in addition to an emphasis on college-track courses, led to a significant increase in college enrollment in the 1960s and 1970s.

More systemic outcomes resulted from the effort to develop an intellectual elite that would achieve our Cold War objectives and guarantee a continuous supply of academics and technicians. The perceived need to establish an intellectual elite firmly placed control of curriculum and instruction in the hands of the government, the university, and the research centers. Also, academic subjects once again became the foundation of the school curriculum. The need for an intellectual elite prompted a "discovery" of the talented and gifted, which led to legislation and regulatory policies identifying and funding the specialized learning activities needed to develop these human resources. In a sense, this outcome can be seen as the government's effort to channel students (human resources) into different occupations, which in turn would reinforce established social classes.

Another outcome was the shift in control of the curriculum from local control to control by a central authority—in this case the national government and government-sponsored universities and research centers. This shift of control involved the entry of the federal government into education on a massive scale.

In the context of the events before the 1950s, what occurred in the 1950s indicates a pattern in which educational policy reacts to the events that befall the nation and to the beliefs and agendas of interest groups. A related aspect of this pattern is that consequently curriculum, instruction, and more generally the purpose of education are instruments to be used to achieve policies constructed by those who are not professional educators. Another pattern that became obvious at this time is that educational reform is based on which of various conflicting views on the purpose of education and on how society should be defined is dominant, rather than on the utilization of diverse research methods to develop new ways of understanding the purpose of education and understanding how to create an effective and equitable educational system. Also, the old adage that education isn't about children, it is about adults, takes on added validity in light of the reforms of the 1950s.

The Beginning of the Quest for Equity

Another direction of reform, which bore fruit later and significantly affected education in the rest of the twentieth century, began in the 1950s. As the nation hotly pursued excellence, the issue of equity officially became part of the national education agenda in 1954. In a landmark decision, *Brown v. Board of Education of Topeka*, the U.S. Supreme Court decided that the practice of providing "separate but equal" schooling to black and white students was inherently discriminatory. This decision facilitated the equal rights efforts of individuals and groups, and eventually fueled the civil rights movement of the 1960s and 1970s. This Court decision and the ensuing struggle for equity had enduring effects on American educational reform.

THE 1960s AND 1970s

As in the previous decades, the educational system in operation at the beginning of the 1960s, which essentially was a compilation of the previous reforms, was soundly criticized. Also as in the previous decades, new challenges faced America, and again the country looked to education to answer these challenges. Just as the reforms of the 1950s were focused on one theme, excellence, the reforms of the 1960s and 1970s were focused on another theme, equity.

Striving for Equity in American Education

Brown v. Board of Education of Topeka was followed by a series of ineffectual civil rights laws. However, in 1964 the Civil Rights Act became the most significant attempt in American history to ensure racial equity in America. In addition to addressing voting rights, the use of public accommodations, and employment, the act also attacked the segregation of the schools. A very significant aspect of this civil rights initiative was the use of federal appropriations as a lever to achieve educational goals. To receive federal funding, schools had to comply with federal regulations. Title IV of the Civil Rights Act of 1964 empowered government officials to facilitate desegregation. In addition, Title VI allowed the government to withhold federal funds from schools who did not comply.

The Elementary and Secondary Education Act and Compensatory Reform

After President John F. Kennedy's assassination, Lyndon B. Johnson and the Eighty-eighth and Eighty-ninth Congresses passed unprecedented laws that aimed at achieving equity in society through educational reform. The Elementary and Secondary Education Act of 1965 (ESEA) was a part of President Johnson's war on poverty, in which the federal government sought to improve education for the economically disadvantaged and thus break the cycle of poverty. The ESEA provided over $1 billion in federal funds for this purpose. The ESEA provided money for library and instructional resources, the establishment of educational research and development centers, and the strengthening of state departments of education. One of the most famous and enduring programs sponsored by Title I of the ESEA was the Head Start program, which attempts to break the cycle of poverty of disadvantaged children by providing social services as well as early education experiences. During the 1960s and 1970s additional federal monies were allocated for this purpose through the Manpower Development and Training Act of 1962, the Vocational Education Act of 1963, the Civil Rights Act of 1964, the Bilingual Education Programs of 1967 (Title VII), the Economic Opportunity Act of 1968, and the Emergency School Aid Act of 1972.

The term used to define this federal effort was compensatory education. Through federal spending on education, the government aimed to compensate for the economic disparities that existed between the social classes. Title IV of the Civil Rights Act of 1964 authorized a survey to examine the equality of educational opportunity in America. The result of this survey, which was directed by James Coleman, became know as the Coleman Report, submitted to Congress in 1966. This report appeared to undermine the idea of compensatory education as a panacea for inequality, when it reported that there appeared to be no relationship between the quality of facilities and curriculum and student achievement. Therefore, the reason for poor student achievement, which contributed to the unequal status of some groups, could not be corrected by compensatory measures. One outcome of this report was the resurgence of the view, expressed most forcefully by Arthur Jensen, that I.Q. was the reason some people were poor and others rich and that no amount of special support could change intelligence because intelligence was genetic. This view resurfaced in 1994 (during the conservative restoration, as it is known in the scholarly community) with the publication of *The Bell Curve: Intelligence and Class Structure in American Life* by Richard Herrnstein and Charles Murray.

Subsequent reanalyses of the Coleman data indicated that inequality was not racially centered but was the result of socioeconomic status. Since the poor were largely minority students, some individuals used this conclusion to support the federal busing program. One belief underlying busing and various other compensatory programs was that if minority children could acquire the same cultural capital as white mainstream children, then they also would find success in school and in later life. Others pointed out that until adult inequality was resolved, more funding for education would not be an effective way to increase student achievement.

Continuing Federal Reform into the 1970s

Federal involvement in civil rights and economic reforms of education continued in the 1970s with Title IX of the 1972 Education Amendments to the Civil Rights Act. Title IX prohibited discrimination against women in any educational programs that received federal aid. This prohibition included discrimination in all school programs, including curriculum and interscholastic athletics. This support of women's rights in education continued with the passage of the Women's Educational Equity Act of 1974. In addition to women's rights, the Education for All Handicapped Children Act (PL 94–142) reformed the access that handicapped children had to equitable educational opportunities in the mainstream or regular classroom.

Aside from legislative action in the form of compensatory education, the Supreme Court in successive decisions continued to promote desegregation. In 1968, in *Green v. County School Board of New Kent County*, and in 1971, in *Swann v. Charlotte-Mecklenberg*, the Court pushed to have segregation achieved immediately, even if the busing of students was necessary. Further decisions in the 1970s led to court-ordered desegregation of several large metropolitan school districts nationwide. One outcome of these desegregation efforts was the promotion of the magnet school concept, in which certain schools could focus on special programs and so draw a diverse student population.

New Reforms, the Fate of Previous Reform, and the Critics of Education

With the dissent over the Vietnam War and the deteriorating economic system, educational reform in the 1970s faced a new climate. The idealism of the reformers in the 1960s was tempered by national concerns about law and order and unemployment. Also, America was changing. The home and the church, historically two social institutions that provided education and supported the schools, were changing. The supportive relationship between the home and school was declining. In addition, within the schools, teachers were forming labor unions and collectively bargaining with the school districts. Reform was affected by these changes.

An Emphasis on Individualism

In retrospect, some scholars claim that the reforms of the 1960s were focused on the individual rather than on society. Thomas Popkewitz argues that the reforms of the 1960s and 1970s were based on the belief that individuals are independent and that therefore their success depends upon their own efforts (1991). Contrary to this view is the argument that the organization of schools, curriculum, and knowledge handicap some and benefit others. This view argues for a recognition that neither poverty nor low student achievement is an individualistic phenomenon, that rather all members of society share responsibility for these conditions. Systemic discrimination and an inequitable distribution of wealth are as much to blame for an individual's social status as the motivation of that individual.

Innovations in Curriculum, Instruction, and Assessment

The 1960s were a hotbed of innovation. Educational innovation included diverse organizational structures, curricula, and methods of instruction.

Open schools in open space facilities were promoted, along with individualized instruction, as well as small-group learning. Innovations in assessment included pass-fail grades, continuous progress, and mastery learning. Interdisciplinary team teaching was the vogue, with an awareness of the effects of the curriculum, instruction, and assessment on the child's self-esteem. Critical thinking, problem solving, and the use of the scientific method were infused in the entire curriculum. In the 1970s values clarification brought moral development into the curriculum. Mini-courses sprouted in disciplines that formerly consisted of yearlong courses. Advanced placement and college-level courses remained in the curriculum but were diminished in their importance. Student interest was a consideration in any curriculum planning. However, as quickly as these innovations burst upon the educational scene, critics rose to contest them.

Critics of the Innovations

The essentialists saw these innovations as excellence for a few students and mediocrity for the rest. As mentioned in Chapter 1, a radical view maintained that these liberal innovations not only failed to provide appropriate educational experiences but also repressed the children's natural ability to learn. Others saw these innovations as liberal Band-Aids, which did nothing to change the inherent structural and organizational flaws of an oppressive school system. Some critics advocated making fundamental changes in the current structure but keeping the idea of a common school as a free school; however, others felt that compulsory education should be terminated after the primary grades, or that compulsory schooling should be completely abolished.

Stages of Reform

In an attempt to understand the reform initiatives of the 1960s through the 1980s, Michael Fullan and Suzanne Stiegelbauer (1991) have described this period as having four stages. They describe the first stage, during the 1960s, as the adoption stage, during which a plethora of innovations were adopted for use. This was followed by the implementation failure stage, which occurred during 1970 to 1977. During this time the innovations were soundly criticized, and in many cases for good reason. The period from 1978 to 1982 is seen as the implementation success period, in which lessons learned from the failures of the previous stage facilitated pockets of success. As will be explained in the next section of this chapter, the last stage they describe, that between 1983 and 1990, is the intensification versus restructuring stage.

The Failure of the Innovations

What prompted the failure and eventual demise of these innovations? Undoubtedly, many of them were quick-fix, piecemeal changes that did not address the systemic aspect of educational change. As will be explained in Chapter 5, change cannot be viewed as an isolated and decontextualized phenomenon. Any change will affect all other parts of the educational environment and all the individuals connected with the educational system. Piecemeal change and quick fixes cannot offer what is required to sustain educational change. As the 1970s drew to a close, a final attempt was made by President Jimmy Carter to guarantee the reform of our schools. In 1979, President Carter signed into law the creation of the Department of Education as a cabinet-level executive agency. Unfortunately, this act was as controversial as were the other innovations of this time period.

Reform Outcomes and Patterns of the 1960s and 1970s

Keeping in mind that present-day education and educational reform are constructions that comprise the reforms of the past, the reforms of the 1960s and 1970s greatly contributed to our current construction. One significant pattern that emerged in the 1950s, was strengthened in the 1960s and 1970s, and has continued to the present is the ascendancy of the federal government and its related regulatory agencies and research centers as the entities that define educational reform and determine the purpose of education. A significant aspect of this pattern is the use of federal money to force compliance with reforms endorsed by the government. During the 1960s and 1970s, this pattern was based on the belief that the problems of society could be solved through social engineering supported by large amounts of government money.

Another component of this pattern was the shifting of control from the professional educators to the academic expert, again something that started in the 1950s and was strengthened in the 1960s and 1970s. These experts consisted of authorities from other fields such as psychology, science, math, and business, in addition to university professors. A final outcome of the reforms and a related part of the overall pattern of reform activity was the acceptance and promotion of positivism, or the sole focus on the use of scientific reason in the solution of problems, as the dominant cognitive view. One effect of this dominance was the de-emphasis and denigration of indigenous knowledge. Indigenous knowledge is the knowledge gained by educational practitioners and laypeople through their trial-and-error experience with education.

Decisions based on indigenous knowledge are usually intuitive instead of based on research. In a positivistic view there is no room for intuition; only results obtained through the rational application of the scientific method are considered valid.

THE 1980s AND 1990s

After the enervating malaise of the late 1970s, the 1980s started no better. In fact an economic recession achieved unemployment figures of the kind found in a depression. On the global scene America's pride was assailed on numerous fronts. In the 1980 presidential election, the nation overwhelmingly turned to Ronald Reagan to lead them out of this malaise. With Reagan's election began the conservative restoration that reoriented the purpose of education and the definition of reform. Excellence, not equity, was the catchword. Other beliefs that guided the reform of education included a belief in individual responsibility and accountability rather than in collective responsibility for individual and societal problems. Also, a belief in a new federalism attempted to decentralize not only the control of the national government over domestic policy but also controls over the educational system. Finally, there was a return to the belief that the purpose of education is directly linked to the economic and business needs of the nation.

The Influence of Business in Educational Policy

As the nation languished, some individuals and groups targeted education as both the cause and the solution. Many agreed that public education was essential for the well-being of our nation, and many suggested that the purpose of education was to help America compete in the global marketplace. The purpose of education began to shift, from the development of citizens to the development of the human resources needed to regain our place as the world's economic leader. As this economic purpose became entrenched in the minds of the people, businesspeople naturally assumed a larger leadership role in planning the reforms that would take American education into the twenty-first century. With the central goal of preparing workers for our industrial labor force, education once again acquired the trappings of the business world. Total Quality Management techniques and philosophy rapidly spread through the educational community. Business leaders such as Ross Perot in Texas became the leaders of reform commissions and used business beliefs and practices to restructure educational systems and policy.

The specific details of the influence of business on education in the latter part of the twentieth century will be presented in Chapter 4. The involvement of business in education proved profitable for business in many ways. With education focused more on vocational and occupational training, business had to spend less on worker training. Also, to maintain an adequate supply of labor in different business sectors, business could influence the channeling of America's human resources into a service industry pathway, a technical pathway, or an academic and managerial pathway. This channeling was aimed at assuring an adequate supply and distribution of labor. The pathways movement in the early 1990s encouraged children to make career decisions in middle school and follow a related pathway into a job, a technical school, or a university. In addition, schools provided a market for certain businesses. Sports, food, entertainment, and educational support industries were able to secure a foothold in the daily lives of many children while at school. A related outcome was the opportunity for business to train students to be consumers even while attending school. The influence of business in education quickly became an ongoing reality during the 1980s, and it has continued to the present.

Compensatory Education

Compensatory education continued during the latter part of the twentieth century. In 1981, the ESEA was reorganized through the Education Consolidation and Improvement Act (ECIA). The original ESEA programs were maintained in ECIA Chapters, which were organized around such ESEA programs as bilingual education, vocational education, and programs for the educationally handicapped. The most significant change was the consolidation of ESEA funding into block grants to be given to the states. This change ensured more local control over the spending of federal money for educational purposes.

Commission Reports and Reform Initiatives

A Nation at Risk

Fears of the apparent decline of America in the global economy, coupled with the conservative goals of minimizing government control and reproduction of a common culture, led to a plethora of educational commissions that assessed and criticized education. The definitive report of the reform movement of the 1980s was *A Nation at Risk: The Report of the National Commission on Excellence in Education*. The dramatic title emphasized the commission's assessment that the security of the

United States was at risk because of the poor performance of American schools. The commission described the "rising tide of mediocrity" that they declared was now characteristic of American schools. The commission proposed that the threat was so great from this mediocrity that "if an unfriendly foreign power had attempted to impose on America the mediocre educational performance that exists today, we might well have viewed it as an act of war" (National Commission on Excellence in Education 1983, 5).

The commission proclaimed that this "rising tide of mediocrity" threatened not only our very future as a nation and a people, but also undermined our "prosperity, security, and civility" (5). The reference to prosperity in the latter statement was clarified in a report by the Carnegie Forum on Education and the Economy: "America's ability to compete in world markets is eroding. The productivity growth of our competitors outdistances our own. The capacity of our economy to provide a high standard of living is increasingly in doubt" (1986, 2).

The data used to support this assertion were primarily based on student achievement on standardized tests, literacy rates, and the decline in course offerings in the academic disciplines. The commission declared that the school curriculum had become homogenized, diluted, and diffuse to such an extent that schools offered a cafeteria-style curriculum devoid of substantial main courses. Consequently, a foundation of five basic courses was recommended: English, math, science, social studies, and computer science. In addition, instruction in a foreign language was recommended. The commission also recommended that expectations and eventually excellence could be raised by setting clear standards for student achievement and student conduct that could be assessed. Also, more homework and longer school days and years were essential to counteract the perceived mediocrity. Teachers were to be paid more, but in turn they were to work eleven-month contracts. Also, teacher certification needed to be upgraded, and teacher preparation programs needed to be held accountable for their students' achievement.

Commissioned in 1981 by Secretary of Education Terrel Bell, this call for reform unleashed a torrent of criticism of the liberal reforms begun in the 1960s and became a clarion call for a move back to the academic basics and the promotion of a common culture. *A Nation at Risk* was a conservative call to arms for basic skills, national goals and standards, standardized testing, more educator accountability, partnerships between the private sector and public education, and more control of education by state government and business interests. Another effect of *A Nation at Risk* was that it marked the beginning of a plenitude of reports on education that were issued by numerous organizations during the 1980s. The following is a list of the better-known reports:

- ➡ The National Science Board, in *Educating Americans for the 21st Century,* called for more school time allocated for math, science, and computer technology.
- ➡ The College Entrance Examination Board, in *Academic Preparation for College,* called for improvement in reading, writing, speaking, listening, reasoning, math, and study skills.
- ➡ The Education Commission of the States, in *Action for Excellence,* called for minimum competencies in the basics, strengthening gifted education programs, and raising college entrance standards.
- ➡ The Carnegie Foundation for Achievement in Teaching, in *High School,* called for mastery of the English language and basic skills, expanding the academic curriculum, helping students transition from school to work, and strengthening graduation requirements.

Other Reports on Educational Reform during the 1980s

Other reports from the secretary of education, the National Association of Secondary School Principals, The Twentieth-Century Fund, the National Alliance of Business, the National Governors' Association, the Carnegie Foundation for the Advancement of Teaching, the U.S. Department of Labor, and the U.S. Department of Education all called for a diversity of reforms, which included, in addition to those already mentioned, school choice through voucher programs, an emphasis on thinking skills, improvement of textbooks, improving the condition of at-risk children, attending to teenage pregnancy, reducing school dropout rates, increasing adult literacy programs, improving educational leadership, increasing state involvement in education, increasing the quality of the nation's workforce, increasing business support of education, developing national educational goals, and providing a safe school environment (Ornstein and Hunkins 1998).

Mortimer Adler and the Paideia Proposal

In addition to commission reports, there were proposals for action by individuals. In 1982, Mortimer Adler published his *Paideia Proposal,* which proposed a course of study that framed the high school curriculum within the three goals of learning: acquisition of organized knowledge, development of intellectual skills, and enlarged understanding of ideas and values. All students would move through this curriculum, which would be instructionally supported through textbooks, laboratory activities, coaching by the teacher, and use of Socratic questioning.

John Goodlad and A Place Called School

In 1984, John Goodlad reported the findings of a large research project funded by numerous philanthropic foundations and the United States Office of Education. Overall, Goodlad saw a need for a general restructuring of schools as the only way to remedy education's deficiencies. Some of his findings included the need for state governments to clearly articulate academic, vocational, social, civic, and cultural goals with the needs of children in mind, not the needs of adults. He also proposed a decentralization of the school district into a network of self-directing schools, or schools within schools. In this structure, each school in a district would have a significant degree of self-government. Also, individual schools could contain programs that would be different from the curriculum, instruction, and operation of the larger school in which the program would be nested. Goodlad even suggested a restructuring of the beginning and ending ages for children, having children start school at age four and end at age sixteen.

Theodore Sizer and the Coalition of Essential Schools

Another reformer advocated a restructuring of schools. In 1984 Theodore R. Sizer, the head of the Coalition for Essential Schools, proposed a different plan. In a series of books based on the experience and reflections of a fictional teacher named Horace, Sizer discussed the dilemma of the American high school and proposed a redesign of that institution (1984, 1992). Sizer made the following recommendations:

- The central focus of the school for all students should be on the intellect.
- Education should be personalized, in the sense that the strengths and needs of all students should be understood and taken into account.
- The curriculum would consist of three academic areas: Math/Science, the Arts, and History/Philosophy.
- Two diplomas would be offered—a Diploma of Secondary Education and an Advanced Secondary Diploma.
- Students would be required to demonstrate their knowledge

and skills by performing a holistic graduation project called an exhibition. The exhibition would be interdisciplinary, monitored by the whole faculty, and of sufficient size and complexity to showcase the knowledge and skills learned in the academic areas.

•• Program and student assessment would include standardized tests for diagnostic purposes, a student portfolio showing achievement over time, and an outside review or audit of the school's performance.

•• The school would be divided into decentralized and autonomous schools within schools, or houses, with the purpose of promoting personalized interactions between faculty and students.

•• The role of teachers would be to coach more and direct less, in order to encourage students to develop the habit of learning on their own.

Sizer utilized the phrase "less is more" to articulate his basic assertion that the current schools were spread too thin in what they were asked to accomplish and what they offered. Sizer promoted a more intense concentration of intellectual activity, which would result in the child's ability to develop habits of learning and inquiry. Essentially, quality not quantity of learning would guide the development of curriculum.

William Bennett and James Madison High School

In 1987, U.S. Secretary of Education William Bennett, in a book describing a fictitious American high school, proposed a curriculum of high academic standards for all students, except those who would track into vocational and other specialized curricula. Bennett proposed that students should learn a common body of knowledge and skills, develop proficiency in the English language, and learn a common moral and ethical code. Bennett's curriculum was humanistic, in that it required learning the basic disciplines within the context of Western civilization. At this time, Bennett's book aligned with the proposals of other conservative reformers such as Chester Finn and Diane Ravitch.

The Forgotten Half

Another study in 1988 impacted education in the 1990s by suggesting that education had forgotten those students who did not go to college. A report by the William T. Grant Foundation Commission, *The Forgotten*

Half: Pathways to Success for America's Youth and Young Families, focused on the need to train workers for the economy of an information society. This commission proposed that merely providing students with basic skills is not enough to prepare them for the new economy. Instead, the commission maintained that the "forgotten half" needs support from adults and the community, but most important, schools need to provide training opportunities that will help these students transition into the workforce. One result of this report was the creation of the pathway curriculum, in which students in middle school make a career choice and pursue a curriculum track through a post–high school vocational or technical college. The public schools and the two-year technical colleges could form a partnership, in which the high school curriculum would articulate with the college curriculum.

America 2000

By the end of the 1980s, the restructuring of education that was proposed by the previously presented commissions and individuals appeared to have resulted in little or no real change. The term "restructuring" had become a catchall phrase for a myriad of reform initiatives. Schools were burdened with numerous state regulations, and the implementation of mandated reforms appeared to be superficial in many cases. As a response to this criticism, President Bush in 1989 called an education summit of the nation's governors at Charlottesville, Virginia. From this meeting and from a similar one five months later, President Bush proposed six national goals. These goals were to be achieved by the year 2000:

- All children will start school ready to learn.
- The high school graduation rate will increase to at least 90 percent.
- American students will leave grades four, eight, and twelve having demonstrated competency in challenging subject matter, including English, mathematics, science, history, and geography; every school in America will ensure that all students learn to use their minds well, so that they may be prepared for responsible citizenship, further learning, and productive employment in our modern economy.
- U.S. students will be first in the world in science and mathematics achievement.
- Every adult American will be literate and will possess the knowledge and skills necessary to compete in a global

economy and exercise the rights and responsibilities of
citizenship.
➥ Every school will be free of drugs and violence and will offer
a disciplined environment conducive to learning.

The 1989 Charlottesville conference became the basis for *America
2000: An Education Strategy* (Alexander 1991), which was the Bush administration's plan to implement the six goals. The strategy included creating New World Standards and assessing these standards in a nationwide standardized test. Also, 535 New American Schools were to be
created that would spawn a new generation of schools. These schools
would be designed by experts from business, universities, think tanks,
and the professional development industry, and would be funded
through a nonprofit corporation called the New American School Development Corporation. In relation to adult education, business and labor
were asked to identify the skills and knowledge necessary for adults in
the twenty-first century to be productive members of the workforce and
society. Communities were challenged by President Bush to become
America 2000 Communities by achieving the six national goals.

In addition to the six original goals, in 1994 President William
Clinton proposed, as part of the Educate America Act, two more goals:
that parent involvement in their children's education increase, and that
teachers continue to increase their professional skills throughout their
career. One change from the Bush educational initiative was the elimination of the concept of federally supported school choice. Generally,
the Clinton educational strategy continued the promotion of a national
emphasis on meeting the global economic challenges through the development of national standards and accountability measures.

Restructuring, Educational Standards, and Accountability

Waves of Reform

Much of the reform movement during the 1980s has been labeled restructuring because of the attempt to alter basic structures that make up
the educational system. For example, one such structure deals with the
power relationships between the stakeholders within an educational
system. In the factory model of education, power is clearly delineated
and hierarchical, in that it is in a top-down arrangement with school
boards over administrators, administrators over teachers, teachers over
students, and parental involvement limited and controlled by the educators. Some of the restructuring initiatives of the 1980s promoted the

idea of empowering teachers and including parents and the community in educational decision making. Obviously, this kind of change would affect the traditional structure of power arrangements.

Joseph Murphy (1990) identifies three waves of reform in the 1980s—Wave I (1982–1985), Wave 2 (1986–1988), and Wave 3 (1988 into the 1990s). To understand the distinctions between these waves, Murphy uses three metaphors concerning improving transportation. In this metaphor, Wave 1 would consist of fixing the old clunker (repair); Wave 2, getting a new car (restructuring); and Wave 3, rethinking transportation (redesign). According to Murphy, Wave 2 thinking assumes that all of the problems with education are attributable to the structure of schooling and that if the system can be changed, then the problems will go away. A complementary perspective is provided by William Lowe Boyd (1990), who saw the first wave as an emphasis on centralized control by the state governments and the second wave as an attempt to create teacher autonomy, supported by efforts to professionalize teaching through the restructuring of schools. Boyd saw the third wave as a move to more nationalizing and centralizing forces. Boyd proposed that the answer to the dilemma of education in the 1980s was to find a balance between control and autonomy.

Restructuring versus Intensification

Fullan and Stiegelbauer (1991) identify reform in the late 1980s and into the 1990s as a contest between the proponents of restructuring and intensification. Like Murphy, Fullan and Stiegelbauer see a major aspect of restructuring as empowerment of teachers through the development of new teacher roles as mentors, coaches, and teacher leaders. Another essential component of restructuring as they see it was the empowerment of parents through their inclusion in school-based management. In this view, the educational practitioners and community in partnership with the university and business would generate reform.

Intensification involves the "increased definition of curriculum, mandated textbooks, standardized tests tightly aligned with curriculum, specification of teaching and administrative methods backed up by evaluation, and monitoring, [and] all serve to intensify as exactly as possible the what and how of teaching" (Fullan and Stiegelbauer 1991, 7). Restructuring and intensification are philosophically and politically contradictory in relation to the power arrangements within the reform initiative. Unlike the restructuring move to lessen external or centralized control, intensification only empowers educational stakeholders within a tight and restrictive context, with decision-making control firmly in the hands of a central authority. According to this view, more control rather than empowerment assures credible reform implementation. A current example of an intensification strategy is the use of curriculum in which scripts are provided for teachers to recite as they conduct the lesson. The justification for this practice is that the expert-created lessons containing research-based best practice will not be diluted or disrupted by idiosyncratic teacher behavior.

As education moved into the 1990s, through initiatives like America 2000, intensification became the dominant reform philosophy. This philosophy became embodied in the standards and accountability initiatives sponsored by states and the federal government. Through the 1980s and 1990s, Texas developed a highly centralized and intensive standards and accountability system that includes a high-stakes standardized test that all students are required to pass in order to graduate. In the presidential election of 2000, George W. Bush proposed the Texas system as the model for the nation. The fact that the democratic candidate, Albert Gore, did not contest this proposed reform direction indicates that intensification is here to stay for at least some time into the twenty-first century.

Outcomes of the Reforms of 1980 to the Present

School Choice

The differences underlying the reform initiatives of the last two decades of the twentieth century represent a continuation of the philosophical and ideological differences that were evident from the late 1800s up to the 1980s. Because of the inherent political nature of educational reform, critics of the reforms of the last two decades focus not only on the efficiency and effectiveness of educational practice but also on the political effects of both restructuring and intensification. For instance, the school choice movement promoted by the Reagan and Bush administrations has been seen as an attempt to weaken the free common school by channeling public funds to private schools. Some critics claim that America 2000's promotion of school choice will result in a two-tier system of public and private schools, with the private schools funded in part by taxpayer money, a system that will ultimately favor economically privileged students (Brady 1995).

The recent advent of cyber schools is another reform situation that is viewed by some as a threat to the common school. A cyber school is one in which home-schooled students can receive instruction at home through the Internet. Typically, a cyber school is an organization that provides asynchronous programmed instruction via computer. The location of the school can be anywhere. In some states, if a cyber school is chartered by the state, the school districts whose resident students become cyber school students must pay the cyber schools for their services.

Resegregation

One result of the educational reforms during the 1980s and 1990s is the trend toward resegregation of many U.S. schools. Critics of the latest reforms point out that urban schools have been especially affected, with the growing Hispanic student populations becoming as isolated as the African American populations. This resegregation also occurs in rural areas when middle- or upper-class whites move their students into private and parochial schools. Critics call for more emphasis on the establishment of federal magnet schools and federally supported charter schools. They add that government-supported school choice programs would greatly increase the racial and economic isolation of individuals, as well as even further diminish the economic and cultural support for those left in the public schools.

A Culture of Sameness

As previously mentioned, recent intensification reforms have taken the form of the standards and accountability movement. A multitude of standards currently exist in education. The professional organizations of the major disciplines have created their own standards. In addition, some states have mandated standards and accountability measures. Also, to become certified and accredited, universities and colleges must show evidence that they have incorporated in their curriculum, instruction, and university structure the standards of the certifying or accrediting agencies.

The essential outcome of this intensification of knowledge, skills, values, and organizational structure has been a pervasive sameness. The whole point of this kind of technical standard setting and rigidly focused accountability is to create a homogeneity of practice that will allow easy comparison of schools and individuals. The institutionalization of a common core curriculum and its consequent values leads to a common culture.

Critics of this sameness see the end result as a lessening of diversity and creativity, and a return to expert-driven curriculum and instruction, which diminish teacher spontaneity and intuition. In an intensely defined learning environment, there is less personalization of instruction, due to the need to cover the material and the need to teach to the test. Autonomy is lessened and control is heightened when those who are external to the classroom, school, and community define the knowledge base. The focus of schooling shifts to the individual and collective student achievement on the test, away from the needs of the students and the art and craft of the teacher.

Some critics of intensification propose standards of complexity and multiple assessments rather than technical standards and standardized tests. The distinction between these two types of standards and assessment strategies will be discussed in detail in Chapter 7.

A Narrow Focus: The Promotion of Individualism

One foundational belief of the reforms of the last two decades of the twentieth century is the belief in the efficacy of the individual. Whether in a reform context of restructuring or intensification, the belief that the individual is the central focus of reform dominated the reforms of the 1980s and continues to the present. In the restructuring efforts designed to empower educators and community members, the focus of the reform was on the individual. In a standards and accountability system, change occurs due to individual responsibility for student achievement. The individual school districts, administrators, teachers, students, and parents are held accountable for the performance of the students. The problems of education and the solutions for these problems are focused on the innate abilities and performance of individuals. For example, from the mid-1990s to the present, many states have instituted new procedures for the certification of administrators and teachers. The more restrictive process to attain a credential related to education is indicative of the focus on the individual element of the reform process.

Critics of this inordinate focus on the individual claim that old problems will continue to be reproduced and that viable solutions will never be found unless the larger context, in which education is nested, becomes part of the reform effort. This larger context must include the ideological, social, economic and cultural conditions that directly affect communities, schools, teachers, and students. The argument is made that the economic disparity between rich and poor significantly affects the ability of the individual student to learn and to want to learn. The pervasive and intense child poverty throughout the United States also impacts the education of many children and later their performance in the American workplace. The institutionalized racism that persists along with other manifestations of inequity is also part of this expanded context.

The critical point is that those in control of educational reform seldom address this larger societal context, which contributes to the quality of education as much as the motivation and effort of an individual. Dealing with this context would require recognition of education as a political and ideological football, and require a reprioritization of national goals. These critics often claim that throwing more money at education will not significantly change the end result. On the other hand, analyses of successful schools do in fact indicate that they are adequately funded, that the school structure is equitable, that attempts are made to ameliorate the intrusions of the larger context on the school, and that the welfare of the children is the focus of the school.

The proposed educational goals of Presidents George Bush and William Clinton were revolutionary in the sense that they assumed that every child can learn basic skills, essential knowledge, and higher-order thinking skills. The phrase "leave no child behind" became the educational mantra in the presidential election of 2000. However, as we move into the twenty-first century, many critics of current reforms believe that achieving these revolutionary goals is impossible, given the insistence on technical standards and rigid accountability systems and the inability of the reformers to tackle the issues that involve the larger context of educational reform.

REFERENCES

Adler, Mortimer. 1982. *The paideia proposal: An educational manifesto.* New York: Macmillan.

Alexander, Lamar. 1991. *America 2000: An education strategy.* Washington, DC: U.S. Department of Education.

Bennett, Kathleen P., and Margaret D. LeCompte. 1990. *The way schools work: A sociological analysis of education.* New York: Longman.

Bennett, William. 1987. *James Madison High School: A curriculum for American students.* Washington, DC: U.S. Department of Education.

Bennett, William. J., Chester. E. Finn, Jr., and J. T. E. Cribb, Jr. 1999. *The educated child: A parent's guide from preschool through eighth grade.* New York: The Free Press.

Boyd, William L. 1990. Balancing control and autonomy in school reform: The politics of perestroika. In *The educational reform movement of the 1980s: Perspectives and cases,* edited by Joseph M. Murphy. Berkeley, CA: McCutchan Publishing.

Carnegie Forum on Education and the Economy. 1986. *A nation prepared: Teachers for the twenty-first century.* Washington, DC: Author.

Coleman, James. 1966. *Equality of educational opportunity.* Washington, DC: U.S. Government Printing Office.

College Entrance Examination Board. 1983. *Academic preparation for college: What students need to know and be able to do.* New York: College Board.

Conant, James B. 1959. *The American high school today.* New York: McGraw-Hill.

Education Commission of the States. 2002. *Action for excellence.* Online: *http://www.ecs.org.*

Fullan, Michael G., and Suzanne Stiegelbauer. 1991. *The new meaning of educational change.* New York: Teachers College Press.

Goodlad, John I. 1984. *A place called school: Prospects for the future.* New York: McGraw Hill.

Herrnstein, Richard J., and Charles Murray. 1994. *The bell curve: Intelligence and class structure in American life.* New York: The Free Press.

Hirsch, E. D., Jr. 1988. *Cultural literacy: What every American needs to know.* New York: Vintage Books.

Kliebard, Herbert M. 1995. *The struggle for the American curriculum: 1893–1958.* 2d ed. New York: Routledge.

Murphy, Joseph M., ed. 1990. *The educational reform movement of the 1980s: Perspectives and cases.* Berkeley, CA: McCutchan Publishing.

National Commission on Excellence in Education. 1983. *A nation at risk: The report of the national commission on excellence in education.* Washington, DC: U.S. Department of Education.

National Science Board. Commission on Precollege Education in Mathematics, Science, and Technology. 1983. *Educating Americans for the 21st century.* Washington, DC: National Science Board Commission on Precollege Education in Mathematics, Science, and Technology.

Ornstein, Allan C., and Francis P. Hunkins, eds. 1998. *Curriculum: Foundations, principles, and issues.* 3d ed. Needham Heights, MA: Allyn and Bacon.

Paris, David C. 1995. *Ideology and educational reform: Themes and theories in public education.* Boulder, CO: Westview Press.

Popkewitz, Thomas S. 1991. *A political sociology of educational reform: Power/knowledge in teaching, teacher education, and research.* New York: Teachers College Press.

Postman, Neil. 1995. *The end of education: Redefining the value of school.* New York: Alfred A. Knopf.

Sizer, Theodore R. 1984. *Horace's compromise: The dilemma of the American high school.* New York: Houghton Mifflin.

———. 1992. *Horace's school: Redesigning the American high school.* New York: Houghton Mifflin.

Taylor, Frederick W. 1911. *The principles of scientific management.* New York: Harper and Brothers.

Tyler, Ralph. 1949. *Basic principles of curriculum and instruction.* Chicago, IL: University of Chicago Press.

Chapter Three

⚫ Chronology

1837 **Horace Mann.** Horace Mann was an extremely influential educator in the 1800s who championed the creation of schools that would be supported and controlled by the general public. In this year Mann became a member of the newly formed Massachusetts Board of Education. This was the beginning of Mann's efforts to promote the development of free public common schools in America.

1893 **Report of the Committee of Ten.** Charles W. Eliot, president of Harvard University and chairman of the National Education Association's Committee of Ten, issued what has become known as the Report of the Committee of Ten, consisting of recommendations for a national curriculum consisting of a mixture of classical and modern courses for all students. This report is considered the most important manifesto of the early stage of what is called the humanist movement in education.

Early 1900s **John Dewey.** Dewey was an influential philosopher and educator from the late 1800s through the 1930s. Essentially, Dewey was a pragmatic progressive, in that he proposed that children learn most effectively through their own interaction with the environment. Life experiences are an essential element not only in a child's learning but also in the development of citizens for a democratic society. Three of Dewey's better-known books are *School and Society* (1899), *Democracy and Education* (1916), and *Experience and Education* (1938).

Dewey and Thorndike. In the early part of the twentieth century, a debate occurred within education concerning

65

Early 1900s, *cont.*

the foundational nature of educational research. The opposing sides in this debate were represented by the distinctively different views of John Dewey and Edward Thorndike. The outcome of this debate set the tone for the way research, scholarship, theory, and practice have been defined and valued in education. Thorndike, a behavioral psychologist, advocated an experimental scientific and statistical basis for educational research. According to Thorndike, educational research was to follow the established scientific procedures of psychology, and only knowledge gained through quantifiable and statistically verified procedures conducted by certified experts would be considered appropriate as a basis for educational decision making. Dewey envisioned teachers-as-researchers who would generate theory, incorporate it into their practice, and evolve their teaching through an ongoing critique of their theory and practice. In Dewey's vision, teachers would be empowered to scientifically add to the educational knowledge base through their own research. Research conducted by experts external to the classroom would have less value than that of the teachers. Also, qualitative research methods would be appropriate to allow a better understanding of the breadth and depth of an educational phenomenon. Some scholars claim that because the position held by Thorndike prevailed, education has become expert-driven and rigidly hierarchical, and teacher knowledge has been devalued. Also, they claim that another outcome was the separation of the scholar and the practitioner, of theory and practice.

The Laboratory Schools and School-Based Experimentation. In the early 1900s, educational research occurred in university- and school-sponsored laboratory schools. This type of research was supposed to create knowledge about education from the concrete experiences of scholars and teachers in a natural educational setting. Teachers College established the Horace Mann, Lincoln, and Speyer schools to provide an experimental environment that could be used to generate educational theory and train teachers. In 1896, John Dewey established an experimental laboratory school at the University of Chicago. Along with Ella Flagg Young, Dewey promoted a research environment in a naturalistic setting in which teachers could construct, implement, and critique educational theory as it would apply to the practical problems of education. Experimental schools that promoted experimentation in the school environment were sharply criticized by those scholars who saw research as a process that should occur exclusively in the laboratory and be conducted by experts in quantitative research and statistical analysis. Another large school-based research project occurred in the Denver, Colorado, school system under Superintendent Jesse H. Newlon. The focus of this reform was the revision of the curriculum by teachers instead of external curriculum experts.

Early 1900s to the mid-1900s
Child Study and Child Development Movement. During this time period the intellectualism of the humanist movement was countered by the beginning of the child study and child development movement. Led by individuals such as G. Stanley Hall, Charles Francis Adams, and Colonel Francis Parker, the movement advocated application of scientific principles to the study of children. One outcome of this application was the view that children go through developmental stages, and that education should accommodate these stages.

1912
The Principles of Scientific Management. This book by Frederick Winslow Taylor has influenced the structure and administration of American schools for over eighty years. Many reform efforts have attempted and failed to lessen the influence of scientific management on American schools.

1917
Smith-Hughes Act. An act of Congress mandating federal support for vocational education, home economics, and agricultural education in the public schools. This legislation moved the American curriculum away from the academic emphasis advocated by the Committee of Ten.

1918
The Cardinal Principles of Education. Commissioned by the National Education Association in 1913, a committee presented seven principles that came to guide secondary education curriculum for most of the twentieth century.

1918,   These principles were focused on individual develop-
cont.   ment and the socialization of the individual into American society.

1919   **Establishment of the Progressive Education Association.**
This professional organization was devoted to the promotion of the ideals of the progressive movement in education. Members of the organization represented different
beliefs about education, but their commonality lay in their
focus on the child instead of on academic disciplines.

1930s   **The Great Depression.** The collapse of the American economic system resulted in an educational emphasis on life
skills instead of academics. The movement to promote content and skills that would help students survive the economic hard times was called the life adjustment movement.

1938   **The Essentialist Manifesto.** In 1938, at the annual meeting
of the American Association of School Administrators, a
group of educators criticized progressive education and
child-centered activity education. In addition, they advanced the idea of essentialism as the alternative to progressive and child-centered education. They proposed
that essential education involved a focus on the traditional
content disciplines, academic achievement, and systematic and organized learning. They charged that American
education had become ineffective and weak in relation to
academic achievement in other countries.

1947   **Establishment of the Educational Testing Service (ETS).**
The establishment of the ETS solidified the idea that standardized testing should be the primary means to determine admission to undergraduate and graduate university
and college programs. It reinforced the belief that achievement in academic subjects, as measured by a standardized
test rather than other achievement criteria, solely and accurately measured the success of student learning and indirectly the success of the students' schools. The creation
of the ETS also supported the educational reforms that
promoted the idea that school should be focused on the
knowledge provided by the academic disciplines, instead
of on the more progressive foci such as child development,

citizenship development, or life adjustment. In addition, with the advent of the GI Bill and the subsequent increase in the number of individuals who wanted to go to college, ETS provided an efficient way to rank and sort these prospective students into different levels and types of colleges and universities.

1949   **The Tyler Rationale.** Ralph Tyler theorized that all educational activity needed to include setting clear and specific educational purposes, determining the educational experiences necessary to achieve those purposes, creating an organizational plan to enact the experiences, and evaluating whether the purposes had been attained. The Tyler Rationale continues to influence educational practice.

1950   **The Establishment of the National Science Foundation (NSF).** Established by the federal executive branch, the NSF was to grow to be a significant influence on curriculum and instruction. The NSF guided the national educational effort to compete with the Soviet educational system and overcome its perceived superiority.

1954   ***Brown v. Board of Education of Topeka.*** This Supreme Court decision fueled the quest for racial equity that resulted in the civil rights movement. The struggle to remedy the discrimination of the old policy of "separate but equal" education had a profound effect on education. Most obviously, this ruling started the desegregation of American schools. Desegregation directly affected the quality of education for black Americans, whose segregated schools were severely underfunded and inferior to white schools.

1957   **Sputnik.** The successful launching of the first satellite by the Soviet Union provided a focus for the claims already being made by numerous groups during the 1950s that American education needed substantial reform. In addition to the arms race that was part of the Cold War, there was also a race to produce an intellectual elite that could ensure American superiority.

1958   **The National Defense Education Act (NDEA).** The NDEA was America's immediate response to the Soviet threat

1958, cont. embodied in the successful launching of sputnik. The NDEA linked the security of the nation to America's ability to develop math, science, and language skills in American students. Much of the money appropriated for the NDEA was channeled through the National Science Foundation. From a curriculum perspective, the NDEA represented a return to the humanistic and essentialist emphasis on intellectual training.

1959 *The American High School Today.* This report by James Conant supported the humanist position, which promoted the centering of school curriculum on academic disciplines. Conant's report thus supported the Cold War reforms that reemphasized the academic disciplines. Also, in this report Conant called for the consolidation of small school districts, which resulted in many school districts combining into larger districts.

1960 *The Process of Education.* A report by Jerome S. Bruner on the findings of the Woods Hole Conference sponsored by the National Science Foundation. This conference supported the idea of activity learning in children, as opposed to the transmission of knowledge from teachers to passive students. These findings became foundational for activity learning, discovery learning, and constructivist learning.

1962 *Education and the Cult of Efficiency.* Raymond E. Callahan's study of the scientific management of American schools became the basis for subsequent reform attempts involving the structure and administration of schools. Callahan critiqued those practices of school administrators that sacrificed educational goals for the advancement of business practices and purposes.

1964 **The Civil Rights Act.** A broad attempt to ensure racial equality in America, which also included the desegregation of American schools. This act allowed the government to withhold federal funding for education if a school did not comply with both nonbinding and binding federal regulations.

The Great Society. The name given to President Lyndon B.

Johnson's program to promote equality and eradicate poverty in the United States. Out of the Great Society came the legislative reforms of education that created a greater role for the federal government in education. The liberal philosophy of the Great Society became the target of the conservative restoration of the 1980s.

1965   **The Elementary and Secondary Education Act.** Legislation that provided federal funding for schools for the purposes of improving education for all children, helping children break the cycle of poverty, and fighting inequality in the schools. This compensatory program continues to the present, with Head Start as one of the most high-profile ESEA programs.

Mid-1960s   **Man: A Course of Study (MACOS).** In 1959, Harvard psy-
to the mid-   chologist Jerome Bruner led a National Academy of Sci-
1970s   ences study group in the development of this curriculum, based on the findings of the Woods Hole Conference. Intense political resistance developed to MACOS and its attempt to institute a research-based best-practice curriculum. The higher-order critical thinking, collaboration, student participation, inherent constructivism, and general questioning of traditional thought and values involved in MACOS created an intense conservative reaction. Criticism from textbook publishers, anti-Communist zealots, religious fundamentalists, and conservative politicians eventually doomed the project. The MACOS situation impacted educational research, in that a major government research organization, the National Science Foundation, was censored for its initiation and implementation of a politically incorrect research-based educational reform. Because of this political pressure, future reforms were scrutinized for potential political reactions as well as for their validity and effectiveness.

1966   **The Coleman Report.** Authorized by the Civil Rights Act of 1964, James Coleman headed a commission to study inequality in American schools. The resulting report indicated that there was no relationship between student achievement and the quality of school resources and curriculum. This meant that improving schools would not ef-

1966,
cont.   fectively raise student achievement without addressing the issues of poverty. Later interpretations of the report's data continued to indicate that socioeconomic status or social class were better indicators of differences in student achievement than race or minority status. Refer to Berliner and Biddle's 1995 book, *The Manufactured Crisis,* for a detailed critique of the Coleman report.

1969   **The Establishment of National Assessment of Educational Progress (NAEP).** This federally funded program periodically surveys student academic achievement. Designed to be the "nation's report card," the test is given to national samples of students aged nine, thirteen, and seventeen. The test includes mathematics, science, reading, writing, geography, and computer skills, and is administered by the National Center for Education Statistics of the U.S. Department of Education. In 2001, the Bush administration and Congress mandated statewide assessment of educational standards. Each state retained the right to create its own test; however, the NAEP for reading and math would be administered to a sample of fourth- and eighth-grade students in each state every other year in order to verify the results of the statewide assessments.

1960s
and Early
1970s   **Liberal Curriculum Reforms.** This time period was characterized by a liberal vision of curriculum and instruction (C&I). Reforms of C&I included reducing traditional courses to several mini-courses, which students could elect, small-group learning, individualized learning, mastery learning, continuous progress assessment, interdisciplinary team teaching, simulation gaming, and the open classroom. These reforms were supported by open space buildings, open campuses (where students could come and go as on a college campus), and flexible modular scheduling.

1971   ***Swann v. Charlotte-Mecklenberg.*** In this decision the Supreme Court empowered federal district courts to take necessary action to speed up the desegregation of schools. This action allowed the courts to order the busing of students to achieve desegregation.

1972   *Inequality: A Reassessment of the Effect of Family and Schooling in America.* After a reanalysis of Coleman's data, Christopher Jencks argued in this book that poor academic performance was not the result of racial inequality but rather of the social class of the family. The significance of Jencks's argument was that providing more money for schools would not correct the problem of inequality. His argument suggested that the solution lay in a redistribution of wealth in society. Jencks's study has been criticized for its exclusive use of quantitative analysis, ignoring the qualitative aspects of the educational experience.

Education Amendments to the Civil Rights Act. Title IX of this act prohibited discrimination against women in education in schools receiving federal funds. If schools did not comply with federal regulations, they would not receive federal funds. This prohibition included all aspects of the school, such as curriculum offerings and interscholastic athletics.

Creation of the National Institute of Education. The NIE was established to perform the same research function for education that the National Institutes of Health (NIH) perform for the sciences. The NIE was to help solve the problems of education by promoting the establishment of an educational research system and base. Initially, the NIE was adequately funded and assumed the duties of a number of other federal programs; however, the NIE quickly succumbed to the constraints of the 1970s economy and the political manipulation of federally funded research. Almost immediately, the NIE's budget was reduced, and much of the money was micromanaged by Congress, which appropriated the money for specific mandated projects. Because of its initiation by Republican president Richard Nixon, Democratic members of Congress attacked the NIE. The consequence of all these problems was that the NIE never achieved the status or power of NIH or the National Science Foundation. In 1985, the NIE ceased to exist when the Office of Education Research and Improvement absorbed it.

Mid-1970s   **Beginning of the Reconceptualization of the Field of Curriculum.** In the mid-1970s, the reconceptualist movement began in the field of curriculum. These scholars reconceived the study of curriculum as a study of the understanding of curriculum instead of as a study of how to develop curriculum. This movement opposes the narrower technical view of curriculum fostered by the influence of the scientific management of education. One result of the reconceptual view of curriculum is the broadening of the definition of curriculum to include not only curriculum within schools but also curriculum generated by societal organizations and individuals that are external to the schools. Reconceptualists are concerned about the interconnectedness of curriculum within and outside of schools, the hidden curriculum of values attached to all formal curriculum, instruction, and assessment, and how curriculum affects the power arrangements in schools and in the general society.

1975   **Education for All Handicapped Children Act (PL 94–142).** This act established a national policy that guarded children with handicaps against discriminatory policies. This law emphasized the mainstreaming of handicapped students in regular classrooms, and required schools to meet the needs of handicapped students.

1979   **Creation of the Department of Education.** Amid much controversy, President Jimmy Carter signed into law the Department of Education, which had a secretary of education who had full cabinet status. One intent of the department was to give the federal government more voice in education. Prior to 1979, the federal government had an Office of Education within the Department of the Interior; however, its function was essentially to collect and disseminate educational statistics. The elevation of this agency to cabinet status created fears among the conservatives that the federal government would now intervene even more directly in the state and local operation of public schools.

Creation of the Office of Education Research and Improvement. The OERI assumed the research duties and responsibilities of the NIE, which ceased to exist in 1985. Created in a time of budget cuts for education, the OERI never assumed the status of research organizations in other fields. Much of the operating budget goes to specific tasks identified by Congress, with little money going to basic research. In 2000, only 15 percent of OERI's budget went to research.

1981   **The Educational Consolidation and Improvement Act.** The ESEA was revised by Congress to address concerns about waste, inefficiency, program effectiveness, and the growing bureaucracy needed to administer this program. The basic elements of the ESEA were maintained; however, federal funds were consolidated into block grants to the states, which assured greater state control over the disbursement of the federal funds.

1983   *A Nation at Risk: The Report of the National Commission on Excellence in Education.* President Ronald Reagan's Department of Education issued this report on education in America. The National Commission on Excellence in Education determined that many aspects of American society were in jeopardy because of a "rising tide of mediocrity" in education. This report identified problem areas such as lower achievement scores, lower testing requirements, lower graduation rates, lower expectations of students by teachers, and a decline in focus on academics. Essentially, the report proposed that there was an absence of standards in American education, a situation that led to mediocrity instead of excellence. This report set the tone of educational reform for the last two decades of the twentieth century.

1984   **Perkins Vocational Education Act.** This act extended the vocational education reform that began with the Smith-Hughes Act for Vocational Education in 1917. In addition, it extended funding to individuals with handicaps, single parents, and homemakers.

1986   *A Nation Prepared: Teachers for the Twenty-First Century.* The report of the Carnegie Forum on Education and the Economy. This task force, sponsored by the Carnegie Cor-

1986,
cont.   poration, issued a report that was a continuation of the
themes expressed in *A Nation at Risk.* It also called for a restructuring of schools, the establishment of national
teacher standards, the development of lead teachers, aid
for minorities in becoming teachers, and an increase in
teacher salaries. This report contributed to the justification of the current standards and accountability movement.

1989   **Charlottesville Education Summit.** A meeting between
President George Bush and the National Governors Association, which was followed by Bush's response to the in-
adequacies of educational practice. This response was a
six-goal statement covering ensuring children's readiness
for school, increasing graduation rates, insisting on
demonstration of competency in core courses, making
U.S. students first in science and math achievement, increasing adult literacy, and creating schools free of drugs
and violence.

1980s to   **The Standards and Accountability Movement.** As a re-
the present sponse to the perceived decline of American education
and as an extension of the back-to-basics movement of the
1980s, a major reform of education was undertaken. This
reform called for the establishment of technical standards
that would be assessed through the use of standardized
testing. Professional organizations representing the academic disciplines and professional accreditation and certification organizations responded by establishing a diversity of standards for universities and practicing educators.
Most states established content and skill standards for students that were measured by a standardized test. The educational effectiveness of schools and educators on all levels was defined by the results of the standardized tests.

1990s   **Total Quality Management (TQM).** TQM is a business
strategy, whose adoption in education means the incorpo-
ration of business-oriented change techniques in educational change. The purpose of adopting this strategy is to
create an efficient and effective change environment in a
school system. TQM relies heavily on goal setting, periodic
testing to determine goal implementation, and "customer"

(students, parents, community) feedback. TQM is based on the ideas of W. E. Deming.

Professional Development and Teacher Empowerment. During the 1990s, many scholars and professional development consultants promoted the idea of teacher empowerment as an essential educational improvement strategy. Teacher empowerment was defined in various ways, such as teacher collaboration, teacher collegiality, sharing power and authority with teachers, recognition of the complexity of teacher work and roles, and educating teachers as reflective practitioners, teachers as researchers, and teachers as transformative intellectuals. This program of teacher empowerment recognized the importance of involving the local context in educational reform efforts. The teacher empowerment effort was blunted by the technical standards and standardized test movement that began in the 1990s and continued into the early twenty-first century.

1991   **America 2000.** The strategy set by the Bush White House to implement the six goals articulated after the Charlottesville Education Summit. National standards were to be developed, which were to be assessed by a national standardized testing system. Also, 535 new American Schools were proposed that would implement curriculum and instruction developed by research experts, business, and labor. America 2000 set in motion the current standards and accountability movement in American education.

1993 and 1995   ***The Sandia Report* and *The Manufactured Crisis.*** Two major reports that criticized the conclusions of *A Nation at Risk* and other reports critical of public education. These independent researchers challenged the assertions that today's students are less intelligent and know less than those in the past, that the Scholastic Aptitude Test scores have dropped because of the failure of American education, that illiteracy is rising, and that increased funding of education has no positive effect.

1994   **Educate America Act.** President Clinton added two more goals to America 2000 dealing with increased parental in-

1994,
cont.

volvement in education and the continuing professional development of teachers. In addition, federally supported school choice was set aside.

2000

The Presidential Election. This election established that the standards and accountability movement was the politically recognized reform that would dominate education at the beginning of the twenty-first century. Both candidates agreed that education was in need of reform and that a system of testable standards was the key to successful change. The advocacy of this reform by both political parties and their candidates prevented a public conversation about the complexity of the problems of American education and the nature of reforms needed.

2001

National Education Summit. Governors, business leaders, and educators made a commitment to develop more and better standardized tests, establish more stringent accountability measures, and improve teaching. The summit, which was organized by IBM chairman and CEO Louis V. Gerstner, Jr., called for raising academic achievement while closing the achievement gap separating the educational haves from the have-nots. To accomplish this dual purpose, the summit called for the creation of new tests, providing curriculum to teachers, paying accomplished teachers more to work in low-performing schools, and creating high standards for those who want to become teachers.

The Bush Education Plan. With support from both parties, Congress passed the education plan of President George W. Bush. Known as the "Leave No Child Behind Act," the plan required millions of school children to take annual standardized tests; for the first time their scores would affect how much federal funding schools would receive. Supporters of the plan reiterated their assertion that public education had failed. The law also required schools to create plans that would close the achievement gap between students. Schools are to be compared through "report cards" that will show the schools' achievement on standardized tests. The law contained specific language, to the point that one section mandated that students with limited English skills would have to be tested in English after living in the United States for three consecutive years, and another mandated a reading program favored by Bush. Despite a tutoring addendum that required schools to fund the tutoring and transportation to agencies and schools that provide tutoring for students with persistently low scores, some conservatives criticized the exclusion of federal support for private school vouchers. Opponents of the law, such as the National School Boards Association, the National Conference of State Legislatures, the American Association of School Administrators, and the National Education Association, criticized the law because of the overall lack of federal funding. Critics claim that the low level of funding, combined with the increased costs to school districts to meet the program demands of the law, will force states and school districts to spend millions more at a time when their revenues are shrinking. In addition, the act attempts to define quality educational research as solely science-based quantitative research.

2002   **Landmark Supreme Court Decision on School Choice.** In June 2002, the U.S. Supreme Court in a 5 to 4 split decision along ideological lines upheld the school choice program of the Cleveland public schools. The Court's conservative majority upheld the constitutionality of Cleveland's use of public funds to provide vouchers to children to attend private or religious schools. The Ohio plan is a six-year-old pilot program that provides $2,250 in tuition assistance to 4,000 elementary students to attend private schools or suburban public schools. None of the suburban schools agreed to participate in the program, and according to an editorial in the June 28 edition of the Harrisburg *Patriot News*, 99.6% of the students participating in the program attend religious schools.

REFERENCES

Berliner, David C., and Bruce J. Biddle. 1995. *The manufactured crisis: Myths, fraud, and the attack on America's public schools.* Cambridge, MA: Perseus Books.

Bruner, Jerome S. 1960. *The process of education.* Cambridge: Harvard University Press.

Callahan, Raymond E. 1962. *Education and the cult of efficiency: A study of the social forces that have shaped the administration of the public schools.* Chicago: University of Chicago Press.

Carnegie Forum on Education and the Economy. 1986. *A nation prepared: Teachers for the 21st century.* Washington, DC: Author.

Conant, James B. 1959. *The American high school today.* New York: McGraw-Hill.

Jencks, Christopher. 1972. *Inequality: A reassessment of the effect of family and schooling in America.* New York: Basic Books.

National Commission on Excellence in Education. 1983. *A nation at risk: The report of the national commission on excellence in education.* Washington, DC: U.S. Department of Education.

Sandia National Laboratories. 1993. Perspectives on education in America: An annotated briefing. *Journal of Educational Research* 86 (5): 259–310.

Tyler, Ralph. 1949. *Basic principles of curriculum and instruction.* Chicago: University of Chicago Press.

Chapter Four

☙ The Politics of Educational Reform

As discussed in Chapter 1 and as is evident in the history of educational reform given in Chapters 2 and 3, education has always been viewed by political, economic, and ideological interests as a means of promoting their agendas. Whether for profit, equity, national security, or the reproduction of the status quo, the youth of America have been and continue to be seen as part of a possible solution to the problems of others. To enhance an understanding of the historical and current efforts of these interests, as they attempt to influence society through education, and for the sake of a deeper understanding of the framing questions posed in Chapter 1, this chapter will go more deeply into these interests and their respective agendas. First a more detailed account of the three basic perspectives, conservative, liberal, and radical, will be given, and then the agenda of each will be considered in the context of the culture wars, market-based reforms, and school choice. Also, the political role of the teacher unions will be discussed.

CONSERVATIVE, LIBERAL, AND RADICAL PERSPECTIVES ON EDUCATION AND REFORM

The Conservative View

Sometimes the best way to define a position is to identify those who support that position. In this case, the high-profile politicians and intellectuals who promote the conservative view of education include numerous individuals with ties to the Reagan and Bush administrations of the 1980s and early 1990s, and to the current Bush administration. Some of the more vocal proponents include Terrell Bell, William Bennett, Alan Bloom, John E. Chubb, Chester Finn, E. D. Hirsch, Jr., Terry M. Moe, and Diane Ravitch.

The conservative view of society and education that all these individuals share is focused on the development of a common culture and advocates a minimalist role for the federal government in society and education. They also share a primary foundational belief in individual responsibility and accountability. A common culture entails a society that has an agreed-upon set of values, beliefs, and knowledge, to such an extent that homogeneity is prized and difference devalued. Cultural uniformity of this type implies the acceptance and reproduction of traditional values, as defined by those individuals who hold power and constitute the mainstream. Those who differ from this mainstream are considered of marginal importance.

The values, beliefs, and knowledge involved are essentially Judeo-Christian, Eurocentric, and patriarchal. Conservative educators, such as Edward A. Wynne, Kevin Ryan, and William K. Kilpatrick, are vociferous and direct in their promotion of a tradition drawn from Western Europe, a culture that is essentially Christian and historically male-dominated. The promotion of these values and this knowledge base is facilitated by a reliance on positivistic methods that adhere to the reason and rationality that have characterized Western enlightenment thought. The lack of a scientific foundation for non-Western cultural traditions and knowledge results in a devaluation of indigenous knowledge (see Glossary).

The common culture promoted by conservatives when they are in control defines the purpose of education, educational reform, and the need for education in terms of that common culture. Thus the conservative definition of the common culture shapes students' understandings of non-Western cultures and different viewpoints. For example, in *High School,* a report published by the Carnegie Foundation for the Advancement of Teaching, Ernest L. Boyer (1983) devotes a chapter to the core curriculum, which is defined as the Western canon. Boyer promotes the need for a common cultural literacy similar to that later defined by E. D. Hirsch, Jr. (1988), in his *Dictionary of Cultural Literacy.*

Along with the conservative belief in individual responsibility and accountability and in accordance with a strict interpretation of the U.S. Constitution is the belief that the involvement of the federal government in the lives of individuals is supposed to be minimal. The social reforms and compensatory educational initiatives promoted by the federal government during the 1960s and 1970s were especially antithetical to the belief in the primacy of individuality and personal accountability. This belief in the efficacy of the individual is rooted in the rugged individualism, Social Darwinism, and capitalism that were especially characteristic of the United States in the 1700s through the early 1900s and which had a resurgence in the late twentieth century. In the context of this individualism, educational problems are individual and intellectual in nature and should be dealt with on an individual level.

This narrow focus minimizes the larger and systemic social context in which a problem is nested. Proponents of this view argue that progress in society and in education occurs when individuals are held accountable for their actions and learning. In this view, the focus of reform is on the individual, not on government involvement. Likewise, the interplay of free market forces, such as competition, is appropriate for education as well as for society as a whole.

According to the conservative view, the organization and operation of schools and educational systems should be hierarchical in organization with clearly defined roles, should contain transmissional curriculum and instruction (see Glossary), and should be precise and accountable in their assessment of stakeholder performance. A hierarchical organization implies a chain of command that extends from a state education regulatory agency to the school board and eventually to the students, who are the least empowered and the most controlled. Power arrangements are clearly delineated so that all know their place, and one's identity is linked to one's position in the hierarchy. The nature of authority at every level in the school system is authoritarian, rather than a facilitating, empowering, negotiating, and sharing leadership model. The hierarchy approximates the social class arrangement of society, in that students are tracked according to future occupational roles and according to academic and social performance. Some degree of heterogeneous grouping may occur in the less essential courses within tracks, but an emphasis on tracking in math, science, and English means a course-scheduling situation that inevitably creates a degree of tracking within other disciplines.

The transmissional nature of a conservative view of curriculum and instruction requires the teachers to emphasize a core curriculum that promotes the values, beliefs, and knowledge that are acceptable to the dominant culture. Teachers are seen as technicians, with clearly defined and limited power over the determination of curriculum and instruction. Their primary responsibility is to effectively transmit the core curriculum to the students. Paulo Freire called this transmission of knowledge the banking method of education, in which facts are deposited by the teacher into the minds of the students (1996). To ensure the effective transmission of the core curriculum, teacherproof curriculum packages are developed, scripts are prepared for teachers to use, and professional development is geared to the best instructional practices in line with this view of curriculum and instruction.

Within a transmissional model of schooling, assessment relies upon empirical data gotten through quantitative methods that can be used to rank and sort students. Standardized tests can conveniently provide this type of data, which then can be used for placement within the hierarchically organized school. Decisions about placement in course tracks, matriculation within the system, and future occupations can be expedited with test results. In addition, test results can be used to assess the performance of individual teachers and schools. From this rating, teachers, administrators, and schools can be compared and ranked.

The alignment of core curriculum content with the test questions helps define classroom curriculum and instructional procedures. In this system, proponents of standardized testing suggest that the most efficient pedagogical strategy is to teach to the test and to use instructional techniques that best accomplish the transmission of the content. The ideal pedagogical situation is one in which the curriculum that is written is the curriculum that is taught and tested. If a high-stakes exit-level test were used, a test that must be passed by the student in order to graduate from the program or school, the scope and sequence of the entire curriculum would be aligned to maximize student performance on the exit-level test. The success of the alignment would be determined by student performance on the exit-level test.

Within this conservative view of schooling, when is reform necessary and how will this reform be defined? Simply, reform would be necessary when current curriculum does not reflect the core curriculum of the dominant culture, when instructional and assessment procedures are deemed ineffective in promoting the core curriculum, and when social, economic, or political situations provide a window of opportunity to further the general conservative view.

The Liberal View

Using the conservative view as a basis for comparison, certain similarities and differences become apparent that help explain the liberal view. Immediate differences become apparent in liberal beliefs concerning culture, government involvement, and responsibility and accountability. The liberal view values cultural diversity, in that racial, ethnic, and gender differences are perceived as valuable influences on American culture. Like the conservatives, however, liberals believe that a common culture exists and that all can participate in it if there are equal social and educational opportunities. Liberals believe that a common culture can be constructed that is devoid of race, gender, and class inequality. This common culture is again based on a Eurocentric view of values, beliefs, and knowledge.

Liberalism is based on the faith in reason and reverence for rationality of the Age of Enlightenment. The end result, belief in the desirability of a common culture, is the same as the conservative view, but the reasons that result is seen as desirable are different. Liberal educators argue that a common culture is needed to unify the diversity that is always inherent in American society and to maintain the Western values, beliefs, and knowledge that have always dominated American society. The difference between the liberal and conservative position lies in the liberal belief that there is a social responsibility to remedy the inequitable differences in the ability of people to become part of and gain the benefits of the common culture, whereas conservatives believe that progress is achieved through the personal actions of an individual within the context of a common culture.

A shift in focus from the individual to the group or society is one of the main differences between the conservative and liberal views. The social and educational reforms of the 1960s and 1970s were based on the liberal view that society is responsible and should be accountable for the inequalities that inhibit individuals who are different from the dominant group from becoming part of the common culture. Another major difference between the two views is the role played by the federal government in dealing with inequality. In the liberal view, the government should be directly involved in helping individuals attain common culture status. This view was represented in the Great Society endowment programs of Lyndon Johnson and in the compensatory educational initiatives of the 1960s and 1970s. Unlike the laissez-faire beliefs of the conservatives, the federal government is seen as ideally an active participant whose responsibility is to equalize the playing field for all and provide assistance to those who are disadvantaged and underprivileged. (Ironically, in the conservative administration of George W. Bush in the beginning of the twenty-first century, the intensive intervention in education by the federal government has resembled the intervention of the liberal administrations during the 1960s.) In any case, the goal of the liberals is the same, to promote a common culture, albeit one that recognizes the diverse cultural heritages of the various groups in America.

Conservative curriculum instructs students about other cultures with the focus of the instruction on the implications of the non-Western culture for the dominant Western culture. The non-Western culture is studied within the context of and compared to the values, beliefs, and knowledge of Western culture. The non-Western culture only has value in relation to the West. A liberal curriculum instructs students about other cultures in a similar manner but also promotes a broader awareness of the non-Western culture. Cultural elements such as dress, food, music, and language are celebrated. However, the liberal assumption is that although non-Western individuals should value their historical heritage, they should adhere to American values, beliefs, and knowledge, as defined by the dominant culture. The primary educational goal for both liberals and conservatives is for non-Western individuals to become Americans, as defined by those who control society.

Within the liberal view, the organization and operation of schools and educational systems remain hierarchical in structure and organization but tend to promote more empowerment opportunities for the stakeholders. Even though the principal is the primary individual who is held accountable for the school, power is shared with the teachers, students, and parents. These individuals are allowed limited voice and decision-making opportunities. This was evident during the curriculum reforms of the 1960s and 1970s in the promotion of mini-courses, flexible school schedules, elective courses, open campuses, parent involvement initiatives, and student rights initiatives. Instructional activities, such as team teaching, teacher-generated materials, discovery learning, cooperative learning, values clarification, individualized instruction, inquiry methodology, simulation gaming, and high-interest educational materials, all reflected this attempt to interest, empower, and involve students. However, the goal of these practices was to help individuals assimilate the common culture as represented by the values, beliefs, and knowledge that would lead to cultural uniformity at the cost of the richness provided by diversity. Also, policy decisions were still made by those individuals at the top of the hierarchy.

Assessment during this liberal period of education included empirical testing (i.e., standardized tests) but also included multiple assessments that included mastery learning, peer- and self-evaluation, pass-fail grading, and portfolio assessment strategies. Student assessment included grade point average, class rank, SAT scores, and performance on a myriad of diagnostic tests, but also included more subjective measures characterized by less scientific, mathematical, and verifiable analyses and reports. However, the object of assessment was still to measure the attainment of the values, beliefs, and knowledge of the core curriculum proposed by the dominant culture, and to allow the ranking and sorting of students.

Liberals believe that reform is necessary whenever individuals fail to become part of the common culture due to inequities created by society. In this view, reform is defined as the necessity for all Americans to eradicate this inequity, especially through the involvement of the federal government in educational policy and practice. Individual responsibility is recognized but is viewed as secondary to the responsibility of society to correct lack of progress toward cultural uniformity.

Once again, the liberals share with the conservatives the same historical view of what it means to be an American—a view that is essentially Western, patriarchal, and Judeo-Christian. The version of the liberal view just described is characteristic of the progressives during the first half of the twentieth century. Those who focused on child development, or the solution of societal problems through a progressive view of education, were working to promote the melting pot idea of American society, an idea that was based on the development of a common American culture that would reproduce an inherently Western culture. In the liberal progressive view of society, educational reform would result in a uniformly Western American culture in which individuals of all races, ethnicities, and genders would have equal opportunity to reap the benefits and rewards of a common American culture.

The Radical View

As suggested in earlier discussions of radical ideas about educational reform, the radical view is not a uniform view. The radical view of education encompasses a diversity of views that range from those who would deschool society, lessen the capitalistic and market-oriented influences on education, promote an egalitarian and emancipatory systemic view of education, to those who would promote a pluralistic and critically multicultural society through common public education. The following are some commonalities in the contemporary radical literature and research, all found more in the conversation of the scholarly educational community than in the educational practice of the public schools.

Concerning the purpose, necessity, and definition of educational reform, the radical view significantly differs from the conservative and liberal views. The basic beliefs of the radical position create a totally different vision of what ought to be the purpose of schools and educational reform. One fundamental belief is that all meaning is constructed through social interactions within the setting or place where the interactions occur. In other words, during these interactions the participants create their own reality. Radicals contest the idea that meaning or reality can be transmitted by teachers to students. Proponents of this view argue that students create their own meanings, not only from the formal school curriculum, but also from the hidden curriculum they encounter within the school and from other sources in society. This view not only opposes the idea that values, beliefs, and knowledge can be transmitted to students from teachers, but also proposes that students and teachers need to develop critical and reflective skills that allow them to identify and critique the transmitted curriculum. Put simply, radical reformers see culture as something that is produced, and they oppose the reproduction of the dominant culture.

The radical view proposes that if schools are sites where meaning is negotiated, than how power is arranged between the stakeholders is a critical concern. They argue that if schooling serves the purposes of the dominant class (for example, the reproduction of Western, white, patriarchal culture), then oppression will occur. They propose that not only are those individuals who represent subordinate groups (for example, nonwhites, females, the poor) oppressed, but that the oppression extends to all other students. All students are viewed as oppressed when a cultural transmission model of education is employed. In this case, radical reformers see the current purpose of schooling as serving the interests of the dominant class. Therefore, educational reform is necessary to offset the oppressive tendencies of schooling. A radical definition of educational reform involves action that will counteract this oppression.

The purpose of education, according to the radical view, is emancipatory: Because schools are sites of cultural struggle, students and educators can be empowered to resist the oppressive tendencies of the dominant culture. Radicals maintain that schools can become sites of social change rather than sites where one cultural view is oppressively reproduced. They argue that this emancipatory purpose can be achieved through a curriculum that promotes a critical consciousness through the development of collective and self-critical skills in students and educators.

Ira Shor refers to critical consciousness as the way that we see ourselves in relation to knowledge and power in society (1992, 129). Shor identifies four qualities of critical consciousness: power awareness, critical literacy, permanent desocialization, and self-educational organization. Shor proposes that through critical thought, writing, reading, and speaking in which they go beyond the surface meanings of what is presented to them in schools, educational stakeholders can become aware of all aspects of how power is arranged and how it affects their lives. He proposes that the development of these skills will allow stakeholders to understand and challenge the artificial and political limits on their development. In addition, these critical skills and the awareness that informs them will facilitate self-organized cooperative action against the oppressive structures in the school.

Another aspect of radical reform is the importance of developing the ability to critique history and its connection to popular culture. Radicals argue that oppression is rooted in how history is constructed and presented to students by those who are in control of the curriculum. To radicals, history is critically important because they see no separation of history and contemporary social conditions. History permeates all human activity. Radicals argue that to become empowered requires a critical knowledge of the foundations of the present, and the acquisition of the critical skills that can facilitate a deconstruction of the past and the present.

Radicals also attempt to uncover, through cultural studies, how popular culture is used to reinforce oppressive beliefs. The radical position maintains that current representations about the past and present need to be critiqued to allow an emancipatory future. Radical critique of the past and the present is intended to uncover the contradictions inherent in an oppressive society. For example, radicals see a contradiction when mainstream groups contend that their actions are creating an equitable mainstream culture, when in actuality their actions create marginalized subordinate groups who experience discrimination in some way.

Another basic belief of radical reformers is that understanding cannot occur when only positivistic techniques are used. Since positivism assumes an objective and verifiable reality, positivistic thinking devalues subjective ways of understanding and explaining reality. Positivistic investigations into the identification of truth and meaning are usually quantitative in nature rather than qualitative. Consequently, they tend to deal only with facts, rather than drawing on intuition built upon individual and collective experience. Chapter 6 goes into detail on this difference between positivistic and radical views of research.

Another radical belief mentioned above is that schools can be sites of transformation. Henry Giroux (1988) argues that through the development of a critical consciousness, teachers and students can transform themselves and their schools into agents of radical change. As transformative intellectuals, these stakeholders can uncover oppression in their schools and create schools as sites of participatory democracy. As transformative intellectuals, they will have the critical ability to see the complex political, economic, and cultural structures that contribute to the oppressive tendencies of their school and society.

As mentioned, there are different radical positions. Some radicals criticize others as critiquing society from a Western patriarchal position, and in doing so, perpetuating Western oppression of non-Western cultures. Others maintain that it is not possible to transform existing schools, and therefore the current public school system needs to be dismantled. Others emphasize the importance of the individual in combating oppression, while yet others argue for a greater federal presence.

However, all radicals view current education as being held captive by the dominant culture, which oppresses those individuals who are different.

The radical position concerning educational reform differs markedly from the liberal position. Radicals value diversity and promote a pluralistic society in which the common good is a dynamic and continuously negotiated concept. Like conservatives and liberals, the radicals recognize that education is the critical institution in the promotion of their definition of society. Contrary to the Western, patriarchal, and Judeo-Christian vision of society promoted by the conservatives and liberals, radicals see a pluralistic society in which all individuals—regardless of race, gender, social class, lifestyle, sexual preference, religion, and age—share power and equitably reap the benefits of a participatory democracy. Therefore, their definition of educational reform is constructed to promote their unique view of what the common culture should be.

THE CULTURE WARS

Culture *wars?* The military metaphor may be a bit melodramatic; but for a decade these so-called wars have indeed agitated the American educational scene, remolding curriculums, revising canons, perplexing administrators, infuriating alumni, and otherwise disturbing the peace. (Schlesinger 1998, 149–150)

Arthur M. Schlesinger, Jr., is describing a major aspect of the politics of educational reform. Since the 1960s, educational reform in America has been and continues to be greatly affected by the culture wars, which continue to rage. In this war, each person's position on this issue, wherever he or she is situated, on the right (conservatives and reactionaries) or on the left (liberals and radicals), represents a different purpose for education and a different definition of educational reform. This section will bring out the common ground between liberals and radicals, and the opposition of conservatives and reactionaries to both liberal and radical reforms.

This political activity is referred to as the culture wars because the battle is over which vision of culture will dominate American society. As previously explained, the fundamental difference between left and the right involves whether a common culture, which assimilates groups who differ from the established culture, or whether a multicultural view, which values difference and diversity, becomes the dominant culture. The issue of the promotion of a common or diverse culture becomes even more complex because of the different positions of the liberals and radicals on the issue of multiculturalism. Joe L. Kincheloe and Shirley R. Steinberg (1997) detail the distinctions between conservative multiculturalism/monoculturalism, liberal multiculturalism, pluralist multiculturalism, left-essentialist multiculturalism, and critical multiculturalism. On the political spectrum, the right and the left represent many different degrees of reactionary, conservative, liberal, and radical thinking.

During the ferment of the 1960s and early 1970s, those on the left gained influence and subsequently promoted liberal reforms of education. As previously described, increased federal involvement, especially in the area of compensatory educational reform, characterized the liberalism of the time period. In addition, the thriving radical counterculture greatly influenced all aspects of the status quo, including not only music and dress but also fundamental values, beliefs, and concepts of the nature of knowledge. All of the primary societal institutions were affected, including religion, family, and education.

As the liberal agenda played out in relation to race, gender, social class, and environmental and global consciousness, one consequence was that the educational reforms of this time period became associated not only with the mainstream liberal agenda but also with the intentions of the radical counterculture. Reforms such as the open classroom, open campus, flexible scheduling, individualized instruction, minicourses, interdisciplinary teaching, whole language, the New Math, and inquiry methods were viewed as radical, as revolutionary and culture-changing reforms. From a pedagogical perspective, the efficacy of traditional schooling was challenged and, in many cases, the liberal reforms replaced traditional methods. Concurrently, the acceptance of conservative views declined in the face of the ascendancy of liberal influences on American culture.

The economic malaise of the 1970s after the end of the Vietnam War facilitated the conservative restoration and the rise of the new Right. With the conservatives firmly in control of the government, the liberal elements in American culture were attacked. In 1983, *A Nation at Risk* spread the battle between conservatism and liberalism to education. The prolonged and significant control of the government by the conservatives during the 1980s and early 1990s forced the Democratic Party to move toward the right in its political platforms. Seen in relation to the liberalism of the 1960s, the Clinton administration successfully gained and retained control of the executive with a less-than-liberal position. The significance of this Democratic position was that educational reform continued a conservative direction, which has been maintained by the George W. Bush administration. Individuals on the left, both liberals and radicals, argue that during the last two decades the purpose of educational reform has been to purge education of the liberal reforms of the 1960s and promote conservative values, beliefs, and knowledge in the schools.

Aspects of the liberal agenda influencing American culture through the curriculum of education that many conservatives found unpalatable were humanitarianism, globalism, and multiculturalism. Two different factions emerged on the political right to oppose these tendencies, one consisting of mainstream conservatives and the other aptly named the religious right.

Mainstream conservatives, as well as some mainstream liberals who had become more conservative, were concerned about the threat to the perceived continuation of a common culture with uniform values, beliefs, and knowledge. Their criticism of the schools focused on the pursuit of excellence in a competitive global market, but it also focused on the perceived threat posed by multiculturalism. Some argued for a strict return to a curriculum that promoted only "American" culture, while others argued for a curriculum that would teach a respect for other cultures but result in a uniform culture. Books espousing these views had titles like *The Menace of Multiculturalism* by Alvin J. Schmidt (1997) and *The Disuniting of America* by Arthur M. Schlesinger, Jr., quoted above, the first edition of which appeared in 1992.

Proponents of a return to traditional American culture focused a great deal of their activity on education. Two books that are characteristic of this position and their subsequent reform initiatives are *Learning from the Past: What History Teaches Us about School Reform,* edited by Diane Ravitch and Maris A. Vinovskis (1995), and *New Schools for a New Century: The Redesign of Urban Education,* edited by Diane Ravitch and Joseph P. Viteritti (1997). In these books, the basic themes of conservative educational reform are presented in chapters promoting the privatization of public schools, the reduction of the role of the federal government in education and the ascendancy of state and parental control, various forms of school choice, the proposition that professional educators are the problem, the promotion of individual responsibility and decision making, the promotion of assimilation into a uniform culture, the establishment of national goals, and the promotion of various kinds of standards and accountability procedures. The same themes are reiterated in *Education Reform in the '90s,* edited by Chester E. Finn, Jr., and Theodor Rebarber (1992).

Another aspect of the culture wars of the last two decades has involved a more reactionary group called the religious right. Members of this conservative faction have directed their activity toward the reestablishment of Protestant Christianity in the public schools and the channeling of taxpayer dollars to private and parochial schools. To the religious right, current educational practice shaped by liberal reforms have promoted secular humanism and multiculturalism. The religious right argues that both are a threat to the traditional Protestant Christian values, beliefs, and knowledge that should be inculcated in students. They argue that multiculturalism is especially threatening, because the tolerance required for different races and ethnicities would be extended to gays and lesbians. Some of the major proponents of this position, organizations that have provided leadership in defining the agenda of the religious right and focusing political activity, are Phyllis Schlafly's Eagle Forum, Pat Robinson's Christian Coalition and American Center for Law and Justice, Citizens for Excellence in Education, and Mel and Norma Gabler's Educational Research Analysts. *School Wars: Resolving Our Conflicts over Religion and Values,* by Barbara Gaddy and her colleagues (1996), is a book that provides comprehensive information on this topic.

The religious right has aggressively moved to block even moderately liberal educational reforms. Their political activity has been directed at numerous targets, ranging from censoring school library books and influencing textbook selection and course content to organized opposition to outcome-based education, an initiative proposed by Theodore Sizer, head of the Coalition of Essential Schools, and to any other curriculum or form of instruction that they see as threatening their values.

One example of a major battle in the culture wars involved the national history standards developed by the National Council for History Standards (NCHS) (1996), and the standards for social studies developed by the National Council for the Social Studies (NCSS) (1994). In 1994, both sets of standards were issued, after being created over a period of years with input by classroom practitioners and university professors. For various reasons both were immediately targeted by the religious and mainstream right as containing inappropriate content and skills. The right objected to references to multiculturalism, globalism, and critical thinking. The history standards were criticized for "rewriting history." Opponents to the standards supported this accusation with an analysis of the standards, in which they claimed that too much attention was given to individuals and groups who played an insignificant role in American history and that many of America's traditional heroes were shortchanged. The opposition of the right to the history and social studies standards gained national prominence through the news media. Their opposition resulted in revisions of the standards and a limited use of the standards by school districts. One detailed perspective on this battle is presented in *History on Trial: Culture Wars and the Teaching of the Past* by Gary B. Nash, Charlotte Crabtree, and Ross E. Dunn (2000). Sources representing the view of the right are listed in Chapter 10.

In this culture war, opponents of the right are an eclectic group that includes radical university scholars, professional educational organizations, and liberal and radical interest groups that seek to promote their agendas in the public schools. The right also opposes groups who promote sex education, environmental education, the teaching of evolution (in the case of the religious right), bilingualism (see Glossary), whole language (see Glossary), critical thinking, and multicultural education. Language is a key issue in this war. Proponents of English-only immersion strategies contest the landscape of language in public schools with the proponents of bilingualism. Related to the issue of language is the issue of learning styles. Proponents of multiculturalism propose curriculum and instructional strategies that enhance indigenous culture and promote the development of a pedagogy that also develops the students' thinking, speaking, and learning in their home language or dialect. In this context, learning becomes a political issue that both sides contest. Additional references concerning the position of both sides are available in Chapter 10.

MARKET-BASED REFORM

Another component in the understanding of the politics of educational reform involves the influence of business and industry on educational reform. The issue is not whether business is an influence on educational reform but rather the extent and purpose of the involvement of business in American educational reform.

Throughout the years, business and industry have contributed time and money to public education. From large foundations to small local businesses, the economic sector has been represented on educational commissions, university boards of trustees, and local school boards. Those who view the purpose of education as a support institution for business and industry support this involvement. Those who see the purpose of education as preparing critical citizens for involvement in a participatory democracy find elements of business involvement problematic.

In the last two decades, beginning with the conservative restoration, business and industry have forged new relationships with education. Besides performing an advisory function, providing student scholarships, and engaging in local curriculum efforts such as the Junior

Achievement Program, business has come to more aggressively see education as a market, and educators and students as consumers. In addition, since the 1980s, change strategies and techniques used in business and industry have been applied in attempts to change education. One example of this influence of business ideas on educational reform is the Total Quality Management (TQM) initiative.

Total Quality Management

In the early to mid-nineties, hundreds of schools adopted what were considered state-of-the-art business management procedures packaged as TQM. Based on the ideas of W. E. Deming (1986), TQM is considered a double loop system, in which schools set goals, implement them, evaluate them, and use the evaluation feedback to make adjustments to the reform initiative. In this linear change system the direct connection of goals and results is critical. The nature of the goals and achievement of the results are mediated by stakeholder or customer feedback loops, in which data are solicited from the stakeholders of the system. In TQM systems, administrators become quality control engineers, and teachers and students are held responsible for their part in the achievement of the reform. In the 1990s, the techniques of TQM were seen by some as efficient strategies in the implementation of the outcome-based assessment reform and the standards and accountability initiative. TQM's focus on efficiency and accountability in the reform process is better facilitated by objective forms of assessment such as standardized tests, rather than subjective forms of assessment such as portfolios and journals. In a TQM system, decisions are solely based on data rather than relying on intuition based on experience. Rational decisions (based on statistical theory and techniques) must be routinely made that control for any variations in the implementation of the reform.

Proponents of TQM claim that this system can effectively solve both instructional problems (such as low student academic achievement), and noninstructional problems (such as student attendance problems, vandalism, and school dropouts). TQM proponents see schools as systems in which all aspects of the environment can be defined, quantified, and controlled. Opponents of TQM argue that successful schools are vibrant communities that are complex in their nature and activity, and evolve through trial and error rather than through a completely conscious decision-making process. A comparison of TQM systems thinking and community building will be detailed in Chapter 5.

The Influence of Business Consultants on Education

Business influences on educational reform have continued through the application of the ideas of business consultants such as Peter M. Senge, the director of the Center for Organizational Learning at the Massachusetts Institute of Technology. Senge represents an established trend in which the ideas about how to create change come from business and management experts and are promoted as viable change strategies for public schools. For instance, in 1990 Senge published *The Fifth Discipline: The Art and Practice of the Learning Organization.* This highly popular book promoted a change model that was heavily business-oriented, and it quickly became a staple in many education courses. In 1999, Senge's *Fifth Discipline* franchise continued with a more detailed how-to-do-it book entitled *The Dance of Change: The Challenges to Sustaining Momentum in Learning Organizations.* Other examples of the influence of business consultants on educational change include Margaret J. Wheatley, *Leadership and the New Science: Learning about Organization from an Orderly Universe;* Jeffrey Goldstein, *The Unshackled Organization: Facing the Challenge of Unpredictability through Spontaneous Reorganization;* and Ken Baskin, *The Corporate DNA: Learning from Life.* Occasional best-sellers from the business sector that are used by some educators to understand change include *Zapp! In Education* by William C. Byham and *Who Moved My Cheese?* by Spencer Johnson. The previous examples are a small sample that illustrate the highly lucrative incursion of business and management consultants into education.

The Privatization of Public Schools

Another example of the invasion of the schools by business practice is the involvement of business in the conservative attempt to privatize public schools. Traditionally, some businesses, such as Sylvan Learning and Kaplan, have provided remediation services for students who have academic difficulty, who desire to accelerate their learning, and who need to prepare for standardized tests required for entry into college programs. Recently, in concert with the current privatization movement, businesses have expanded the services they offer to the degree that some public schools have been placed under the control of educational businesses.

One high-profile educational business is Edison Schools, Inc., operated by Whittle Communications. Edison, a for-profit school organization, which included Chester Finn as a founding member and which was initially supported by Time Warner and Phillips Electronics, proposes that through the use of efficient business procedures, education not only can be better but also economically profitable. Edison Schools has approximately 75,000 students in its more than 130 schools in 22 states. One current example of the politics behind the use of for-profit businesses in educational reform is the hostile takeover by the state of Pennsylvania of the Philadelphia public school district. The Philadelphia public school system is currently the largest school system ever run directly by a state government. It is the nation's seventh largest system, serving approximately 200,000 students, with an annual budget over $1.5 million. Prior to the Philadelphia school takeover, the Harrisburg public schools and the Chester-Upland school district in suburban Philadelphia were taken over by the state. The Harrisburg schools were placed under mayoral control, and nine of ten Chester-Upland schools are under the control of Edison.

In Pennsylvania, two laws enacted by the state legislature provide the legal basis for the takeover of schools by the state. Act 46, passed in 1998 when the former superintendent of the Philadelphia School District threatened to close the schools if the state did not provide more funding, empowered the state of Pennsylvania to hire for-profit and nonprofit organizations to take over the administration of low-performing schools. In addition, the Pennsylvania Education Empowerment Act, passed in 2000, set a three-year limit, after which low-performing schools that had not improved their test scores would be taken over by the state.

The Republican governor and Republican-controlled legislature of Pennsylvania base their assumption that for-profit schools can provide a better education than some current public schools on the claims of for-profit companies like Edison Schools, Inc. Chris Whittle, the CEO of Whittle Communications and Edison Schools, Inc., argues that Edison has the capacity for cutting-edge research, administrative efficiency, and long-term stability. Edison claims that technology can be provided for the schools at a level above current use, and that back-to-basics programs can raise academic achievement as measured by standardized testing. In addition, higher test scores and financial stability can be achieved through more frequent teacher evaluations, intensified training of teachers in test-related basic skills, a longer school year, and a longer school day. Administrative efficiency is achieved through the reduction of teaching staff, hiring low-wage replacements for unionized workers, and the privatization of noninstructional services.

In the Philadelphia situation, Edison has claimed that $40 million can be saved through the privatization of noninstructional services.

They further argue that additional efficiency can be achieved through the elimination of unnecessary expenses and nonessential services, both of which would be defined by Edison. As an example, in their assessment of the Philadelphia schools, Edison reported that significant money could be saved if the district's cleaning staff would cover more square footage per person. Opponents of the takeover indicated that the Edison data were based on a national average of an eight-hour workday instead of the five-hour workday of the Philadelphia staff.

One example of the Edison strategy in the Philadelphia situation is Edison's proposal to use a reading program called Success for All. In this program, all teachers receive intensive training in phonic skills and age-appropriate writing and reading skills. Then each day for ninety minutes all teachers, regardless of their discipline, engage students in small groups in structured reading-related activities. Opponents of the takeover of the Philadelphia schools claim not only that there is nothing cutting edge about this reading program and that results are inconclusive, but that more affluent suburban school districts do not use the program because they do not consider it a quality program. Henry Giroux, a leading radical critic of the politics of market-based initiatives, characterizes this type of curriculum and instruction as a return to the authoritarian classroom, characterized by transmission, standardization, and control.

The conditions that led to this state action were low student test scores, a chronic teacher shortage, deteriorating school buildings, and a $216 million budget deficit, expected to reach $1.5 billion by 2006. The demand by the city for additional state funding prompted the legislative action by the state government. Besides enacting the 1998 and 2000 laws, then governor Tom Ridge hired Edison, for $2.7 million, to make recommendations for the improvement of the troubled 264 schools containing 210,000 students, of which 80 percent are minorities.

Based on the Edison report, Governor Mark Schweiker first recommended that universities, community groups, and private companies run approximately sixty of the worst performing schools. He proposed that a private company should administer the school district, a change that would have led to the privatization of about fifty-five top administrative positions within the district. He also proposed that Edison would be the ideal company to run the district. In addition, Schweiker also asked the state and city to contribute an additional $75 million to offset the deficit. His plan also asked the city to commit to a $300 million bond issue to offset future deficits. In the event of a takeover, state law required a five-member school-reform commission to replace the elected school board, in which the governor could appoint four of the five members.

The Republican governor's plan, made possible by the legislation of the Republican-led legislature, immediately drew opposition from many sources, including the democratic mayor of Philadelphia. Besides the very vocal and tenacious opposition of Mayor John F. Street, organized opposition also arose from the city council, the school board, community groups, parents, students, a service employees union, and the teacher union. Over a period of weeks hundreds of students marched in protest. Two lawsuits were filed, by the Coalition to Keep Our Public Schools Public and the Philadelphia chapter of the National Association for the Advancement of Colored People, challenging the constitutionality of the legislation and attempting to block the takeover. As a result of this protest, Schweiker amended his proposal to hire Edison as the central administrator. Under the revised recommendations Edison would function as a consultant to the administration, provide services, and be hired to run some of the schools. It has been estimated that Edison could receive as much as $40 million for its role.

The Deeper Issues of the Privatization of Public Schools

An examination of the politics of the privatization reform of public schools uncovers deeper political issues. First, in the Philadelphia case study, opponents of the reform questioned what would happen if another company absorbed Edison, which is a common occurrence in the corporate world. Those opposed to the takeover noted that Edison had recently absorbed another for-profit company, Learning Now, and that a third company, Mosaica, had dropped out of the Chester-Upland takeover. The result, they reported, was a monopoly of services by Edison. They used these events to contest Edison's assertion that long-term stability could be maintained by privatization. A second problem involved the membership of the five-member commission. Opponents cited the fact that one member of the control board over the Chester-Upland district was a lawyer and businessman who financially contributed to the campaign of former governor Ridge and then lieutenant governor Schweiker. They pointed out that the names being suggested to make up the board consisted of businesspeople, lawyers, and politicians, but no educators.

More foundational issues were also brought up by the opposition. Numerous groups cited the inherent disparity between the funding of schools representing a lower socioeconomic constituency and those that were more affluent. Their oppositional commentary stressed that in a democracy, education is a right, not a privilege, and that there was a substantial lack of commitment on the part of the state to equitably fund education for all children, whether rich or poor. Some critics cried "taxation without representation" in relation to the Schweiker-appointed commission's ability to levy taxes without any accountability to state and local elected officials, taxpayers, and parents. Also, opponents of privatization note the whole justification for privatization is based on the need to improve academic achievement as measured by performance on standardized tests. In this context, school success does not include how effectively the public schools meet the social service functions that are required of them or the academic objectives that cannot be adequately assessed through standardized testing.

In a critique of the restructuring movement, of which privatization is a central theme, Joseph Murphy and Philip Hallinger (1993) provide this analysis: They maintain that privatization as a reform of education focuses on the apparent dysfunctional nature of public schooling, promotes the power of competition as a panacea, promotes the deregulation of public education, and attempts to transfer billions of dollars from the public to the private sector. Murphy and Hallinger further note that "the glue that holds all of the components in this theme together is accountability" (9).

Channel One: Students as Consumers and Schools as New Markets

The politics of market-based reform also means that businesses have targeted students within the confines of the school environment, treating them as potential consumers. Corporate logos abound in schools, with Coke and Pepsi vying for soft-drink monopolies in public schools on all levels. The Nike swoosh is ubiquitous on sports uniforms, and the winning soft drink is prominent on sports scoreboards and in the school cafeteria. Product advertisement dots school corridors, lunchrooms, and school stadiums. The major benefit for the school is an additional source of funding.

In addition to funding, the case of Channel One illustrates how schools can receive free technology by allowing advertisers access to the students. Channel One is a commercial venture founded by Chris Whittle that provides schools with free VCRs, televisions, and satellite dishes if the schools guarantee that all students will be required to see a daily ten-minute news program consisting of reporting on current events and advertisements geared to the youth market. Proponents maintain that this is a viable way for cash-strapped schools to gain needed technology. Opponents criticize this attempt to sell products to captive student audiences. They argue that students are uncritically exposed to the hidden curriculum, which accompanies the selected news and consumer products.

Neil Postman (1995) characterizes this invasion of consumerism in the public school as worship of the god of consumerism. Postman argues that this market intrusion in the public school is not an educational reform, as proposed by the proponents of market-based reforms, but a reinforcement of the message of the need to consume that bombards students before entering school and continues in their lives outside of school. From his radical position, Postman contests the message of consumerism, which postulates that you are what you accumulate. Postman further argues that education does not serve a public but creates a public. If Postman is correct, then the involvement of business in public schools greatly reinforces the market orientation of our society.

The positions of Whittle and Postman are obvious examples of the values, beliefs, and knowledge earlier discussed in the sections describing conservative and radical ideology, and of how these ideologies play out in the public schools.

SCHOOL CHOICE AND THE POLITICS OF EDUCATIONAL REFORM

As indicated earlier, school choice was suggested as a viable reform of education as early as the 1960s. In 1962, the conservative economist Milton Friedman, in *Capitalism and Freedom,* advocated a voucher system that would allow all parents to select their child's school. At this time, Friedman's position was supported by the radicals who saw the deschooling of society as the only viable reform of education. Choice initiatives continued during the 1970s, but they only gained wide currency with the conservative restoration of the 1980s. With the support of the Reagan administration, the idea of school choice as a substantial and probable educational reform became a mainstream possibility and a staple of right-wing political platforms.

Generally, school choice proposals fall into three categories: districtwide, statewide, and private school choice (Carlson, 1996). Districtwide school choice allows parents to select schools within their school district. Magnet schools, charter schools, and cyber schools are examples of the kind of alternative schools that can be chosen with districtwide choice. These schools can accommodate a mix of student abilities and interests, or provide a specialized educational experience for a particular kind of student, such as gifted students or dropouts. Statewide school choice allows parents to select schools within the boundary of their state. Private school choice allows parents to send their children to nonpublic schools, such as independent schools, Catholic schools, Protestant Christian schools, and home schools. With the recent Supreme Court decision upholding the right of public schools to initiate voucher systems that allow public money to pass to private schools, many states are poised to implement voucher systems that will make possible private school choice.

School choice reform initiatives are financed by taxpayer dollars. With school choice funded by voucher programs, parents are given a stipend from the federal, state, or local government, which can be used to offset the tuition of the school of their choice. Another form of financing parental choice involves the establishment of tax credits. In the case of choice within a public school system, as with charter and magnet schools, there are no additional costs for parents, since these schools are already publicly funded. In relation to vouchers, the bottom line is that public tax money would flow from the public schools to the private schools.

The issue of school choice is highly political. A quick search of any of the media will uncover a plethora of sources explaining and supporting all of the positions on school choice; the underlying basis of all these arguments is purely ideological in nature. For the purposes of this book, instead of a detailed analysis of all the various arguments for and against school choice, the essential points will be made by contrasting the right-wing, or conservative, position with the left-wing, or liberal and radical, position.

The arguments of the conservatives who are for school choice and against the existing public school structure coalesce into the patterns of thought previously discussed. The competition inherent in the free enterprise system and a market economy is proposed as the solution to the perceived shortcomings of the current public school system. To bring the competitiveness of the market system into education requires a reduction in the control of education by the national government. For instance, instead of allocating dollars for specific federally directed compensatory programs, educational efficiency would grow as a result of competition between the schools for taxpayer dollars, which would now be controlled by the parents instead of doled out by the federal government. Also, in keeping with the philosophy of individualism, parents should have the right to decide what their child learns, how their child learns that curriculum, and where that child learns it. Those on the right further maintain that if parents want to sustain a Eurocentric belief system and to incorporate religion in their child's education, then they should have that right and therefore should have the ability to place their child in an educational situation conducive to their desires.

Finally, if parents believe in the efficacy of a transmissional curriculum and instructional pedagogy, then they should have the opportunity to enroll their child in a school that provides that type of pedagogy.

Left-wing arguments against school choice follow a similar ideological pattern. Liberals and radicals argue that market forces are inappropriate for education and inevitably result in social and economic inequity. Government influence in education is necessary because without it not all children will have an equal education, which will have deleterious effects for our democratic society. They argue that America has a collective social responsibility for all Americans, and that the national government must be a powerful advocate for the disenfranchised and marginalized. Liberals argue that without a well-funded educational system and without the federal government as an overseer, our common American culture will not be maintained. Radicals argue that school choice will lead to a two-tiered society, divided between the economically affluent and the economically disadvantaged. They propose that the result of a two-tiered society will be the establishment of an elitism that privileges those in the dominant tier over the others. In addition, instead of embracing the strength that can be derived from cultural diversity and difference, society will be Eurocentric and patriarchal, thus losing the richness provided by a multicultural society. True, the two-tiered society and the Eurocentric and patriarchal perspective are already present, but they argue that this situation is exacerbated when elite students are able to go to schools that reinforce Eurocentric and patriarchal values. Finally, radical educators decry regressive transmissional curriculum and instruction and see the public schools as the appropriate venue for the promotion of progressive curriculum and instruction that will facilitate the kind of society they envision.

The basic foundation of the school choice issue is ideological. Both sides are ardent in their beliefs and aggressive in their attempts to attain the type of schools that can lead to a society that mirrors their beliefs. This ideological contest involves one important question: Will the common public school remain in its current form, or will school choice change what has been the fundamental structure of American education for the last 150 years?

TEACHER UNIONS AND THE POLITICS OF EDUCATIONAL REFORM

Teachers are also participants in the politics of educational reform. As representatives of teachers, teacher unions extensively lobby on their behalf on the national and state levels. However, the impact of teacher unions on local education is chiefly mediated by the collective bargaining process. The two main organizations that support collective bargaining for teachers are the National Education Association (NEA) and the American Federation of Teachers (AFT). Established in 1870, the NEA was primarily concerned with curriculum until the rise of the teacher unions in the late 1960s and early 1970s. While still considering itself a professional association, the NEA does engage in union activity. The AFT was established in 1916 as an affiliate of the American Federation of Labor. The AFT gained significant power as a union when laws were passed allowing teachers to bargain and strike. Currently, approximately 90 percent of all teachers belong to either the NEA or the AFT. The AFT alone has a membership of approximately 875,000 teachers.

Despite the large membership and elaborate organizational structure of the unions, some argue that unions have had little impact on educational policy outside the area of teacher salaries, benefits, and working conditions. The teacher contracts negotiated by the NEA and AFT are still largely like those produced by the industrial unionism of the early 1900s. The contracts are periodically negotiated by district bargaining units and result in comprehensive legal agreements, dealing only with economic issues and working conditions, that are binding for a fixed period of time. In addition, they contain grievance procedures and spell out some kind of arbitration that can be used to resolve disagreements between the teachers and the school district. These contracts rarely deal with curriculum, instruction, or school community issues.

Despite the adversarial nature of collective bargaining, this process of negotiation is looked on favorably by many in positions of power in the educational system because it reinforces the top-down hierarchy of management and power arrangements, and guarantees the district a stable workforce. In addition, financial compensation for all employees of the district, including administration and support staff, is indirectly efficiently regulated by the negotiated teacher contract. However, despite the relative stability fostered by collective bargaining, many argue that it is not really being well used, because it has had no effect on other educational outcomes.

This lack of influence over issues unrelated to teacher economic needs is the result of the continued lack of empowerment of teachers. Many individuals have pointed out that this lack of power in the workplace is reinforced by the inability of the unions to expand their negotiations to noneconomic issues such as curriculum and instruction. Traditionally, unions have accepted the exclusion of teacher involvement in policy making because conventional wisdom has been that policy is the job of the administration. Therefore, as waves of reform have washed over education, teachers have only been participants in a limited and contrived manner dictated by district administration. The argument has been made that teacher associations and unions have had little impact on educational policy because of this lack of empowerment.

Recently, the NEA and AFT have been calling for a "new unionism." The purpose of this initiative is to enhance the professionalism of educators, and to focus on student achievement. Throughout the United States, there are numerous professional development initiatives sponsored by the unions. One such initiative is the Teachers Union Reform Network, which is a consortium of union leaders dedicated to creating union involvement in professional development. Traditionally, school administration has been responsible for planning and implementing professional development, and for requiring teachers to be accountable for implementing what they learn. To change this situation and to empower teachers, this network is proposing union-sponsored training and evaluation of the implementation. Some schools in this network are working with districts to develop and incorporate in their teacher contracts core concepts that will improve teacher quality and empower teachers in curriculum-related decisions. Unions are also looking at accountability measures such as peer review to create teacher-generated accountability.

Despite this recent movement toward union involvement in non-economic areas of teaching, unions still have little impact on educational policy making. Occasionally, local unions will become politically involved in a local or state issue; however, the educational policy decisions that have resulted in the cycles of reform have largely been initiated by world events, politicians, university scholars in diverse disciplines, and individuals in the private sector. The result is that, collectively, teachers are generally not participants in policy decisions.

To put the matter in its political context, teacher unions represent labor, and their school districts represent management. As in all labor and management contexts, teacher unions are part of the constituency of moderate and liberal Democrats. Teacher interests inherently mediate teacher union political positions on all issues. However, as the "new unionism" shows, teacher unions are sensitive to the changing conditions of their profession as well as to the political positions of the general public. Also, just as the political influence of labor has declined within the last two decades, so has the influence of teacher unions in the national and state political arenas.

In conclusion, this chapter has described the political context of educational reform, showing the ways groups on all points of the political spectrum attempt to promote their religious, ideological, economic, or cultural agendas through their control of education. The target of this control is the process of educational reform. In order to realize its political goals, each group needs to control the process of reform. Control over the process of reform means that the group is in position to initiate reform that is beneficial to the group's agenda, and select the object of reform that can best result in outcomes favorable to the group. The complexities of the reform process and the attempts to control this process are the subject of the next chapter.

REFERENCES

Boyer, Ernest L. 1983. *High school: A report on secondary education in America.* New York: Carnegie Foundation for the Advancement of Teaching, Harper and Row.

Carlson, Robert V. 1996. *Reframing and reforming: Perspectives on organization, leadership, and school change.* White Plains, NY: Longman Publishers.

Deming, W. E. 1986. *Out of the crisis.* Cambridge, MA: MIT, Center for Advanced Engineering.

Finn, Jr., Chester E., and Theodor Rebarber, eds. 1992. *Educational reform in the '90s.* New York: Macmillan.

Freire, Paulo. 1996. *Pedagogy of the oppressed.* New York: Continuum.

Friedman, Milton. 1962. *Capitalism and freedom.* Chicago: University of Chicago Press.

Gaddy, Barbara B., T. William Hall, and Robert J. Marzano. 1996. *School wars: Resolving our conflicts over religion and values.* San Francisco: Jossey-Bass Publishers.

Giroux, Henry A. 1988. *Teachers as intellectuals: Toward a critical pedagogy of learning.* Westport, CT: Bergin and Garvey.

———. 1994. *Disturbing pleasures: Learning popular culture.* New York: Routledge.

Hirsch, E. D., Jr. 1988. *Dictionary of cultural literacy: What every American needs to know.* New York: Vintage Books.

Kincheloe, Joe L., and Shirley R. Steinberg. 1997. *Changing multiculturalism.* Philadelphia: Open University Press.

Murphy, Joseph, and Philip Hallinger. 1993. *Restructuring schooling: Learning from ongoing efforts.* Newbury Park, CA: Corwin Press.

Nash, Gary B., Charlotte Crabtree, and Ross E. Dunn. 2000. *History on trial: Culture wars and the teaching of the past.* New York: Vintage Books.

National Center for History in the Schools. 1996. *National standards for history.* Los Angeles, CA: National Center for History in the Schools.

National Council for the Social Studies. 1994. *Curriculum standards for social studies: Expectations of excellence.* Washington, DC: National Council for the Social Studies.

Postman, Neil. 1995. *The end of education: Redefining the value of school.* New York: Alfred A. Knopf.

Ravitch, Diane, and Maris A. Vinovskis, eds. 1995. *Learning from the past: What history teaches us about school reform.* Baltimore: Johns Hopkins University Press.

Ravitch, Diane, and Joseph P. Viteritti, eds. 1997. *New schools for a new century: The redesign of urban education.* New Haven: Yale University Press.

Schlesinger, Arthur M., Jr. 1998. *The disuniting of America: Reflections on a multicultural society.* 2d ed. New York: W. W. Norton and Co.

Schmidt, Alvin J. 1997. *The menace of multiculturalism: Trojan horse in America.* Westport, CT: Praeger.

Shor, Ira. 1992. *Empowering education: Critical teaching for social change.* Chicago: University of Chicago Press.

Senge, Peter M. 1990. *The fifth discipline: The art and practice of the learning organization.* New York: Currency Doubleday.

Senge, Peter M., Art Kleiner, Charlotte Roberts, Richard Ross, George Roth, and Bryan Smith. 1999. *The dance of change: The challenges to sustaining momentum in learning organizations—A fifth discipline resource.* New York: Currency Doubleday.

Sizer, Theodore R. 1984. *Horace's compromise: The dilemma of the American high school.* New York: Houghton Mifflin.

———. 1992. *Horace's School: Redesigning the American high school.* New York: Houghton Mifflin.

Chapter Five

●◆ The Process of Educational Reform

Previous chapters have made clear that a study of the history of educational reform reveals the inherent and pervasive political activity involved in the perception of a need for reform, in the way reform is defined, in the selection of the object of the reform, and in whether a reform is sustained. This chapter considers the process of educational reform: who initiates reform, how reform is implemented, and what the basic elements of the reform process are.

INITIATING EDUCATIONAL REFORM

In the previous chapters, we have seen that numerous groups attempt to promote their own interests by influencing the purposes, the organization, and the structure of schools. However, once those who can mandate the reform agree upon a reform, who then initiates the implementation of the educational reform? This question is an important one because the beliefs, knowledge, and skill of those who will have to implement the reform will alter the original intent of the reform. In other words, the original nature of a government mandate will change to accommodate individual interpretations and local contexts. In some cases, those who must implement the reform may disagree with the purpose of the reform and therefore implement the reform in such a way as to dampen the intended effect of the reform. Even if those who must implement the reform agree with the reform, they may still modify the intended effect as they strive to accommodate the idiosyncrasies of their local educational environment. Those individuals and organizations who hold the responsibility for initiating a reform are as important in the realization of the purpose of the reform as are those who mandated the reform. Historically, many reforms have been mandated, but few have been sustained for any significant period of time. Understanding the process of reform is the key to sustaining a reform.

Who then is responsible for initiating reform? Those who have the most direct responsibility for initiating a reform include national and state governments, statewide regional educational support groups, individual schools, universities, and textbook publishers. Those who have a more indirect effect on the initiation of reform include private interest groups and the media.

As seen in the history of educational reform, the national government has been an active agent in the promotion of educational reform. Its involvement in the actual process of reform implementation has varied throughout the years. In some instances, the role of the government in reform implementation has been restricted to merely providing statistics and information that could be utilized by state, local, and private reformers in their attempt to implement reform. In other cases, the federal government has provided funding earmarked for specific reform purposes but has left the actual implementation of the reform to others, as in the case of the establishment and funding of the National Science Foundation (NSF).

In relation to reforms dealing with equal opportunity, the federal government has, in some cases, been more directive and controlling in how the funds should be disbursed. In these cases, the federal government has affected the implementation of a reform by mandating the withdrawal of funding if the implementation does not follow the federal guidelines attached to the funding.

More recently, under the George W. Bush administration, the government has provided more specific direction about the exact nature of a reform and how to implement it. In the educational reform legislation of 2001, the federal government identified specific reforms (for example, mandating annual testing of all children in grades three to eight, providing tutoring for children in persistently failing schools, and setting a twelve-year timetable for closing chronic gaps in student achievement) and expanded government influence in implementing the reform. This expanded influence is given effect by tighter and more specific government regulations monitored by the Department of Education. In addition, federal influence in implementing the reform is also transferred to the states, by allowing the states considerable discretion in managing the federal money provided for the reform.

The initiation of educational reform is more directly the constitutional responsibility of the states. Historically, state governments have established the general parameters for the educational missions of their school districts and have allowed the local districts the freedom to implement the state regulations within the context of their local communities. States have traditionally established specific regulations and monitored their implementation in areas such as teacher and adminis- trator certification, student attendance, and the election of school boards. More recently, states have sought more control over the initia- tion and implementation of educational reform; for example, many states have mandated educational reform in the form of a standards and accountability program. At the turn of the twenty-first century, state- initiated reform in many states has been characterized by an identifica- tion of basic skills and knowledge that all students should know, to be assessed by a standardized test.

In addition to the national and state governments, local schools can initiate educational reform. The school board and superintendent may establish a reform as districtwide policy, or the principal and fac- ulty of a specific school may initiate reform in that school. Also, local reform can be initiated by regional educational support organizations established by the state. Whether initiated by the local school or a re- gional support organization, these reforms are usually geared to chang- ing specific instructional techniques, rather than to making more sweeping changes in the purpose and the organizational structure of a school.

Universities also can initiate reform through the curriculum pro- vided in teacher and administrator certification programs, and in the graduate programs that provide professional development courses for practicing educators. In addition, through their own research projects, university educators can attempt to initiate change in local schools. Some universities attempt to initiate change by example, through the innovative practices found in university-sponsored private laboratory schools and charter schools, and by direct action, in university and school partnerships.

Textbook publishers are also a source of reform. How the text- books are structured, the curriculum that is included, the skills that are promoted, and the hidden curriculum of values and beliefs attached to the text content may all be elements in reform promoted by textbook publishers. In most cases, the reforms that are promoted by the pub- lishers are affected by the demands of the consumer. In some cases, the textbooks used in all of the schools in a state are purchased by the state. This practice provides that state with an inordinate amount of leverage in determining what content is appropriate and, more specifically, what content should not be included in the text. Providers of educational re- sources other than textbook publishers also can promote their view- points through their materials.

Also, private interests and professional organizations may at- tempt to initiate reform through the direct lobbying of government agencies and officials. However, they are more likely to be effective if they establish organizational networks that have the resources to provide professional development services and materials to schools and individual teachers. They may also provide instructional materials that promote their reform ideas.

On a personal level, individual teachers and parents may also initiate reform. Through their own professional development, action research, and cumulative experience, teachers may attempt to incorporate new content, instructional techniques, and values in their own classroom. Due to the isolated work environment of teachers, these reforms are invariably limited to the individual's classroom. Of course, the ability of teachers to initiate reform is severely constrained by the mandates of those who are more powerful, and by the diverse requirements placed on the teacher by national and state governments, school district policies, and building principal mandates. Parents, whether as individuals or as a member of a parent-teacher organization, are even more limited in their ability to initiate reform. Parental involvement in reform tends to be restricted to reactions to reform initiated by the previously mentioned groups, or to providing support through parent-teacher associations.

Governments, schools, universities, textbook publishers, private interests, and individual educators—some educational scholars argue that the serious initiation and subsequent implementation of educational reform requires a coalition involving all or at least a majority of these groups, a coalition in which each member is a willing, empowered, and committed member of the change initiative. Any analysis of the history of education will show that this vision rarely becomes a reality on a large scale. Some reformers propose that educational change is a process, not an event. Therefore, they view reform as a process that requires a long-term shared commitment on the part of all of the stakeholders in the educational system that is undergoing the change. In addition, they believe that the process must become institutionalized in order to accommodate the length of time required to initiate and implement educational change.

Private interest groups also can directly and indirectly initiate change. Indirectly, they can lobby all other stakeholders (students, parents, teachers, administrators, school board members, and community members) to promote their private agendas. In a more direct way, private interests can initiate change by providing instructional materials to educators that are biased in favor of the interest group's position. Also, they can initiate change by challenging textbooks and other instructional materials that do not support their view. The book-banning activity of conservative interest groups has been a common example of the initiation of reform by private interest groups. In addition, content in the school's curriculum guides, instructional techniques, and assessment strategies, as well as the way a school is organized, have been challenged by diverse groups.As an example, the scientific theories of evolution and the Big Bang as well as multicultural content has been challenged. In the 1960s and 1970s, liberal private interest groups promoted changes in school curriculum, which ranged from the addition of environmentalism in the science curriculum to giving a more prominent position to women and minorities in the social studies curriculum.

Mass media also can initiate change. Editorial policies may create a conservative or liberal bias in print and nonprint media. Television and radio news and talk shows may be utilized to act as infomercials for various reform agendas. The motion picture industry may also affect the initiation of reform through its portrayal of the effectiveness and operation of the educational system and the individual stakeholder groups in schools. Unlike print media, which can directly promote a reform position, celluloid media is subtler in its impact on educational reform. The cumulative effect on viewer opinions about education of the way education, educators, and students are represented over time in movies and television shows may be a powerful influence on reform.

Generally, the initiation of educational change may involve bottom-up or top-down strategies. Mandates or school takeovers by the state, a federal decree, a school board's directive, or a principal's order are all examples of top-down reform strategy. Depending on their political orientation, reformers support either the one or the other. Those who desire more control over the reform process or event advocate a top-down initiation strategy that establishes clear goals and clearly defined power arrangements that limit the ability of individuals to make decisions. In a top-down strategy, individuals who are on the lower rungs of the hierarchical ladder are allowed some degree of decision-making power; however, they are usually empowered only to carry out the dictates of those who are in control of the reform. For example, in Texas, the state maintains total control over the reform process. In Texas, state officials make all decisions about the nature and direction of educational reform. Their mandates are then given to the universities and schools for implementation. Basically, as long as the schools respond appropriately, they can do as they want; if the results are not good, then the state steps in.

Empowerment of stakeholders in a top-down reform situation is usually contrived, given by those who hold the real power, but limited, constrained, and situational. In a reform initiative driven by a bottom-up change strategy, all stakeholders in the system being reformed share the actual decision-making power. An example would be a school in which the administration and faculty collegially craft the reform vision, mission, and implementation strategies. Proponents of this strategy would argue that students, parents, and other community members would also have to have a significant role in the change process—even, in some cases, be equal partners in the process. Historically, most educational reform has employed a top-down strategy. Proponents argue that top-down strategies are more efficient, more accurately represent the hierarchical nature of society, and can utilize the expertise of individuals from the private and political sectors who are seen as having more valuable experience and knowledge than educational scholars and practitioners.

Reform processes that involve a bottom-up strategy are characterized by the empowerment of most, if not all, stakeholders in decisions concerning the initiation and implementation of educational reform. The use of a bottom-up strategy implies that those closest to the educational process (teachers, administrators, students) know best what is necessary to ensure relevant and quality education. When this strategy is employed, stakeholder roles change. Faculty and administration become active participants in the determination of viable reforms for their local context, while regional support centers, universities, private consultants, and governments facilitate the reform initiatives of the practitioners. Bottom-up reform strategies represent a flatter and more collegial decision-making structure, in contrast to the vertical and authoritarian structure of a top-down strategy.

IMPLEMENTING EDUCATIONAL REFORM

Once a commitment is made to initiate a reform, how is that reform implemented? Each of the groups who have the potential to initiate reform may implement it in various ways.

Implementation of Educational Reform
by State Governments

As previously mentioned, state governments can be very directive or can allow school districts a degree of latitude in complying with the state reform mandates. A specific example of a very directive and controlling state reform implementation process would be the implementation of the Texas standards and accountability system.

The Texas Education Agency (TEA), a regulatory agency established by the Texas legislature, is responsible for implementing the state-mandated educational reform of Texas public schools. The State Board for Education Certification (SBEC) controls the higher-education certification process for teachers and administrators. Both the TEA and SBEC have adopted a comprehensive and tightly controlled implementation strategy, so that together they control all aspects of educational reform from kindergarten through educator certification. The TEA and SBEC have established standards and accountability procedures for each educational level. The primary accountability tools are a series of high-stakes exit-level tests that must be passed by high school students to receive a diploma, by prospective teachers to be certified to teach, and by prospective administrators in order to become principals and superintendents. School districts and universities are held accountable for student performance on these tests. Accountability in Texas schools also extends to school board members, who are also given standards that must be met. The main accountability measure for public schools in Texas is the Texas Assessment of Academic Skills test (TAAS)—a high-stakes exit-level test that must be passed if a student is to receive a high school diploma.

Chronically poor student performance on the TAAS can lead to a state takeover of a school district. On-site monitoring of campuses and school districts by the TEA is conducted through the District Effectiveness and Compliance (DEC) visitation system. Due to the possibility of a state takeover and to the publishing of the TAAS scores, the job security of administrators and teachers is related to student performance on the TAAS. In addition, prospective teachers and administrators must pass the Examination for the Certification of Educators in Texas test (ExCET). If performance on the ExCET does not meet state performance standards, colleges of education can be stripped of their ability to certify teachers and administrators.

In Texas, TEA accountability measures supersede all other public school and university assessments. Grade point average, class rank, and any other indicators of student achievement are all secondary to the TAAS and ExCET. In addition to student achievement on standardized tests, TEA supervision and control extends to other aspects of Texas education. Annual public school teacher evaluation and professional development must comply with the Professional Development and Appraisal System (PDAS). The key component of the PDAS system is that teacher appraisal is directly linked to student achievement on the TAAS. Also, state control extends to the beginning teacher. The Texas Beginning Educator Support System (TxBESS) is a mandated support system for beginning teachers. In addition, a new program, the Beginning Teacher Activity Profile in Texas (BTAPT), is an evaluation of the competence of beginning teachers within the first semester of their teaching career. The data accumulated by state-certified evaluators is not intended to serve as a basis for evaluation of beginning teachers, but rather to provide a direction for professional development of the teachers by their schools and to evaluate the effectiveness of the university teacher preparation program. The BTAPT holds the universities accountable for the behavior of their graduates.

The state's control of education is facilitated by the Public Education Information Management System (PEIMS). PEIMS is a statewide computerized data management system that all public schools are required to supply with data. They must submit organizational, budget, financial, and staff development information, student demographics, program descriptions, and student attendance, dropout, retention, and graduation data. Each year an Academic Excellence Indicator System Report (AEIS) based on PEIMS data provides comprehensive details on all aspects of each school district. This management system is so comprehensive and inclusive that a principal can track an individual student's performance on a given test item back to the teacher who had the responsibility for teaching that content.

The Texas standards and accountability system is an example of how a state can retain complete control over the implementation of an educational reform initiative. The state of North Carolina also established standards that were assessed through student performance on end-of-grade and end-of-course tests. Like Texas, in the 2000–2001 school year North Carolina made these tests a factor in the promotion of students in grades three, five, eight, and twelve. Similarly, North Carolina linked student achievement on these tests to the determination of teacher and administrator effectiveness. The North Carolina law allows special assistance teams to replace principals and teachers in low-performing schools. In addition, the law allows any tenured or untenured teacher to be terminated if a ninety-day professional development plan does not result in improved teaching.

North Carolina also focused on the beginning teacher. To upgrade teacher licensure and to support beginning teachers, North Carolina mandated a Performance-Based Licensure program (PBL) that was to be implemented in the 1999–2000 school year. This program eliminated principal participation in the review and evaluation process, and adopted the Interstate New Teacher Assessment and Support Consortium (INTASC) standards. Assessors were trained in these standards, and the state proceeded with implementation of the PBL system. However, unlike the situation in Texas, teachers and principals resisted the reform, and the state listened. The North Carolina Department of Public Instruction met with elected officials, teacher associations, state board representatives, and regional implementation personnel to modify the reform.

The reform initiatives of Texas and North Carolina are just two examples of the processes that many states are utilizing to implement educational reforms. In both cases, these states took an active and controlling part in the reform process, using government regulation as a means of control over the local educational system. Also, they both focused on students, teachers, and administrators as the primary individuals who are responsible for successful implementation of the reform. In both cases, the implementation process is focused solely on individuals as the primary targets of the reforms, instead of focusing on the broader societal issues that affect education, such as the equitable funding of all schools and the poverty level within a state.

Implementation of Educational Reform by Universities

Universities and colleges can implement reform in two basic ways. First, they can implement reform theory in their degree programs and in the professional development provided to practicing K-12 educators. Second, they can develop theory and present it to the educational community through scholarly publication and presentation. In addition, individual professors can attempt to implement change through their service to professional organizations. Obviously, dealing directly with future and current practitioners has greater potential for the more immediate implementation of reform. On the other hand, even though attempting to initiate reform through the publication and presentation processes employed by the scholarly community is a lengthy process that significantly delays any attempt to implement the reform, it subjects the reform idea to a rigorous interrogation that may significantly increase the long-term success of a reform.

Since universities and colleges are still the main instructional agencies for educators, they have the potential to promote reform in education through the curriculum and instruction of their degree programs. Institutions of higher education have the potential to influence educational practitioners by providing degree programs for entry-level teachers and administrators, advanced degrees for practicing educators, and through nondegree professional development opportunities offered to practicing educators. Reform ideas can be embedded within the curriculum of the associate, bachelor's, master's, and doctoral programs, and of certification programs. In addition, another powerful reform implementation strategy is the demonstration of reform ideas through the modeling of the idea by the professor in the college classroom. Universities can implement reform in their degree programs by infusing the reform ideas in the course content, as well as in the required internships, observations, and student teaching. However, there are situations that limit the effectiveness of university reform implemented through these activities.

For instance, if a reform is promoted in the course content but the professor's instructional practice is opposite to what the reform proposes, the students may be influenced more by what the professor does than by what the professor says. Likewise, when students participate in field experiences, such as internships, observations, and practice teaching, they may encounter practices that are in opposition to the reforms learned in the university classroom. Also, reforms promoted by a university may be in opposition to the practice required by a public school to meet state mandates. In Texas, constructivist teaching strategies and critical thinking are promoted in prospective teachers as best practice. However, when these future teachers engage in their practice teaching, many find that because of the intense focus on student achievement on the TAAS, the instructional reality is not constructivism and the development of critical thinking. Instead, teaching to the test by demanding rote learning and memorization is the norm.

This incongruity between what is presented in the university and what occurs in the school can effectively negate implementation of the university's reform. Some universities attempt to offset this incongruity by working closely with the local school districts through a professional development school (PDS) system. PDSs have the potential to combine teacher certification activity with the professional development of practicing teachers. In this way, a university can attempt to implement a reform through the certification of beginning teachers and through the professional development of practicing teachers within the same school district. The implementation strategy is to introduce the reform at the same time to both the pre-service teacher and the practicing teacher. A basic PDS format involves a partnership between the university and the school. The school opens its doors to the university, and in turn the university supplies pre-service teachers, professional development for practicing teachers, and an infusion of new ideas. In some cases, university professors not only teach pre-service classes on-site but also become engaged in the curriculum and instruction of the school.

Use of the PDS model is an attempt to recombine educational theory and educational practice. Some research universities also attempt to achieve this goal through the use of laboratory schools. Laboratory schools may be private schools funded by a university or charter schools sponsored by the university. In any case, they are intended to be experimental schools where new curriculum and instructional theory can be applied and assessed.

Another way in which reform can flow from the university to the public and private schools is through the professional consultation provided by individual professors. In some instances, professors are contracted by local schools to provide professional development or to engage in research. This is certainly an opportunity for ideas to flow from the university to the school; however, in many cases, the potential to facilitate reform is muted by what the school needs. In some cases, the services needed by the schools are created by government mandates, which are tightly focused on specific curriculum or instruction. In cases like these, the educational consultant has less latitude in promoting other reforms.

As previously mentioned, professors can attempt to implement a reform idea in a less direct way—through scholarly writing and presentation. To achieve promotion and tenure, all professors are required to show growth in scholarly activity, teaching, and service. All three categories can be gateways for the promotion of reform. Scholarly activity involves publishing in professional journals and books, and presenting at professional conferences. Professors can promote a reform agenda by engaging in scholarly activity. One drawback is that few public school practitioners engage in professional development on this level. Therefore, reforms presented through scholarly activity are usually aimed at other professors, practitioners who are pursuing advanced degrees, and politicians who are inclined to be receptive to scholarly ideas that serve their political purposes. Indirectly, the promotion of reform through scholarly activity actually reinforces top-down implementation strategies, since those who are doing the teaching lack access to scholarly ideas. On another level, however, professors have the potential to implement reform through their professional organizations. These organizations can function as lobbies to promote or contest reform activity.

Implementation of Educational Reform by Professional Organizations

Professional organizations connected with education can attempt to influence reform through the lobbying of governmental agencies and politicians; however, the most direct way of implementing reform is through their influence on universities. Some professional organizations, either individually or through consortiums with other organizations, have established standards and accountability procedures that promote specific educational reforms. These standards have been advanced as best practice, as determined by the educational experts in a particular discipline. These standards then create a competitive environment, in that universities that have met these standards can use that status in the recruitment of faculty and students. The assumption is that universities that are accredited by the professional organization are better than those that are not accredited. The term "accreditation" means that one organization is validating or authorizing another organization or institution because the second organization has met the criteria or standards presented by the accrediting organization. Unlike state mandates, the accreditation process is entirely voluntary.

Educational leadership and administration programs must answer to quite a few outside agencies if they want to be competitive in their acquisition of accreditation. For example, in a highly restrictive environment like Texas, an educational leadership program would have to meet the state guidelines monitored by state agencies such as the TEA, SBEC, and the Texas Higher Education Coordinating Board. In addition, to be competitive with other programs, these preparation programs would have to meet the standards created by the National Council for Accreditation of Teacher Education (NCATE), the Southern Association of Colleges and Schools (SACS) standards, and the Interstate School Leaders Licensure Consortium (ISLLC) standards. All of these accreditation agencies are supported by professional organizations.

The standards promoted by these professional organizations apply to all aspects of a program. The NCATE standards deal with everything from the design of the program, the nature of the faculty, the program content, and the professor's course syllabus to the amount of faculty office space. Each accrediting organization promotes its own position, which creates layers of standards and accountability that a university must meet to be accredited by all of the organizations. A professional organization may decide that one method or organizational strategy is better than another and essentially mandate its implementation to those universities that want to acquire accreditation status from that organization. One effect of this accreditation process is the facilitation of pedagogical and organizational uniformity between universities. Some argue that this process is essentially about who controls the profession.

Another example of the control exerted by professional organizations deals with the appropriate way to present scholarly information. The *Publication Manual of the American Psychological Association* (APA) provides the most common format used in the reporting of educational research. If a professor, journal, or agency requires APA format, before the information will be accepted it must meet the standards of grammar, punctuation, spelling, formatting, and the like of the APA format. Whether provided by the APA manual or the *Chicago Manual of Style,* these formats, created by professional organizations, impact the implementation of educational reforms.

Some argue that the most serious drawback to the mandates of professional organizations is that they stifle innovation and creativity, and facilitate the development of a suffocating uniformity. On the other hand, proponents of these standards maintain that clearly stated standards and accountability procedures are necessary in order to professionalize education.

Implementation of Educational Reform through Professional Development in Schools

Eventually, all reform must be implemented in the schools by administrators and teachers. "Professional development," "staff development," and "in-service training" are terms used to describe ways practitioners learn about the reform to be implemented. Even though they are often used interchangeably, the first two terms will be used here to represent two different approaches used to get teachers to implement reform. The third term, "in-service training," is simply a generic term that indicates that teachers are engaged in either professional or staff development. The staff and professional development processes, as the terms are used here, are nested within two different philosophies concerning the implementation of reform through teachers. These philosophies underlie top-down and bottom-up change strategies.

The purpose of teacher development within the context of a top-down change strategy, or staff development, is simply to get teachers to implement the reform decisions of those outside the school or classroom. Development activities consist of training teachers in the skills, contents, and attitudes that will allow them to accurately and efficiently implement the decisions of others. In this developmental process, teacher empowerment is at best contrived. Power is given to teachers only in highly controlled and restricted contexts, and teachers are not involved in decisions about the purpose, definition, or nature of the reform. In staff development, teacher development tends to be expert driven and presented within limited and restrictive contexts, and it does not allow criticism of the reform.

For instance, if standards assessed by a standardized test were the reform to be implemented, then experts would teach teachers about the standards and how to increase student performance on the test. The in-service time devoted to this purpose would not allow time for teachers to critique the standards or the test, or to bring up the question of whether this particular standards and accountability system was even appropriate for their students. The context in which the material is presented to the teachers would be limited to the generic presentation made to all teachers in all school districts within that state. Teachers would be discouraged from modifying the standards, the test, or the learning activities presented by the experts so that they are more authentic and relevant to their students. In short, teachers become mere technicians who carry out the mandates of the experts.

In contrast, the purpose of professional development, that is, of teacher development within a bottom-up change strategy, would be to foster authentic professional growth that would be relevant to the individual teachers and to their students. In addition, another purpose would be to generate reform that meets the needs of the local educational environment. Teacher development within this strategy would not be directed by those from outside of the school environment, but by the teachers and administrators who work within the school. Development activities of this kind would require egalitarian participation on the part of the teachers, in that they would be empowered to make the critical decisions about reforming their school and would also have the responsibility to develop accountability procedures to assess the progress of their reform. Achieving the purpose of professional development requires a change from the view of teachers as subordinate technicians to a view of teachers' work that includes initiating change based on critical reflection on their practice. Finally, development of this nature is highly context specific, in that the way the learning environment actually functions on a daily basis greatly affects the implementation of reform. The local context continuously mediates and informs the teacher development process.

As top-down and bottom-up reform strategies are different, so are staff development and professional development activities. Staff development generally connotes the expert-driven training of teachers, which is usually focused on one aspect of their pedagogy. Staff development usually involves an outside consultant providing a script, formula, or model that the teachers learn to follow. For instance, if the decision were made to utilize brain-based teaching strategies in the school, staff development would consist of training sessions only on the technical aspects of brain-based pedagogy and conducted by an expert on that subject. The sessions would not devote time to teacher conversation about the need for this training, or about how they can significantly modify the technique to accommodate their local learning situation.

In the context of the true professional development that is possible in a bottom-up situation, teachers may still decide to infuse brain-based learning techniques within their teaching, and may even contract an expert to provide nuts-and-bolts training in this technique. This kind of training may be defined as staff development if that term is used for any development that focuses on improving skills, attitudes, and knowledge in teachers, whether in a top-down or bottom-up situation. True professional development, on the other hand, development whose purpose is to foster the professional growth of teachers and the effectiveness of educational reform that is relevant to their unique place through the empowerment of teachers, can only happen in a bottom-up context.

Professional development differs from staff development in that it takes a broader view concerning the role of teachers in the initiation and implementation of reform. During the 1990s, unlike staff development, which essentially consists of training programs focused on specific instructional techniques, professional development was seen by its proponents as promoting teacher empowerment in educational decision making. In this case, empowering teachers refers to involving teachers in the determination of the purpose, definition, and nature of reform. Teacher empowerment strategies are inherently bottom-up reform strategies. One major difference between staff development and professional development is that the latter focuses on reform through the professional and personal growth of the empowered teacher, whereas the former utilizes experts to deliver the reform package to the teachers. Those who promote professional development argue that better and more relevant curriculum and instruction emerge from more knowledgeable, skilled, and caring teachers.

Proponents of professional development also claim that the involvement of teachers in the formulation and implementation of reform guarantees the inclusion of the local context, which in turn guarantees reform that is authentic and relevant to the local school, reform likely to be sustainable over a longer period of time. Proponents of professional development propose that without the inclusion of the local context and the experiential knowledge of the teachers, reform activities are apt to mean the worst kind of staff development—fragmented, uncoordinated, piecemeal, and ephemeral attempts at a quick and easy fix to the problems of education.

Those who promote professional development that empowers teachers value teacher knowledge gained through the teachers' examination of their beliefs and experience. On the other hand, staff development training programs seek to impose knowledge and skills on teachers that are not significantly informed and mediated by the teachers' understanding of their educational environment. Staff development is usually characterized as the delivery by outside consultants of generalized formulas that are intended to work in any school regardless of the uniqueness of school environments. In a professional development scenario, teachers are seen as producing and utilizing knowledge within their local context that may not apply to other educational contexts.

In the 1990s, professional development scholars who advocated teacher empowerment (to mention some of the most important, Michael Fullan, Thomas R. Guskey, Andy Hargreaves, Michael Huberman, Thomas J. Sergiovanni) identified characteristics of teacher empowerment as teacher collaboration, teacher collegiality, the development of collegial community, shared power and authority within a school, egalitarianism among teachers, teacher autonomy and choice, the integration of teacher work and teacher learning, teachers as learners, teacher leaders, teachers as inquirers, and teachers as reflective practitioners. Individuals like Henry Giroux (1988) saw teachers as potentially transformative intellectuals who, through the attainment of critical skills and knowledge, could become agents for change, who would promote participatory and egalitarian democracy in their classrooms, schools, and communities. Some opponents of this view of teacher development maintain that teachers are technicians whose responsibility is to carry out the reform decisions of others. An extreme form of this view is the development and requirement of scripted lesson plans, which teachers recite as they teach their lessons. The use of scripts is the most extreme form of teacher-proofing curriculum and instruction. Those who support the use of scripts and other teacherproof techniques maintain that the local context and teacher knowledge gained through experience is irrelevant to the implementation of educational reform.

Advocates of professional development focus on the complexity of education. They see education as involving layers of context that include knowledge, skills, local values, values external to the local school, teacher and administrative culture, the local community culture, and variations in funding. These components are seen as dynamic and interrelated. Proponents of professional development argue that universally generalizable reforms cannot be created that effectively address this contextual complexity, and that if this complexity is not addressed, educational reform cannot be effective and most assuredly cannot meet the real needs of the students.

Both staff development and professional development are constrained by real-world situations. Finding time for the teacher development that is essential to reform in an already long and congested workday is difficult for individuals and almost impossible for large groups of teachers. To attempt to provide time for teacher development by hiring substitute teachers to cover the classes of individual teachers, and by scheduling in-service days throughout the school year, is a costly addition to a school budget. Problems with these approaches include finding the funding for substitute teachers and the money to pay teachers for the noncontracted in-service days. In some cases, in-service days are built into teacher union contracts, and reimbursement for in-service time beyond the contracted day is negotiated and included in the contract. Regardless of contractual arrangements, time is always scarce, especially during the school day, and this condition is a major impediment to the effective implementation of educational reform.

Another constraint on teacher development and therefore on the effective implementation of reform is the idea of teacher career stages. These will be explored in more detail in Chapter 9, which deals with resistance to change. Briefly, school faculties consist of individuals who are at different stages of their professional lives, and therefore see and value reform differently. Proponents of professional development and some staff development experts recognize that teacher development initiatives must take into account the different levels of teacher motivation and investment in reform. On the other hand, some top-down staff developers view teachers as industrial workers, seeing individual differences as irrelevant and any attempt to take them into account as a threat to the efficient implementation of a standardized educational system.

A final constraint is the public's need for immediate gratification. In a sound bite world of quick fixes and fifteen minutes of fame, the length of time needed to effectively implement an educational reform is problematic. If reform is as complex as proposed by the proponents of professional development, then the implementation of reform is defined in terms of years, not months. Opponents of the standards and accountability movement argue that its simplistic technical standards and standardized tests only fuel this need for immediate gratification. They argue that by refusing to recognize the diversity and complexity inherent in educational culture and in the process of educational reform, proponents of technical standards and standardized tests promote the idea of simple, low-cost, and quick solutions to highly contextual, complex, and expensive problems.

Any discussion of teacher development is incomplete without the recognition of the teacher development industry, which significantly affects the implementation of reform. Sponsored by professional organizations, commercial publishers, and special interests, a multitude of agencies and individual consultants vie for the money spent on teacher development. National in-service networks, such as the Association for Supervision and Curriculum Development (ASCD), along with the state ASCD organizations, sponsor conferences that promote reform ideas, consultants who will implement the various reforms, and resources (such as books, tapes, videos, posters) that can be purchased by individual teachers and school districts. Organizations like ASCD also sponsor trade journals, such as the *Journal of Staff Development*, which provide opportunities for the marketing of educational consultants, programs, and products. Universities also compete for market share in this highly competitive industry, as they also provide consultation and products to expedite the hot reforms of the moment. All forms of education, including private schools, parochial schools, and home schooling, have their own product lines tailored to their own unique needs.

An analysis of the teacher development industry shows that products with the greater potential for profit dominate the goods and services that are offered for consumption. This means that the mainstream thinking of the dominant culture is almost exclusively represented in the services and merchandise. Traditionally, the teacher development industry includes little in the way of consulting services and merchandise of a critically progressive or radical nature. Thus an important channel of communication is denied to those who promote critical and radical educational reform. In addition, because of the lack of a market for radical ideas packaged in scholarly jargon, the individual educators who encounter and embrace progressive and radical reform ideas in their university courses lack the support from the teacher development industry that is provided for reactionary and mainstream reform ideas.

Implementation of Educational Reform by Textbook Publishers

Due to their pervasive use by educators, textbooks are an integral component in any reform of curriculum and instruction. Since the late 1800s, when textbooks became the primary teaching tool and source of knowledge, any reform of education has had to factor in the content of the textbooks in use, and how the teachers use the texts. For instance, if curriculum was to become either progressive or more traditionally academic, then textbooks have had to be changed to accommodate the intended view. Also, if a school district or a state adopt a standards-based curriculum, only the textbooks that reflect this curriculum will be deemed appropriate by the educators who must implement the standards. The billion-dollar textbook industry understands this dynamic and continuously revises its books and materials in order to stay competitive.

A significant component of a textbook is the accompanying instructional support material. Textbooks not only are a source of knowledge but also provide lesson plans, activities, assessments, and supplemental materials for the teacher. If standards and accountability are the current nationwide reform, textbooks can provide learning tips and activities directly addressing the students' need to master specific standards and to learn how to take a standardized test. Therefore, even though a reform deals exclusively with instruction, those who implement the reform must still take into account the textbooks that are used.

A seldom used alternative to a textbook-bound curriculum is the creation of learning materials by teachers and students, seen by some educators as the most appropriate source of materials and pedagogical activity. Proponents of this approach claim that the process of creating classroom materials involves critically constructing knowledge. The benefit of this activity is that any construction of knowledge requires a critical component that includes higher-order thinking skills such as analysis, synthesis, and evaluation, not only of the information but also of the students' own values and beliefs. This critical outcome is valued by those on the left but decried by those on the right. This critical difference between the left and the right has been and continues to be evident in the struggle to control public school textbooks.

The selection of textbooks is a political activity. Since all textbooks are laden with values, whoever selects the books is actually selecting the values that will be presented to the students as factual information. The selection process varies widely: Some schools allow individual teachers to select their own textbooks; some states mandate textbooks for all students in the state. Typically, building administrators and local school boards have a process that requires justification of the selected texts. However, whether on a local or state level, whereever screening processes are used, some individual's or group's values become the selection criteria.

Textbook publishers are aware of the dynamics of the selection process, and attempt to keep their products aligned with the values that dominate the state and local selection processes. Since the implementation of educational reform is often contingent on the alignment of the reform with the selection of textbooks and supplemental materials, reformers must be attuned to the political climate and the marketing needs of the textbook publishers.

Because values of one kind or another are inherent in all texts, public school textbooks continue to be sites of political battle between the right and the left. Since textbooks are used as the main source of knowledge for students, they also become the main conveyors of values. Science, social studies, and health texts are frequent targets in this battle to implement the values of special interests. In science, topics such as evolution, creationism, relativity, the Big Bang theory, and environmentalism are lightning rods for some interest groups. Social studies texts are under attack from both ends of the political spectrum over how historical racism, sexism, religious beliefs and events, and issues of social class are represented. Controversy over the ways health texts handle sex education and how they represent individuals and families who are atypical makes them a minefield for publishers. All of the textbook controversy, often resulting in the banning of books or the refusal to purchase certain books, is caused by the desire of some on the right and some on the left to promote their interpretation of the past and the present, and their vision of how the future should be.

Historically, textbooks that have not sufficiently straddled the political fence have come under attack. From early attacks on the romanticized Eurocentric and patriarchal presentations of the McGuffey Readers to the most recent clash between evolutionists and creationists, textbooks have been assailed by those whose views are not represented or are challenged by the textbook content. For example, in the 1930s, Harold Rugg, a progressive educator, launched a series of social studies textbooks that contained up-to-date social and economic research, and challenged students to think critically about American history and current American issues. Inspired by individuals such as John Dewey, Harold J. Laski, Thorsten Veblen, Mary and Charles Beard, John Maynard Keynes, and Charles E. Merriam, Rugg's elementary and secondary texts challenged students to think beyond the mainstream and traditional boundaries of the social studies. In the 1930s, Rugg's texts came under attack from conservatives and the more virulent anticommunists. These interests, including the business community, decried Rugg's texts as anti-American and pro-Marxist. This conservative attack included public burnings of Rugg's texts, as well as vitriolic personal attacks. In 1942 a committee of leading historians examined the Rugg controversy and exonerated Rugg's textbooks. However, with the renewed communist threat after World War II, Rugg's publishers no longer included Rugg's books in their product line.

Rugg's situation is an example of how a reformer's view of history and society (in this case a progressive and critical view) can be implemented through textbooks, and then contested by those opposed to that view (in this case conservatives, traditionalists, reactionaries). The anticommunist fervor that fueled the Rugg situation continued in the late

1940s and 1950s. As McCarthyism swept America, public schools were scrutinized for subversive and un-American activity. Central to this crusade was an evaluation of all teaching materials. Guidelines were provided for communities that would aid loyal Americans in ferreting out communist thought in American textbooks. In the early 1950s there were even proposals to require textbook writers to take loyalty oaths.

As the storm of McCarthyism subsided, no respite was provided for textbook authors and publishers. As a result of the findings of the Woods Hole Conference, sponsored by the National Science Foundation, Jerome Bruner designed a curricular program called "Man: A Course of Study" (MACOS). MACOS was a research-based, state-of-the-art instructional program for its time. However, the required higher-order critical thinking, collaboration, student participation, inherent constructivism, and general questioning of traditional thought and values created a firestorm of conservative reaction. Textbook publishers refused to publish the course, and the funding for the project remained with the National Science Foundation. In the case of MACOS, anti-communists were joined by groups on the religious right in their attack on what they characterized as an anti-American, godless, humanistic, anti-Christian, and communistic invasion of American schools. This short-lived reform finally died when conservative congressmen voted to eliminate MACOS from the NSF budget. Two important outcomes of this situation were that a major government research organization, the NSF, was censored for its initiation and implementation of a research-based educational reform, and that since that time government agencies such as the NSF have closely scrutinized educational reforms for potential political reactions as well as for their validity and instructional effectiveness.

Conservative attacks on the implementation of liberal educational reform continue to the present. For example, Mel and Norma Gabler of Texas administer an organization called Educational Research Analysts. This organization reviews educational materials for information that is disrespectful and destructive of traditional American authority, religion, and social and cultural values as defined by the Gablers. As members of the religious right, the Gablers provide support for others to critique the books used in their local schools. Organizations such as the Gablers', Citizens for Excellence in Education, and the Christian Coalition provide detailed information and operational support for local efforts to identify elements of secularism in public school texts. Liberal organizations are also active, engaging the conservatives in battle in the public school arena. People for the American Way, founded by Norman Lear, not only supports school districts in these battles over educational materials but also provides resources that local individuals can use to combat censorship in their school community.

The reality concerning the outcomes of this battle over school textbooks is that the right has been more effective than the left in utilizing the media and in influencing national, state, and local political action to achieve their goals. Whether in relation to responses to attacks on educational materials by the right or attacks by the left on the positions and materials of the right, the left has been largely reactive, not proactive. Some argue that this is in part due to the fact that the more radical liberalism of the 1960s has been subsumed by the neoliberal response to the Reagan victory and subsequent conservative onslaught. Also, some educators point out that radical thought is invariably restricted to scholarly levels of the educational community and small subpopulations of American society. The bottom line is that the right is much more aggressive and effective in getting out its message. This political activity greatly affects the textbook industry. The goal of the industry is to make a profit on the sale of educational textbooks; however, the realization of this goal requires the industry to walk a fine line between these dueling ideological interest groups.

For more detailed discussions on the textbook wars, see Gary B. Nash, Charlotte Crabtree, and Ross E. Dunn's *History On Trial: Culture Wars and the Teaching of the Past* (2000); David C. Berliner and Bruce J. Biddle's *The Manufactured Crisis: Myths, Fraud, and the Attack on America's Public Schools* (1995); Barbara B. Gaddy, T. William Hall, and Robert J. Marzano's *School Wars: Resolving Our Conflicts over Religion and Values* (1996); Herbert M. Kliebard's *The Struggle for the American Curriculum, 1893–1958* (1995); Joel Spring's *Conflict of Interest: The Politics of American Education* (1998); and Diane Ravitch's *Left Back: A Century of Failed School Reforms* (2000). The books by Ravitch, Nash et al., and Kliebard contain detailed descriptions of the attack on Harold Rugg. A detailed description of the activity of the religious right concerning educational materials is provided by Gaddy et al. In addition, three books that comprehensively deal with textbooks in American education are *The Politics of the Textbook,* edited by Michael Apple and Linda K. Christian-Smith (1991); *Textbooks in American Society,* edited by Philip G. Altbach, Gail P.Kelly, Hugh C. Petrie, and Lois Weis (1991); and *The Textbook in American Society,* edited by John Y. Cole and Thomas G. Sticht (1981). Also, for a view from the right on textbook content, see the books and articles of Lynne Cheney, Arthur Schlesinger, Jr., William Bennett, E. D. Hirsch, Jr., and Mary F. Lefkowitz. For a view from the left, see the work of Molefi Asante, Leonard Jeffries, John Henrik Clarke, and James W. Loewen.

The Influence of Mass Media on the
Implementation of Educational Reform

In order for educational reform to be initiated and implemented, there must be a perception that there is not just a need for reform but also a situation dire enough to warrant significant changes in how schools are structured and organized, and in what and how they teach. In our post-modern information society, the nonprint media have extended the power of the mass media industry to affect public understandings and attitudes about education. The mass media industry is an important player in the process that creates perceptions of school effectiveness and quality. Those who are the active decision makers concerning educational policy and practice (politicians, government officials, educators, businesspeople, and special interests) all use the mass media to promote their agendas, and, in turn, are affected by how education is portrayed in the mass media. The general public is not a direct participant in the reform process, but their agreement, or at least their acquiescence, is a necessary condition for a reform to be implemented. Through their tax dollars, election votes, and responses to public opinion polls, the general public ultimately makes the decision. If the reform is not publicly supported, it will not be sustained.

Many reports and surveys have indicated a paradox in public opinion about education. On the one hand, most parents are supportive of their children's schools and generally give their schools high marks. However, these same individuals support general reform initiatives through their direct approval or through their lack of response when the reforms are implemented. Why would parents regard their local school as effective, yet support reform for American schooling in general?

Some educators argue that the image of schools portrayed through mass media greatly affects the opinions of individuals about education in general. However, what the general public sees and hears about American education on the nightly news, in the daily paper, or in movies with educational settings has less effect on their attitudes about their local school because of their concrete familiarity with their local school. For instance, if teachers are portrayed as less than professional and therefore a reform requiring all teachers to take tests to prove that they are knowledgeable professionals is proposed, surveys show that the public is likely to differentiate between the teachers that they know and anonymous teachers in other places. The public is likely to not believe the negative opinions represented in the proposed reform about the teachers that they know, but they are ready to believe them about the others. Why will they not transfer their confidence to other teachers? Some educators argue that the way educators and schools are por-trayed by the media provides the perception that, even though things may be OK in one's own community, they may still be bad in other places.

Public attitudes about education are impacted by two aspects of mass media—the news media and the entertainment industry. The news media, including television and newspapers, have historically been harsh critics of education. Their criticism shows bias in many ways, ranging from not getting the facts straight to reporting only the bad things about education. Also, historically the news media have sel-dom challenged what has been the "conventional reform wisdom" about education. For example, in the 2000 presidential election both candidates agreed that education was flawed and that only a standards and accountability system could fix it. Almost no one in the news media challenged either the assumption that American education was flawed or the belief that the proposed reform was the best solution. One excep-tion was a segment on the news show *60 Minutes* that took a critical look at the Texas standards and accountability system. Despite this provoca-tive report, no other mainstream news show or paper provided a similar critique of what was considered the conventional wisdom concerning American education.

Another way in which the news media are critical of education is through the media's reliance on sensationalism. Sensationalism can take two forms. First, it occurs when situations are reported out of con-text. For instance, many times when the results of a survey on student achievement are released, the media reports only one aspect of the re-port, or reports the main finding without the qualifying information. The lack of qualifying information, or context, replaces the complexity of the situation with a simple and erroneous understanding of the in-formation. Because complex research has been reduced to a sound bite, the general public is misled, and education is unjustly criticized. A sec-ond form of sensationalism is when the media intensely focus on one extraordinary event or situation over a prolonged period of time. Be-cause of the intense viewer interest, the whole educational system be-comes subsumed and subordinate to this event. An additional effect of the prolonged media coverage is to reduce public awareness of other equally serious and significant educational issues. All aspects of educa-tion are now viewed through the lens provided by this one event.

Media focus on recent acts of violence in public schools provides an example of this form of sensationalism. When an act occurs, cur-riculum, instruction, the effectiveness and competence of the teachers and administrators, and the purpose, nature, and funding of schools are all reevaluated in relation to the violence that took place. This myopia preempts considerations of the larger mission and operation of schools. The sensationalism of the media simplifies the public's understanding of the problems that face American education, as well as of potential solutions.

Why have the news media been critical of education? Some argue that one simple but on-the-mark answer is that there is no profit in reporting the good things that happen in schools. The news is profit oriented, and to gain viewers and readers the news is crisis oriented. While problems, scandals, and crises sell papers, the good things that happen in schools become human interest stories relegated to the less viewed portions of the broadcast and the less read portions of the newspaper. Also, the news media industry is a business, and to make a profit, it has to play well to both conservative and liberal viewers. The news media have found that the message about education that appeals to everyone is that the schools are not very good and therefore require reform. This message plays well to viewers of both persuasions because both conservatives and liberals have their own reform ideas. The result is a mutually reinforcing cycle: The viewers hear what they need to hear to reinforce their beliefs, and by reporting what the viewers want to hear, the news media industry makes a profit through the sale of its product.

Schools are complicit in this process because of their inability to counteract their pervasive bad press. Unlike most organizations of the same size, schools do not have an adequate public relations budget. Public schools and universities generally limit their advertising to periodic flyers and news releases, which get a circulation limited to the local area. In many cases, this kind of public relations effort contributes to public support of the local school, but has limited effect on the public's understanding of the larger educational issues presented in the national news media.

As discussed in the context of the news media, individuals see their local schools and educators, with whom they have personal contact, quite differently from the rest. The annual Phi Delta Kappa/Gallup Poll documents this differentiation in the public's perception of education on a yearly basis. For instance, the polls in 2000 and 2001 showed that the public is very satisfied with their local schools and teachers. In the September 2000 poll, conducted during the presidential election in which the failure of American education was considered a fact by both campaigns, the results were especially striking:

> This year's Phi Delta Kappa/Gallup poll shows again what previous polls have shown: the notion that the public is dissatisfied with its

> public schools is based on myth instead of fact. Respondents continue
> to indicate a high level of satisfaction with their local schools, a level
> of satisfaction that this year approaches its all-time high among the
> parents whose children attend those schools. (Rose and Gallup
> 2000, 41)

This disparity between what the public believes about schools and the
conventional political wisdom that gets great play in the news is further
addressed in the same study:

> Public satisfaction is also evident in the fact that 59% of Americans
> believe that reforming the existing system of public schools, rather
> than seeking an alternative system, is the best way to bring about
> school improvement. When given the specific choice, 75% would
> improve and strengthen existing public schools while just 22% would
> opt for vouchers, the alternative most frequently mentioned by public
> school critics. (41)

Some scholars propose that the different ways that the general
public see schools and educators are the result of the tangible and concrete evidence of their experience with the local schools and educators,
and also the result of how schools and educators are represented on the
news and in entertainment media. The argument is made that the public attitudes that tolerate and encourage educational reform, that plays
to the agendas of the economic and political special interests, is created
not only through the one-sided reporting by the news media but also
through the representations of education that appear in television
shows and movies. Scholars in the field of cultural studies believe that
the knowledge that the public has about schools, educators, and students, who are not part of their local experience and environment, is
created by how education and its stakeholders are represented in mass
media. Educators known as critical theorists have documented the recurrent themes and patterns in the way schools, school administrators,
teachers, and students have been (mis)represented in the popular culture media. In particular, Henry Giroux has studied how these celluloid
representations reproduce the political and economic agendas of conservative and liberal special interests. Race, gender, and class implications of these representations are reviewed in books such as Giroux's
Fugitive Cultures: Race, Violence and Youth and *Living Dangerously:
Multiculturalism and the Politics of Difference;* bell hooks' *Reel to Reel:
Race, Sex, and Class at the Movies;* and Mary M. Dalton's *The Hollywood
Curriculum: Teachers and Teaching in the Movies.* In addition, Daniel J.

Boorstin's *The Image: A Guide to Pseudo-Events in America* is an intriguing historical look at the orchestration of actual events and the creation of nonevents to promote political and economic purposes. On a related topic Neil Postman in *The Disappearance of Childhood* and Shirley R. Steinberg and Joe L. Kincheloe in *Kinderculture: The Corporate Construction of Childhood* study the political, economic, social, and cultural effects on children created by the activities of the special interests through their use of popular culture and mass media.

Scholars such as these make the point that public understanding of the way things are educationally, in places other than the public's own locale, is created through a cumulative and continuing exposure to the way movies and television present education and educational stakeholders. Conservative and liberal special interests are adept at taking advantage of these media representations. Driven by the profit motive, the entertainment industry also is sensitive to the political climate. During the educational conservatism of the 1980s, movies such as *Lean on Me* reinforced the opinion, summed up in the title of an influential report, *A Nation At Risk* (National Commission on Excellence in Education 1983), that education had failed, that schools were seriously flawed, and that only an authoritarian return to basic skills could turn the tide.

The crafting of movies like *Lean on Me* made it easy for predominantly white middle-class audiences to agree with the conservative reforms of the time period. For example, this particular movie opens with a school ten years in the past. The school is presented as a clean and well-kept educational environment containing respectful, eager-to-learn, well-disciplined, and nicely attired predominantly white students. Abruptly, the movie moves forward ten years to the present, and the audience is shocked by the overt violence, drugs, disrespect, utter educational chaos, and general ruin of this once beautiful school. This visual assault is supported by a loud, jarring rendition of "Welcome to the Jungle" played as the audience sees the now predominantly minority student body go berserk. To further manipulate the emotional state of the audience and to make the point even more obvious, during this "jungle" scene a white girl is sexually assaulted by black girls in a lavatory and, to the jeering cheers of the minority student population, flees down the hallway half-naked.

Critical theorists examine media representations such as this to determine if there are repeated patterns and themes involving the types of individuals (i.e., students, teachers, administrators, parents, males, females, whites, and minorities), the interpersonal relationships between educational stakeholders, the types of curriculum and instruction portrayed, and the general effectiveness of education. As they discern these patterns, they link them to the reform initiatives of the economic and political special interests of the time period.

Those who study popular culture report that like the news media, television and film representations of education generally sensationalize presentations of atypical events shorn of the context that provides authentic and relevant meaning. Seldom do television representations of education, such as the current show *Boston Public,* deal with the boring but real curriculum and instructional aspects of school that actually dominate almost all of the school time. Teachers and students effectively working and learning together are not as exciting as violence, sex, and interpersonal conflict. This is the distinction between media creations whose whole purpose is to entertain and documentaries. The analyses by critical theorists clearly show that education-as-entertainment is an inaccurate and highly political representation of education. These representations greatly affect the public's understanding of and receptiveness to educational reform. If a reform is to be successfully implemented, those who initiated the reform must garner support for the reform within the local context and also create supportive public perceptions about the nature of education in other locales.

TWO BASIC ELEMENTS OF THE REFORM PROCESS— CONVERSATION AND STAKEHOLDER PARTICIPATION

Two essential conditions of any reform process are conversation and participation. Conversation of one type or another pervades all human experience. The type of conversation that occurs is important in determining the purpose, the nature, and the eventual success of an educational reform. Conversation is not a generic and neutral human activity, but a highly complex, multifaceted, value-laden, and politically charged activity. Another condition upon which the success of a reform is dependent is the participation of the stakeholders in the reform process. As suggested in the discussion of top-down and bottom-up reform strategies, there are different types of participation, each type having significant implications for the purpose, nature, and success of a reform.

Conversation

How people communicate in the reform process can be essentialized into two broad categories of conversation—collegial and conflictual. These categories can be seen in four types of conversation identified by Patrick M. Jenlink and Alison A. Carr (1996): discussion, dialectical, dialogue, and design. Discussion and dialectical conversation are both conflictual and are the most frequently occurring types. In both, the goal is to advance individual or group interests by "winning" the conversation.

The main distinction is that discussion tends to be more emotional and less analytical. An individual or group who relies upon discussion is usually handicapped by a lack of supportive data or by simply being in a weak position in relation to the issue at hand. Ad hominem attacks and the use of propaganda techniques that are not factually grounded are also common in this type of conversation. Dialectical conversation is characterized by the use of well-developed and logical presentations of facts and inferences to advance one's position or opinion. Formal debates in which both sides present a wealth of information supporting their positions are examples of dialectical conversation. In contrast, a highly emotional conversation lacking any substantial supporting information is characterized as a discussion. Invariably, because of the confrontational nature of these types of conversation, the use of both discussion and dialectical conversation results in a polarization or alienation of the involved individuals. Feelings of being threatened and being coerced into thinking a certain way on an issue are common outcomes of either type of conflictual conversation. Individuals and groups who are conversationally adept can utilize both types in the promotion of their interests.

On the other hand, collegial conversational types, such as dialogue and design conversation, facilitate the development of a "oneness"—a shared culture sustained by morally committed people. In dialogue, people examine their personal assumptions and then suspend them, thus opening new spaces where new meanings can be individually and collectively constructed (Bohm 1992; Horn and Carr-Chellman 2000; Jenlink and Carr 1996). The key in these collegial types of conversation is to become open to the possibilities and potentialities of the viewpoints of others. Individuals and groups who are committed to the use of dialogue and design conversation are also committed to the establishment of a shared vision, and perhaps the creation of a collective consciousness.

The distinction between dialogue and design conversation lies in their purpose. Dialogic conversation can be utilized to promote understanding between different individual views, and to facilitate community building (Banathy 1996; Burbules and Rice 1991; Flick 1998; Isaacs 1999; Sidorkin 1999; Yankelovitch 1999). Individuals who engage in dialogue are committed to listening and responding to the views of others, not in a conflictual manner, but in a respectful and collegial manner. Collegiality implies a desire to include elements of all diverse positions in a mutually agreed upon vision and mission. In contrast, the purpose of conflictual types of conversation is to ensure dominance of one's own ideas, even at the expense of others who do not share these views becoming alienated and marginalized. A dominant theme in the use of dialogic conversation is a concern for others, whereas in discussion and dialectical conversation the advancement of one's own interests overrides all other concerns.

In contrast to the collegial purpose of dialogic conversation, the main purpose of design conversation is to create something new when engaged in the change process. When engaged in creating change through design conversation, the participants are committed "to change *of* the system rather than change *within* the system" (Jenlink and Carr 1996, 35). Design conversation can lead to something new, not just a reshuffling of parts resulting in the same outcomes. Bela H. Banathy (1996) identifies two specific modes of design conversation as strategic and generative dialogue. Strategic dialogue focuses on the specific tasks that lead to the design of an ideal change initiative and to the implementation of the change. The purpose of generative dialogue is to generate a common frame of thinking, shared meaning, and a collective worldview.

All types of conversation are evident in any educational community; however, the degree to which each is valued and used is dependent on the purposes of those who control that community. If the school organization is characterized by a well-defined traditional hierarchy, in which power is concentrated at the top and conditionally disseminated throughout the lower positions, then conflictual types of conversation are more effective in maintaining this power arrangement. Dialogic conversation also would be evident; however, the use of dialogue would have to be controlled so as not to promote thinking that would challenge the hierarchical arrangement of power. Design conversation, in its ideal form, would not be appropriate because those who control the school system would not be interested in change of the system because this would challenge their control. On the other hand, organizationally flatter school systems would promote more conversation of the collegial category. Dialogue would be utilized more frequently to promote the development of egalitarian community and to support design conversations about the purpose of the school, the creation of a guiding vision or image of that purpose, and the implementation of change that would promote the ideal image.

In relation to educational reform, the types of conversation align with the processes of reform. Top-down reform initiatives make use of conflictual types of conversation, whereas bottom-up strategies employ collegial types. Top-down change initiatives rely heavily on dialectical conversation, in that well-developed arguments are presented that consist of seemingly logical and consistent data. Discussion is also employed to emotionally charge the dialectical conversation, and to counteract any discussion that arises from dissident groups or individuals. Dialogue is restricted and tightly focused on specific issues that do not threaten the vision that is being promoted or the top-down organization of the school and reform process. In contrast, bottom-up change initiatives rely on dialogue and design conversation to promote collegial change processes and the development of collegial educational environments. Individuals are encouraged to temporarily suspend their preconceived ideas, to listen to and understand the arguments of others, and to work toward the development of a shared understanding of the issue at hand. This type of conversation is not limited to a specific issue or program, but at any time can bring fundamental concerns about power arrangements, school organization, and school and program philosophies into the conversation.

The types of conversation that dominate a school align with the type of interpersonal relationships that characterize that school. Schools that primarily utilize conflictual types of conversation predominantly contain adversarial relationships among individuals and balkanized groups who work toward fulfillment of their own interests. Proponents of collegial conversation and egalitarian community building maintain that the use of dialogue and design conversation result in interpersonal relationships that are more caring and receptive to difference. In fact, the ideal goal is the development of interpersonal relationships that are closer to the I-Thou relationships described by Martin Buber (1988, 1992) than reflecting the instrumentality of a relational structure whose purpose is the attainment of one's own self-interest.

There are significant implications from the use of different types of conversation in educational reform. Essentially, conversation is a political site, which can become a contested site within a reform process. If a reform is being imposed from the top down or from an external source, then conflictual conversation must be used. In turn, if this occurs, then certain types of interpersonal relationships will occur. Also, how individuals will relate to one another will have significant implications for resistance to or compliance with the reform. Furthermore, a message is sent concerning the value of the knowledge, opinions, and experience of the various stakeholders in the system. The history of educational change is replete with examples of externally imposed reform resulting in adversarial relationships, in which key stakeholders oppose the reform and directly or indirectly work against the reform's implementation and potential success. An indicator of this situation and an active agent in this process is the type of conversation that is utilized. Therefore, not only is the implementation of a reform dependent on the type of conversation, but also the sustainability of a reform is affected by conversation.

Some scholars argue that the reforms that are implemented for a period of time have an additional systemic effect. They maintain that the conversational types that are part of the reform process become entrenched not only in the school but also in the larger community. If dialectical and discussion conversations are utilized by the school in implementing reform, then these conversational types will become accepted forms of conversation in the larger community and will be used by community individuals and groups when they interact with the school. Once again, the purposes and processes used in educational reform mediate and inform the nature of the processes used in society.

During the 1990s, dialogue became a significant theme in educational reform literature. Numerous scholars called for the use of dialogue among stakeholders in the reform process. In this scholarly conversation, dialogue was seen as the mechanism that would lead to the empowerment of educational stakeholders who were traditionally powerless or limited in their ability to equitably participate in educational reform. Proponents of this view argued that significant educational change would occur if teachers and, to a degree, parents and students were empowered through the use of dialogue. This view from the scholarly community had little impact on the actual organization of schools and the practice of teachers. Since dialogue and empowerment deal with the arrangement of power, the traditional hierarchical structure of education actively and successfully resisted this theoretical position. In addition, the advent of the externally imposed standards and accountability reforms of the 1990s required a top-down reform strategy that allowed for only a contrived and conditional use of dialogue and empowerment of teachers in the public schools. Design conversation simply was not used on a large scale because of the inherent incompatibility between design conversation and the requirements of an entrenched traditional hierarchy.

Participation

The degree of participation of educational stakeholders in the reform process also defines the nature of the reform process. As previously mentioned, the extent of their participation correlates with conversational types and reform strategies. For example, when a top-down strategy is utilized, dialectical and discussion conversation is the norm, and stakeholder participation is restricted and controlled. Bottom-up strategies rely on collegial conversation to promote an active participation by the stakeholders.

In educational reform, stakeholder participation is dynamically related to the issues of community and stakeholder empowerment. As mentioned, in the 1990s many education reformers ardently promoted a reform scenario that included teachers as active and empowered participants in the reform process. Michael Fullan and Andy Hargreaves declared that "where change is concerned, the teacher is clearly the key. Leadership that neither understands nor involves the teacher is therefore likely to be leadership that fails. Excluding teachers from the task of leadership or the process of change is in this sense neither practical nor politic" (1996, 14).

This comment by Fullan and Hargreaves echoed that of numerous other reformers, some of whom further advocated the participation of students, parents, community groups, and business in the creation and implementation of reform. Proponents of this view argued that empowered stakeholder participation would result in more effective educational reform that would be more authentic and relevant to the actual needs of the community and general society. They furthered argued that participation of this nature in education would promote the principles of a participatory democracy. Another anticipated outcome was that societal diversity could be utilized effectively and equitably.

Despite this almost universal call for stakeholder participation, however, the definition of participation was diverse. These diverse definitions of participation can be arranged on a continuum ranging from a situation in which "subordinates" essentially do what they are told to one in which all are equal participants in all of the reform decisions. Some educators promoted the view that the boundaries between teachers and administrators should be blurred, in that both would share more equitably in decision making as well as in their professional responsibilities. Others attempted to empower teachers within the traditional hierarchical structure by expanding their participation, but still limiting it to mentoring, peer coaching, and leadership in the implementation of reforms in curriculum and instruction.

A main factor that promoted this definitional difference was the issue of empowerment. Allowing participation requires changes in the power arrangements of an organization. Full and unequivocal participation infers a flatter organizational structure, in which the decision-making boundaries are blurred between the stakeholders. Some educators have documented the systemic resistance to this participation/

teacher empowerment movement. For instance, Gary L. Anderson (1998) reported that despite the widespread call for empowerment and authentic participatory reforms, most actual reforms were bogus, superficial, or ineffective. Anderson identified the main reasons for this failure: Participation was advanced as a form of public relations to actually promote current practice; participation was structured as a disciplinary practice to better control stakeholders; and structures designed to promote participation became sites of collusion between certain stakeholders to promote current practice, organizational structure, and personal agendas.

The degree to which individuals resisted empowered participation coincided with their views on how community should be defined. Those who called for a transcendent community imbued with a spiritual commitment to a shared vision favored the blurred boundaries that are characteristic of a flatter and less authoritarian educational community. Those who desired to maintain the traditional culture and organization of a school supported limited versions of participation. To the latter, schools were way stations in which individuals would acquire what they needed, do what was required, and efficiently function within a well-bounded and well-defined structure. The former believed that schools should be egalitarian communities in which all would work together to transform themselves, their relationships with others, and the larger community.

An example of the interaction between these differing views on participation, empowerment, and community is the way another reform that gained currency in the 1990s was put into practice. To reform the preparation of teachers and administrators, some preparation programs initiated the cohort model. This model gained increasing acceptance in the area of administrator preparation and in doctoral degree programs. Simply, the idea was that preparation could become more efficient and meaningful if a group of students started at the same time, took the same courses, and moved through a structured and invariant program sequence together. Numerous benefits were touted for this cohort model (Barnett, Basom, Yerkes, and Norris 2000; Barnett and Muse 1993; Horn 2001). Students were guaranteed that within a cognitive, emotional, and interpersonally supportive environment, they could complete their coursework and other degree requirements within a specified period of time.

Some proponents of the cohort model also hoped that this structure would better prepare educators to promote and effectively implement educational reform in their schools. However, realization of this outcome depended on how the preparation program dealt with the issues of student participation and empowerment, and the type of community that was fostered between the students and faculty within the program. Some leadership programs promoted the ideas of egalitarian participation, stakeholder empowerment, and the building of egalitarian communities in their course activities. However, since traditional authoritarian hierarchies were maintained in the program as a whole and participatory reforms were not modeled, the extent to which students actually advanced these reform ideas once they became administrators in their own schools was limited. Cases like these illustrate the way participatory reform theories may be subsumed by the persistence of traditional definitions of participation in the minds of those who control the program.

In the promotion of teacher empowerment, two distinct versions emerged. J. Dan Marshall and James T. Sears (1990) give these two versions the names empowerment-as-authorization and empowerment-as-enablement. In the former, teachers and students are given limited power to do what others have prescribed. In the latter, opportunity is provided for teachers and students to create power and to put it into practice. Empowerment-as-enablement is seen as a dynamic process that is started but never completed. Obviously, in this open-ended process, teachers and students can inquire into and participate in the determination of any issues.

As mentioned, participation and empowerment in educational reform are dynamically interrelated to community. The way community is defined affects the definitions of stakeholder participation and empowerment. In the late 1880s, Ferdinand Tönnies ([1887] 1957) distinguished between two types of community: gemeinschaft and gesellschaft. Most basically, he defined gemeinschaft as "community" and gesellschaft as "society." Gemeinschaft, a community, is based on a shared vision—it is a community in which all share a common identity and a concern for other members of the community. Gesellschaft, a society, is based on contractual arrangements, and the relationships between individuals are impersonal and contrived. Sergiovanni maintains that traditional American schooling reflects a gesellschaft mentality, in that we have become conditioned "to adopt an impersonal, bureaucratic, professional, managerial, and technical language" (1994, 29).

In gesellschaft, it is difficult to deviate from the definitions of participation and empowerment that are inherent to this type of community. This conclusion is evident in the example of the cohort model. In that case, proposed reforms that promote significant stakeholder participation and empowerment cannot be realized if the cohort reform model is seen as a way to gain efficiency rather than as a way to build and model egalitarian community.

In the reform process, participation and the necessary collegial conversation are problematic for other reasons. First, time has always been a critical variable in American reform. Quick fixes are favored over lengthy but reasoned reforms. To involve more people in any decision-making process automatically adds time to the process. Also, the additional time required to engage in collegial conversation is frequently viewed as inherently inefficient. A second problem involves issues of trust. Any alteration of a system's power arrangements requires trust—trust in others and trust in the process. In a gesellschaft community, trust is defined by the contractual arrangements and by a willingness to adhere to the established order. To initiate and participate in collegial conversation is a risk by any standard, but in gesellschaft communities it is an unacceptable risk. In theory, an attempt to realize Buber's I-Thou relational level requires conditions that are unacceptable to those who value the conditions that foster a gesellschaft community. Therefore, calls to institute participatory and empowering reforms fail when faced with organizations that are characterized by I-It relationships.

THE DILEMMA OF HOW TO DEAL WITH CHANGE

Once a decision is made that certain conditions require a reform to be crafted and implemented, the actual change process raises a multitude of new challenges. Change in any organization poses significant challenges and problems. However, because of the systemic complexity of education, these challenges acquire a degree of difficulty that confounds the efforts of even the most determined reformers. In his study of educational change from 1880 to 1990, Larry Cuban detailed the lack of significant change in education over that time period and posed the question, "Why do so few instructional reforms get past the classroom door?" (1993, 1). An answer to this question is directly related to the complexity of the change process in education and to the change approach that is used.

The Complexity of Educational Change

Change involving social systems is a complex affair because it involves differentiation, integration, and reorganization (Banathy 1996; Csikszentmihalyi 1990, 1993). "Differentiation means the degree to which an entity, a system, or a society is composed of parts that differ in function and structure" (Banathy 1996, 334). Also in a personal sense, "differentiation implies a movement toward uniqueness, toward separating oneself from others" (Csikszentmihalyi 1990, 41). This aspect of complexity is evident in educational change because schools and educational cultures are only one part of the larger human system represented by what we call society. Words such as "economic," "cultural," "social," and "political" are used to describe the differentiation of society; however, these words only represent a plethora of additional parts of human society that differ in function, structure and purpose.

The idea of integration explains how all of these diverse parts actually are able to function together. Integration describes how well these parts work together in order to attain their own very different goals (Banathy 1996). As Mihaly Csikszentmihalyi puts it, "without integration, a differentiated system would be a confusing mess" (1990, 41). The process of integration includes interaction, cooperation, and communication. How the success of the integration process is measured is determined by how well the parts are able to achieve both their individual goals and the collective goals established by the whole that they constitute. The relationship between differentiation and integration is analogous to a well-functioning human being. An individual's organs, joints, muscles, and glands are all separate, highly differentiated parts of the whole. The brain and nervous system function to integrate all of these parts so that at eight o'clock in the morning when we reach for our coffee, we can successfully get it to our mouths without any spillage.

Complexity is often viewed as a negative phenomenon because of the difficulty and confusion that is created by differentiation without integration (Csikszentmihalyi 1990). The difficulty and confusion arise from the lack of positive cooperation and communication between the autonomous parts in their attempt to attain their individual and collective goals. In our human analogy, disruptions in the central nervous system result from pathologies that disrupt the communication and cooperation functions provided by the integrated parts of the central nervous system. Imagine the complexity involved in an attempt to leave no child behind in education. Each political, economic, social, cultural, and educational organization, along with each family and individual of all ages, has its own needs to achieve within this overall goal. These organizations and individuals face the multiple challenge of not only achieving their own goals but also understanding the goals of others and interacting in such a way as to facilitate goal achievement of all.

The difficulty in integrating all of these autonomous differentiated parts is the crux of the problem with the process of change in education. The breakdown in the change process lies in education's inability to integrate the increasingly differentiated parts of our society. Is the problem that education has not sufficiently evolved to provide successful integration?

The essence of evolution is the ability of an organism to reorganize itself into more differentiated parts that are at the same time sufficiently integrated. In the case of education and the role that it plays in the evolution of society, as society has become increasingly differentiated, education has not been able to provide an integrative function that pleases all of the organizational parts of and individuals in society. One major impediment to education's ability to fulfill its role in this evolutionary process is the dominance of education by political interests. Because education has always been a vulnerable and greatly contested space in the ideological warfare of competing political interests, education has had difficulty in fulfilling its integrative role to the satisfaction of these divergent interests. An important question is whether education can do what it needs to do to serve the evolutionary needs of society in light of this political interference.

The integrative aspect of the process of change is challenging because of the numerous variables that influence change in education. Looking at how the change process is affected by political, economic, cultural, and social factors provides a general glimpse of the complexity of the change process. Political considerations range from divergent ideologies to the different agendas of different levels of government (i.e., national, state, local). Of course, acquisition, maintenance, and use of power are the main foci in the political influences on the educational change process. Economic influences range from the attempts of business and industrial interests to promote their agendas through change in education, to the larger considerations of the necessity to allocate scarce resources.

Cultural issues and cultural change also influence any educational change. The issues involving cultural diversity that result from the changing demographics of the United States greatly impact all aspects of education. Social beliefs, values, norms, and laws all impact education, as well as social priorities that affect the allocation of scarce resources. For instance, the insistence on a large allocation of educational resources for the maintenance of entertainment and leisure activities such as sports, music, and other extracurricular social activities in schools greatly impacts the ability of education to meet academic goals. These broad categories of influential interests in the process of educational change are evident not only on a policy level but also play out in the hidden curriculum of individual classrooms. If individual teachers attempt to incorporate change in their classrooms, they face the same influences in the hidden curriculum that is brought into their class environment through instructional resources, the attitudes and values of their students and the students' parents, and the teachers' own attitudes and values that reflect those found in the broad categories of influential interests.

In addition to these broad categories, variables include interpersonal, intrapersonal, and technological dimensions of change in human systems. The dynamics of working collectively add a level of complexity to the change process. The ability to communicate and collaborate is a vital factor in the success and failure of change efforts. Also, the overall philosophy (whether authoritarian or collaborative and collegial) that guides and structures interpersonal relationships impacts the change process. On an intrapersonal level, change is complicated by the diversity in how well individuals can understand themselves, their actions, and their goals. Mixing technology with these human variables further complicates change.

The rapid rate of technological change adds pressure on the professional, personal, individual, and collective conditions that result from the current inequitable allocation of educational resources. The quantity and quality of the unequal distribution of technology throughout the American educational system confounds attempts to make changes to meet the high rate of technological change. In addition, the relationship between other goals that demand educational change and the goal of creating technological literacy may be problematic. For instance, all change requires the retraining of educators and the reallocation of scarce school funds. If technology is given an equally high priority along with other change initiatives but the funding does not increase, how is this conflict in resource allocation to be resolved? There is only so much time and money available, and much of that is permanently allocated for the basic functioning of the school. To meet additional needs requires more funding, more teachers, and more time dedicated to the school day and year. All of these variables create difficult choices.

In relation to the challenges created by technological change, asynchronous and computer-mediated learning has given rise to another growing and complicating entity—the cyber school. Cyber schools allow instruction to take place over the Internet at any time of day and night. With all traditional instructional constraints thrown aside, education takes on a new organizational meaning. One significant effect of cyber schools is that their funding involves monies that would normally have gone to the traditional public school. Therefore, without additional funds allocated for education, cyber schools further complicate the mission of traditional schools by siphoning funds away from them.

A technical look at the change process as it unfolds within education reveals additional variables. A tool developed by Beverly L. Anderson (1993) of InSites, A Support Network for Educational Change, identifies six elements in the process of change: vision; public and political support; networks, networking, and partnerships; teaching and learning changes; administrative roles and responsibilities; and policy alignment. These elements of change are all involved in progress through the stages of change: maintenance of the old system, awareness of a need for change, exploring the change process and change options, transitioning from the old to the new system, the emergence of a new infrastructure that supports the change, and finally a point where the new system is predominant.

The inherent complexity of educational change is further described in a guidance system for designing new K-12 educational systems proposed by Patrick M. Jenlink and his coauthors (2000). In their change process, they have identified twenty-nine beliefs that are essential components in a successful change initiative. They claim that if all twenty-nine are not in evidence, then the chances for successful implementation decrease. In addition, they describe twenty-six discrete events spread over five phases of a successful change process. They also identify eighteen continuous events that must take place throughout the whole change process if there is to be success. This specific and complex change process proposed by two experienced systems change scholars is a precise and realistic assessment of the complexity of the process of educational change.

Other experts in educational change present similar assessments of the complexity of the change process. Fullan and Stiegelbauer (1991) start with the general observation of six variables in the change process: the soundness of proposed changes, understanding the failure of well-intentioned change, guidelines for understanding the nature and feasibility of particular changes, the realities of the status quo, the deepness of change, and the question of valuing (43). Like many other experts in educational change, Fullan and Stiegelbauer see these other significant variables: the relevance of a change (practicality and need), the readiness of an educational organization to change (capacity and need), and the availability of resources to facilitate the change (63). In classroom and school improvement, they also identify key themes in improvement as vision-building, initiative-taking and empowerment, staff development and resource assistance, restructuring, monitoring the change and coping with problems, and evolutionary planning.

Other related variables identified by numerous change scholars that prove to confound education change efforts are the need to develop a shared vision and the need to empower the administrators and teachers in the development of the vision and implementation strategy. These variables can indeed be confounding if they are at odds with an entrenched view that believes in and wants to promote an authoritarian hierarchy. The proposition by Andy Hargreaves (1994) concerning effective educational change is also problematic for an authoritarian view. Hargreaves proposes that for effective educational change to occur, the educational environment must be a "moving mosaic," not an environment characterized by well-defined and stringently enforced roles and boundaries. Instead, the boundaries that separate administrators, teachers, and parents must be blurred. In addition, roles must be characterized as overlapping in their categories and membership, and all stakeholders must be flexible and responsive to what occurs during the dynamic process of change.

All of these variables are confounding enough by themselves, but gain a heightened degree of complexity when the problems of time and of lack of knowledge of the change process are added to the mix. To take the second element first, how many educators or non-educators who participate in educational policy decisions have any technical knowledge about the process of change? Little if any knowledge related to educational change is imparted to prospective or practicing teachers. In graduate degree and certification programs, change is approached but not its technical nature. In fact, a narrow topical concentration in a doctoral program would even prevent a doctoral student from encountering technical information on educational change. Therefore, the simple fact is that many educators are asked to implement a mandate for change with little if any knowledge of the change process or skill in facilitating it. Also, many educational decision makers mandate changes without a technical understanding of what they are asking others to do. This lack of knowledge and skill makes it yet harder for education to perform an integrative function in the evolution of society.

Finally, the variable of time weighs heavily on those who engage in the process of change. Time is a scarce resource in education, a resource that gets scarcer each time society places another demand on education. Additionally, unrealistic time constraints imposed by decision makers further problematize the change process. How do we increase time for education? What do we cut to accommodate the new mandate? Since time costs money, how do we find the funding to pay for more time? These few questions, in relation to all that is demanded of the schools, poignantly disclose the complexity of educational change.

Approaches to Educational Change

There are three approaches that can be used in dealing with educational change: a piecemeal or incremental approach, a systematic approach, or a systemic approach. These distinctions are based on systems thinking. Systems thinkers see all human activity arranged into systems, each of which has a purpose and structured activities designed to achieve that purpose. Individuals are part of more than one system. One principle of systems thinking is that there are layers of systems nested within one another, and that change in any one system will affect all other systems. For instance, education systems would include an individual classroom, an elementary grade level or secondary department, a school, a school district, the community in which the school district is nested, a state educational system, and government educational systems. Systems thinkers would see this as a very limited list, not only in relation to other education-related systems but also because all other noneducational human activity systems are connected to educational systems. A change in one system reverberates across this web of systems, just as a stone dropped in a pond sends ripples throughout the whole pond.

A change in the political philosophy of the national or state government could start a series of events that could impact all of the educational systems in the nation. On a local level, a teacher's attempt to implement a classroom change could affect many other systems in which the teacher's students play a part. To a systems thinker, systems are everywhere, and they are all interconnected. Therefore, systems thinkers propose that to understand human activity and to bring about effective and purposeful change, individuals need to acquire the knowledge and skills associated with systems thinking. In systems thinking, an understanding of change requires the ability to see the whole as well as the parts—to see how the whole is actually a dynamic web of interrelated, interconnected, and imbedded systems. The extent to which one understands this systems view influences the approach one takes to educational change.

Incremental change occurs when only a specific part of a complex human activity system is the target of a change attempt, without any attention paid to the relationship between the targeted part and the rest of the system. This approach deals with change initiatives as once-and-done occurrences that are divorced from other parts of the educational system. Systems thinkers argue that such disjointed tinkering does not encourage the development of an overall vision. An example of a piecemeal change would be if a school decided to use portfolios to assess the students' progress and implemented a portfolio system without fully understanding the implications of the change for other parts of the school environment and for all of the school's stakeholders. Larry Cuban (1993) identifies incremental change as first-order change. First-order changes attempt to enhance existing arrangements while correcting deficiencies in policies and practices. Such planned changes are efforts to make what exists more efficient and effective without disrupting the basic organizational features of the classroom, school, or district. Also, conversation in incremental change initiatives tends to be of a dialectical and discussion nature. If dialogue does occur, it is tightly restricted and contrived. The purpose of conversation in this approach is to persuade individuals to implement the reform that is generally externally imposed.

Contrary to the seemingly random uncoordinated piecemeal approach, systematic change is characterized by logical, linear, and scientific procedures (Banathy 1996; Carr 1996). Historically, this approach is found in engineering, military, and computer science contexts. Also identified as the functionalist approach (Cunningham 1982; Scheurich 1997) to educational change, systematic change processes emphasize technical knowledge and skill in the change process and control by experts. The change is directed by experts who are trained in change processes such as management by objectives, Gantt charting, Delphi techniques, decision-tree analysis, and a plethora of similar expert-driven tools. A goal of systematic change is to produce results that can be generalized to a larger environment or context. The importance of local or individual situations is secondary to the need to translate a "solution" to a diverse set of school communities. An example would be the implementation of a standardized testing program that could be used in all state school districts. This might be described as a one-size-fits-all strategy of change.

Systematic change tends to be focused on problem solving. A problem is identified, a plan of action is developed, and then the plan is implemented to solve the problem. Systems thinkers argue that the linear nature of systematic change prevents a holistic view of the situation and obscures the understanding that the problem is inherently dynamic and continuous and doesn't really have an end point. Although many systematic change models do encourage feedback in a cybernetic sense, there is rarely a critical concern for the whole environment.

Systematic change typically assumes the ability to resolve a problem by identifying and controlling significant variables, therefore linking the change process to the objectivism of the scientific method. Supported by scientific procedures such as employing experts, quantifying the problem, and devaluing experiential data and indigenous knowledge, systematic change requires a top-down change process. Therefore, systematic change typically does not disrupt existing power dynamics. Typically, this type of change affords students, parents, and teachers a limited voice—often called "input" or "buy-in." Since systematic change is usually expert driven, the conversation that is required is conversation that will achieve the goals of the experts.

In contrast, systemic change is holistic, not reductionist; dynamic, not linear; a critical process, not a mechanical one; and individually and locally relevant, not generalizable. It empowers the stakeholders in the system by allowing them to define and generate the change. Systematic change incorporates process; systemic change additionally requires contextual sensitivity or significant attention to every aspect of the system in which the change will occur. Two additional characteristics of systemic change are that educational systems are understood as embedded within other social systems, and that end points are not recognized due to the constant and recursive nature of change. Because of this embeddedness, school change must involve participation from the larger communities in which the individual school is a part, and also participation of the smaller subsystems within the school system.

This broader view of change, fostered by a systemic or systems-wide perspective, creates the potential for what Cuban refers to as second-order change. In second-order change, there is a fundamental change in the goals, structures, and roles of the educational system. Consultants who specialize in systemic change in the business community and scholars from the field of instructional systems have promoted the systemic view of change in education. A major proponent of systemic change in education from the business community has been Peter Senge (1990; Senge et al. 1999). Senge's version of systemic change is based on the view that schools like businesses are learning organizations, and because of that they need to acquire expertise in the "learning disciplines" of personal mastery, mental models, shared vision, team learning, and systems thinking.

Systemic change is usually a designed change. Systems design employs specialized techniques, generalized rules instead of specific steps, and universal principles that cut across design approaches. "Design is a creative, disciplined, and decision-oriented inquiry, carried out in iterative cycles [that repeatedly explores] organized knowledge as well as testing alternative solutions" (Banathy 1996, 16–17). The design process constantly integrates information, insights, and findings into new potential solutions. Systems design is inherently creative rather than constructive. Instead of focusing on what currently exists, systems designers attempt to facilitate the creation of something new. Also, systems design is not planning. The distinction is that planning is a series of steps taken toward a goal. Design is a thorough and continuous description of the problem, the current system, and the intended system that leads to the creation of a model that is then tested and evaluated

(Banathy 1996). Essentially, the purpose of designed change is not to restructure a system but to create a new system.

One type of systemic design is idealized systems design. In this type of change, all stakeholders participate in the creation of an ideal vision. A model of this vision is constructed through a recursive and comprehensive analysis of the current system and the ideal vision. The model is tested, evaluated, redesigned, and then implemented in the educational system that is to be changed. Because of the stakeholder participation and the modeling process, the chances for a successful implementation of the desired change are high. The downside is the time added to the change process when stakeholders are allowed participation and the time needed for the testing of the model. Designed change is not quick change. Those individuals who are invested in the maintenance of an authoritarian hierarchy would not value the necessity of stakeholder participation in all aspects of the design process—including decisions about the very nature of the change. In addition, this design emphasis on all stakeholders collaboratively creating something new requires conversational expertise on the part of all stakeholders. All individuals need to have a functional awareness of the different types of conversation and to be able to engage in dialogue at critical times in the change process.

Conclusion

There are implications for the use of each approach to educational change. A piecemeal or incremental approach will not provide long-term change because it neglects the other aspects of the educational system that will affect the success of the change. A systematic change can effectively change parts of a system but will not change the basic purpose, function, and organization of the system. Curriculum, instruction, and assessment may change, but the essential boundaries that define roles, functions, and power arrangements remain the same. Therefore, some systems thinkers maintain that if conditions require change that is "new," systematic change will not meet that need. As mentioned, idealized systemic change requires patience and long-term commitment. It also requires a fundamental valuation of stakeholder participation and a willingness to consider questions of equity that arise when stakeholders are allowed empowered participation.

The type of change process used is an important indicator of the purposes, values, knowledge, and beliefs of the individuals who have initiated the change and who are attempting to implement the change. These components further complicate the already complex process of educational reform.

REFERENCES

Altbach, Philip G., Gail P. Kelly, Hugh G. Petrie, and Lois Weis. 1991. *Textbooks in American society: Politics, policy, and pedagogy.* New York: State University of New York Press.

Anderson, Beverly L. 1993. The stages of systemic change. *Educational Leadership* 51 (1): 14–17.

Anderson, Gary L. 1998. Toward authentic participation: Deconstructing the discourses of participatory reforms in education. *American Educational Research Journal* 35 (4): 571–603.

Apple, Michael W., and Linda K. Christian-Smith, eds. 1991. *The politics of the textbook.* New York: Routledge.

Banathy, Bela. H. 1996. *Designing social systems in a changing world: A journey toward a creating society.* New York: Plenum Press.

Barnett, Bruce G., Margaret R. Basom, Diane M. Yerkes, and Cynthia J. Norris. 2000. Cohorts in educational leadership programs: Benefits, difficulties, and the potential for developing school leaders. *Educational Administration Quarterly* 36 (2): 255–282.

Barnett, Bruce G., and I. D. Muse. 1993. Cohort groups in educational administration: Promises and challenges. *Journal of School Leadership* 3: 400–415.

Berliner, David C., and Bruce J. Biddle. 1995. *The manufactured crisis: Myths, fraud, and the attack on America's public schools.* Cambridge, MA: Perseus Books.

Bohm, David. 1992. *Thought as a System.* New York: Routledge.

Boorstin, Daniel J. 1987. *The image: A guide to pseudo-events in America.* New York: Vintage Books.

Buber, Martin. 1988. *Eclipse of God.* Edited and translated by Maurice Friedman. 1946. Reprint, Atlantic Highlands, NJ: Humanities Press International.

———. 1992. *On intersubjectivity and cultural creativity.* Ed. and with an introduction by Shmuel N. Eisenstadt. Chicago: The University of Chicago Press.

Burbules, Nicholas C., and Suzanne Rice. 1991. Dialogue across differences: Continuing the conversation. *Harvard Education Review* 61 (4): 393–416.

Carr, Alison A. 1996. Distinguishing systemic and systematic! *Tech Trends* 41 (1): 16–20.

Cole, John Y., and Thomas G. Sticht, eds. 1981. *The textbook in American society: A volume based on a conference at the Library of Congress on May 2–3, 1979.* Washington, D.C.: Library of Congress.

Csikszentmihalyi, Mihaly. 1990. *Flow: The psychology of optimal experience.* New York: HarperPerennial.

———. 1993. *The evolving self: A psychology for the third millennium.* New York: HarperPerennial.

Cuban, Larry. 1993. *How teachers taught: Constancy and change in American classrooms 1880–1990.* 2d ed. New York: Teachers College Press.

Cunningham, William G. 1982. *Systematic planning for educational change.* Palo Alto, CA: Mayfield.

Dalton, Mary M. 1999. *The Hollywood curriculum: Teachers and teaching in the movies.* New York: Peter Lang.

Flick, Deborah L. 1998. *From debate to dialogue: Using the understanding process to transform our conversations.* Boulder, CO: Orchid Publications.

Fullan, Michael G., and Andy Hargreaves. 1996. *What's worth fighting for in your school.* New York: Teachers College Press.

Fullan, Michael G., and Suzanne Stiegelbauer. 1991. *The new meaning of educational change.* New York: Teachers College Press.

Gaddy, Barbara B., T. William Hall, and Robert J. Marzano. 1996. *School wars: Resolving our conflicts over religion and values.* San Francisco: Jossey-Bass Publishers.

Giroux, Henry A. 1988. *Teachers as intellectuals: Toward a critical pedagogy of learning.* Westport, CT: Bergin and Garvey.

———. 1996. *Fugitive cultures: Race, violence and youth.* New York: Routledge.

———. 1996. *Living dangerously: Multiculturalism and the politics of difference.* New York: Peter Lang.

Hargreaves, Andy. 1994. *Changing teachers, changing times: Teachers' work and culture in the postmodern age.* New York: Teachers College Press.

hooks, bell. 1996. *Reel to reel: Race, sex, and class at the movies.* New York: Routledge.

Horn, Raymond A. 2001. Promoting social justice and caring in schools and communities: The unrealized potential of the cohort model. *Journal of School Leadership* 11 (4): 313–334.

Horn, Raymond A., and Alison A. Carr-Chellman. 2000. Providing systemic change for schools: Towards professional development through moral conversation. *Systems Research and Behavioral Science* 45 (3): 255–272.

Isaacs, William. 1999. *Dialogue and the art of thinking together.* New York: Currency.

Jenlink, Patrick M., and Alison A. Carr. 1996. Conversation as a medium for change in education. *Educational Technology* 36 (1): 31–38.

Jenlink, Patrick M., Charles M. Reigeluth, Alison A. Carr, and Lori M. Nelson. 2000. *Facilitating systemic change in school districts: A guidebook.* Bloomington, IN: The Systemic Change Agency.

Kliebard, Herbert M. 1995. *The struggle for the American curriculum, 1893–1958.* 2d ed. New York: Routledge.

Marshall, J. Dan, and James T. Sears. 1990. An evolutionary and metaphorical journey into teaching and thinking about curriculum. In *Teaching and thinking about curriculum: Critical inquiries,* edited by J. Dan Marshall and James T. Sears. New York: Teachers College Press.

Nash, Gary B., Charlotte Crabtree, and Ross E. Dunn. 2000. *History on trial: Culture wars and the teaching of the past.* New York: Vintage Books.

National Commission on Excellence in Education. 1983. *A nation at risk: The report of the national commission on excellence in education.* Washington, DC: U.S. Department of Education.

Postman, Neil. 1984. *The disappearance of childhood.* New York: Vintage Books.

Ravitch, Diane. 2000. *Left back: A century of failed school reforms.* New York: Simon and Schuster.

Rose, Lowell C., and Alec M. Gallup. 2000. The 32nd annual Phi Delta Kappa/Gallup poll of the public's attitudes toward the public schools. *Phi Delta Kappan* 82 (1): 41–66.

Scheurich, James J. 1997. *Research method in the postmodern.* London: Falmer Press.

Senge, Peter M. 1990. *The fifth discipline: The art and practice of the learning organization.* New York: Currency Doubleday.

Senge, Peter M., Art Kleiner, Charlotte Roberts, Richard Ross, George Roth, and Bryan Smith. 1999. *The dance of change: The challenges to sustaining momentum in learning organizations—A fifth discipline resource.* New York: Currency Doubleday.

Sergiovanni, Thomas J. 1994. *Building community in schools.* San Francisco: Jossey-Bass.

Sidorkin, Alexander M. 1999. *Beyond discourse: Education, the self, and dialogue.* New York: State University of New York Press.

Spring, Joel. 1998. *Conflict of interest: The politics of American education.* Boston: McGraw-Hill.

Steinberg, Shirley R., and Joe L. Kincheloe, eds. 1997. *Kinderculture: The corporate construction of childhood.* Boulder, CO: Westview.

Tönnies, Ferdinand. [1887] 1957. *Gemeinschaft und gesellschaft [Community and society].* Edited and translated by Charles P. Loomis. Reprint. New York: HarperCollins.

Yankelovitch, Daniel. 1999. *The magic of dialogue: Transforming conflict into cooperation.* New York: Simon and Schuster.

Chapter Six

✏ The Dilemma of Educational Research

From the history of education, one thing is certain—education is always being reformed. From the 1800s to the present, not only has there been a continuous perception that education needs to be reformed, but also, to judge from most reform scenarios, education exists in a constant state of crisis. In the earlier chapters, the continuous and compelling need to reform education was discussed in the context of political activity by special interests that were using education to achieve their larger political agendas. However, there is another factor that has contributed to the ongoing need to reform education. This factor is the inability of the field of education to develop an integrated, functional, and publicly acceptable research base. Unlike the fields of math, science, medicine, law, business, and the social sciences, education does not have a research tradition that promotes the reputation of expertise that other fields have been able to achieve. Ellen Lagemann aptly summarizes the "awful reputation" of educational research in her statement that "education research has been demeaned by scholars in other fields, ignored by practitioners, and alternatively spoofed and criticized by politicians, policy makers, and members of the public at large" (2000, 232). How did this situation arise?

An integrated research base implies that professionals in a field have a common language, an understanding of all of the research methodologies employed in their field, and the ability to see how the various kinds of research in their field connect with each other. Even though each discipline within the field has its own conventions and protocols, when the disciplines converge, a reasoned course of action can be planned and implemented that is supported by the collective rigor of all participating disciplines. An example from the medical field of this integration of research is when medical specialists meet to diagnose the patient's illness and prescribe a reasonable remedy that is research-based. This meeting of the minds can occur in a reasonable amount of time because of the shared research tradition, methodologies, and vocabulary, as well as respect for each other's level of professionalism. In the field of education, non-educators, who are generally not knowledgeable about educational research and research methods, are often the decision makers in determining educational reform. In addition, those closest to the students and those who recognize the most relevant needs of the students (i.e., teachers, guidance counselors, and frontline administrators) are excluded from decisions about their students, decisions that they must eventually implement. Some individuals support this exclusion because educational practitioners rarely engage in research, or because the research methods that teachers use, such as action research, are not as valued as more formal and scientific research. In fact, most teachers and administrators are not trained in research methods, or at best receive one general course in research method in their preparation.

Functionality is a critical factor in the public's acceptance of educational research. In the case of the field of medicine, the public is generally satisfied with the research-based decision-making process utilized by doctors because it generally resolves the problem. Consequently, the public accepts the medical practitioner as the primary decision maker, and also indirectly accepts the research base that supports those decisions. In the case of both medicine and education, the public generally has no technical understanding of the field's research base, but due to the perceived functionality of medical research and the perceived lack of functionality of educational research, the public generally accepts the authority of medicine and continuously rejects that of education.

One significant outcome is that educational policy and practice are more vulnerable to criticism from non-educators. Unlike other professions that have developed a sound research base, educational theory and practice are sufficiently fragmented that the dueling theories and instructional practices can be easily utilized by special interests inside and outside the field to discredit specific theories and practices that do not align with their own. This fragmentation provides opportunities for some to exploit education, which in turn diminishes the overall effectiveness of education.

A related outcome is that the general public can easily rely on their own experience-based intuition to criticize the theory and practice of professional educators. Even though education is viewed as one of the most significant institutions in society, it is one of the most easily criticized. Many other fields, as mentioned above, have developed a reputation for professionalism and expertise that makes them resistant to public scrutiny and criticism. Despite the availability of information that could be used by the public to criticize the fundamental theories and practices of other fields, the public rarely critiques these fields with the intensity and tenacity they employ in their criticism of education. Another contributing factor is the continuous perception that schools fail in their purpose and function, and therefore need to be constantly reformed. This alleged ongoing failure serves to diminish the status of educators in relation to professionals in other fields and makes members of the lay public even more ready to rely on their own intuition.

Other factors play a role. Constant changes in society and culture, along with individual diversity and uniqueness, confound attempts to develop foundational theories that can be translated into standardized practice that is appropriate over a long period of time. Human diversity is such that the problems that arise are not simple and straightforward in their representation, but as some systems theorists have noted, are "messy" and "wicked." Messy and wicked problems are inherently complex and are not responsive to simple solutions. In addition, the resolution of these problems requires a diversity of research methods. Also, new knowledge and new ways of looking at reality that are created in other fields, when applied to education, further complicate any attempt to reach an understanding of how individuals learn. In the 1900s, theories concerning relativity, chaos, quantum mechanics, and postpositivistic inquiry further problematized existing educational theory and practice.

Another condition that affects the public perception of the efficacy of education and of the research behind it is the inability of education to impart critical research skills to their students. Some individuals argue that the general public lacks the critical skills necessary to assess and critically analyze the various and competitive theories about educational practice. They maintain that because of this lack of skill in understanding and critiquing theories, the public is susceptible to the hyperbole and propaganda that often surround the theory and practice presented by a special interest group. This lack of criticality in the general public facilitates the public's use of uninformed intuition as the primary basis for their critique of education, and, in some cases, increases their susceptibility to simplistic and politically driven educational reform. Other fields, which are perceived to have a higher level of professionalism than education, are less susceptible to the public's use of uninformed intuition because of the buffering effect of the field's perceived unassailable professionalism. The public's inability to look critically at educational practice and reform policies results in a concomitant inability to understand the enormous and systemic complexity of education, and to discern the political, economic, cultural, and social hidden agendas of those promoting the reforms.

The most significant condition that contributes to the lack of respect for educational research is that there is no consensus in education concerning theory and practice that would lead to a unified structure of educational theory and practice. In other words, when education is assailed by its critics, the idea of educational best practice does not carry the weight that is associated with what is understood as best practice in other fields. What educators propose as best practice is easily contested by others because of the debate within education, each school of thought contending for the appropriateness of its own theories, research methodologies, and practice. The contentious debate within education about theory, practice, and inquiry creates a situation in which any particular version of best practice can easily be challenged.

To understand this dilemma requires an examination of the research methods employed by educators, of the relationship between educational theory and practice, and of the way educators view and attempt to deal with change.

THE DUELING PHILOSOPHIES
OF RESEARCH METHODOLOGY

Any discussion of educational research must first deal with the great divide between two research methodologies—quantitative and qualitative. A research methodology is the overall strategy that is used to seek new knowledge that can be considered trustworthy. Each methodology employed by researchers reflects a philosophy about the kinds of knowledge that are valued and appropriate methods to uncover this knowledge.

Any education graduate student quickly learns that quantitative and qualitative researchers see knowledge in very different ways. Some scholars have identified this distinction in research methodology as the key factor that problematizes how and what we know about all aspects of education. It also contributes significantly to the problems associated with education's professional image. The dilemma that is created by this great divide is not merely about how to do research but also involves the purpose of research, the origins of knowledge, and the subsequent epistemological basis for educational decision making. To fully understand this dilemma requires a look at the current condition of educational research.

The Purpose of Educational Research

The most common perception is that the purpose of educational research is to ensure the effectiveness of educational practice. However, this purpose quickly expands to include the use of research to inform educational policy decisions, to support the political objectives of special interests within and outside the educational community, to guide decisions about local educational initiatives, and to further the careers of educational professionals. Many educators, especially practitioners, argue that the purpose that is least achieved is the use of research to improve teaching in the schools. This argument is supported by the pervasive skepticism that emanates from practitioners when faced with research-based staff development initiatives. As will be discussed in Chapter 9, practitioner resistance to educational reforms is often justified by the tenuous relationship between researchers and practitioners.

Some scholars have focused on the political nature of research methodology. Patti Lather (1999) presents the view that the employment of research methodology is an ideological act. P. C. Sederberg (1984) proposes that ideology and research methodology are similar in that both seek consensus in the knowledge that is uncovered, both promote a shared meaning within their respective communities, both develop accepted procedures for the construction and validation of their conclusions, both attempt to create a foundation for understanding the realities of society, and both attempt to enforce their methods and epistemological philosophies. Acceptance of the views of Lather and Sederberg is an acceptance that research methodologies are neither neutral nor value-free, but inherently biased by the process that emerges from the foundational philosophy of the methodology. Proponents of this view argue that the result is a need for a continuous critique of the methods and intent of all researchers. One implication of this view is that knowledge generated by research must be suspect and critically examined for the effects of the knowledge on the power arrangements within education. A further proposition of this view is that all research has a hidden agenda, which may not necessarily lead to educational best practice for all educational stakeholders.

Like education, research is a complicated affair and potentially has many purposes. Given the many possible purposes of research, the knowledge discovered, constructed, or created by research becomes suspect. To evaluate research requires skill in critical reflection skill and knowledge of research methodology on the part of those who must deal with the research. Proponents of this skeptical view propose that all research is, to a degree, decontextualized, in the sense that not all of the background, conditions, or facts of the case have been disclosed. Therefore, those who must act on the research must have the ability to critique the research in relation to the lack of context provided by the researchers. Nonresearchers also need the critical skills to determine the relevance of the research to their local context.

As previously mentioned, these skills are rarely developed in administrators, teachers, students, parents, and the general public, yet practitioners have to come to some conclusions, since the purposes of the researchers may not be compatible with the purposes of the practitioners. What often happens is that practitioners intuitively deduce a disparity in purpose, drawing on their own professional and personal experience. These intuitive conclusions reinforce the resistance practitioners are apt to feel to research conclusions when they don't really understand them, or don't understand how the knowledge on which they're based was derived. In addition, the contentious debate between the different research methodologies further supports practitioner unease about any best practice proposed by researchers.

The Origins of Knowledge and Educational Decision Making

Knowledge may be based on intuition, on experience, or on research-based evidence. According to some research methodologies, intuition and experience are entirely too subjective to provide knowledge to support credible educational decisions; only empirical research methods give valid knowledge, and only they provide a viable basis for decision making. Other research methodologies maintain that since all reality is subjective, intuition and experience are viable informants of educational decisions. The various attitudes researchers can have concerning the three sources that inform decision making can be seen as falling on a continuum, with objectivism at one end, subjectivism at the other, and constructivism somewhere in the middle.

Michael Crotty (1998) proposes that the great divide in educational research is more accurately defined by an individual's position on this continuum than by whether an individual is a quantitative or qualitative researcher. Crotty explains that some individuals in both research methodologies can share the same epistemological philosophy. An examination of the historical development of qualitative research and the evolution of qualitative methodology indicates that in the initial development of qualitative methodology, most qualitative researchers shared the same objectivist foundations and understandings of the quantitative researchers. In fact, the field of qualitative research can be divided between postpositivistic (see Glossary) qualitative researchers who share the philosophical foundations of quantitative research, and the constructivist and subjectivist qualitative researchers who operate from philosophical perspectives that significantly differ from the objectivist philosophy of quantitative research. The later development of more radical constructivist and subjectivist qualitative inquiry, which sharply contrasts with the objectivist philosophy of traditional qualitative researchers, supports this conclusion. Crotty proposes that what actually separates researchers is their fundamental position on the nature of knowledge and the acquisition of knowledge.

Those who see the world through an objectivist lens fundamentally believe that knowledge is discovered, that meaning exists apart from human consciousness. In other words, objects have meaning in isolation from human thought. Crotty provides the example of the meaning of a tree. From an objectivist's point of view, a tree is a tree regardless of human awareness or interaction with it. This is essentially a positivist position, one that discounts the human dimension in meaning making. If knowledge is external to human awareness, then it is simply a matter of empirically discovering that knowledge and conveying it to those who must act on the knowledge. Quantitative researchers are objectivists in that they believe that, through the rigid application of the scientific method and related scientifically acceptable procedures, they can discover and validate knowledge.

The implication for objectivist knowledge production is that through scientific procedures the whole can be reduced to its parts, which in turn can be quantified and analyzed to discover meaning. This objectivist way of doing research results in hierarchical classifications of knowledge and the belief that knowledge discovered in one context can be generalized to different locations and contexts. Additionally, quantitative research involving individuals objectifies these individuals by eliminating the uncontrollable variables that make up the human condition. In the objectivist view of research, the knower is separate from the known, and the subjective awareness of individuals is discounted. All that counts is the formal knowledge that is scientifically derived by credentialed experts.

Constructivists, on the other hand, believe that meaning is constructed, not discovered or created, when humans engage the realities of the world. Constructivists maintain that there is an interplay between objects (things that exist external to individuals) and human consciousness. In the example of the tree, the tree is a real object, but its meaning is constructed when people become aware of it and think about it. What the tree means is constructed by the individual; however, this construction is affected by the physical nature of the tree. Involved in this act of construction are the individual's unique characteristics, as well as the social and cultural environment in which the individual lives. How the tree is defined, then, depends to some extent on the individual and the individual's culture, not only on the physical characteristics of the tree.

Thus the tree can be seen as having multiple meanings because of the difference in individuals, cultures, and time periods.

Thus, unlike the objectivist view, in which meaning is grounded solely in the object, the constructivist view grounds meaning in the human interaction with the object. One implication of this view is that to know truth requires an ecological view of the interplay between the individual and the object. Meaning cannot be derived solely from an analysis of the parts, but must also include an analysis of the whole. A further implication is that all knowledge is valued, not just formal scientific knowledge. Intuition and experience are relevant areas of investigation. In this view, because of the focus on the individual, the social, and the process of meaning construction, qualitative research methods are as appropriate as quantitative methods in education, if not more appropriate.

This conclusion is supported by the constructivist assertion that an individual's culture and society influence the way that individual constructs meaning, although at the same time the culture makes it difficult to perceive that meanings are actually being constructed about an object or phenomenon. Constructivists see qualitative research as having the potential to move through these masking and filtering layers to more deeply understand the individual's construction of meaning. Critical constructivists (Kincheloe 1993) add a critical dimension of power to the constructivist process. In the critical perspective, how power arrangements affect the human construction of meaning must be assessed in the investigation of meaning making. To fully understand the critical aspect of the construction of meaning requires an investigation of the historical context of the situation. The historical context of every situation and phenomenon becomes an essential element in the understanding of the meanings attached to the situation. The constructivist view also differs from the objectivist in that the knower and the known are intimately connected through the process of constructing meaning.

At the other end of this continuum is subjectivism, the belief that meaning is neither discovered nor constructed but completely created by the individual. In this view, only the individual creates meaning, which is imposed on the object by human thought. All knowledge is considered subjective because all individuals are different, and the meaning that they give an object depends on their personal and cultural uniqueness. There is no interplay between object and subject—there is only the subject. Meaning can come from the individual's thoughts, from dreams, or from Jungian archetypes within the collective consciousness. All meaning is relative. Because of this relativity, predictability is not possible, and one must accept uncertainty. The inherent relativity of subjectivism sharply contrasts with the realism of objectivism, and the interplay of realism and relativity of constructivism. This sharp difference between objectivism and subjectivism can be easily seen in the intense focus on statistical description and analysis provided by quantitative research studies, and in the personally subjective analysis provided in the narrative and theoretical works of previously mentioned authors such as bell hooks and Henry Giroux. In addition, subjectivist qualitative educational research is supported by a body of work by recognized scholars such as Valerie Bentz and Jeremy Shapiro (1998); Michael Connelly and Jean Clandinin (1999); David Cooperrider, Peter Sorensen, Diana Whitney, and Therese Yaeger (2000); Egon Guba and Yvonna Lincoln (1989); Donald Polkinghorne (1995); and Carol Witherell and Nel Noddings (1991).

The work done by subjectivists in educational research is different from the work done by constructivists, as will be brought out later, but both share the conviction that qualitative research is much more likely to be of real use in the field of education. Later in the chapter more will be said about the differences between quantitative and qualitative research, but first it seems useful to provide more background by going into some detail about the current condition of educational research.

These three paradigms are distinctly different in the way they view the nature of knowledge and the processes used to uncover knowledge, as well as in the way they view the decision making based on knowledge. The differences between these three ways of seeing the world are also evident in the ideological differences and subsequent views on the purpose of research held by these individuals. How these differences play out in education can be seen in the current condition of educational research.

THE CURRENT CONDITION
OF EDUCATIONAL RESEARCH

Given the diversity of research purposes, methodological philosophies, and beliefs about what constitutes knowledge, how is this diversity reflected in current educational research? How do these differences inform the current debate about educational research? The answers to these questions can be found in a description of various assessments of the current condition of educational research and of the debate over the creation and implementation of quality research standards, an examination of the political pressures on educational research, and a look at the funding of educational research.

The Current Condition As It Is Assessed

Currently, there is agreement among conservative and liberal educational decision makers that, at best, educational research is uneven in its quality and, at worst, too much research is simply bad. Alexandra K. Wigdor, the director of the study panel for the newly formed Strategic Education Research Program (SERP), points out that despite the large expenditure of money on education (approximately 7 percent of the gross national product), the field is largely uninformed by research (Viadero 2001, paragraph 8). Other scholars point out that only a small amount of educational reform is actually research based. Berliner and Biddle (1995) propose that one of the reasons for this lack of research-based reform is that those who mandate reform do not demand to see the results of research supporting the reform before they implement the reform. One reason action is taken that is not research based is that there is little incentive for publishers who market reform materials to support or pay for foundational research. Rather, the publisher only has to package the reform in such a way that it becomes saleable to those affected by the reform.

Robert W. Carlson (1996) argues that the nature of current school reform inhibits the use of research to inform reform decisions. Carlson states that most studies of organizations tend to be snapshots of one point in time, ahistorical in that they ignore the past experiences that inform the present. Also, most studies are rooted in objectivist methodologies, with other methodologies viewed as unacceptable. This creates a preponderance of positivist studies, which are perceived by practitioners as not providing relevant information. As an example, practitioners who are not skilled in formal objectivist research simply disregard the seemingly esoteric quantitative research. In addition, in many cases the concerns of practitioners are not easily answered by decontextualized scientific studies. Also, Carlson notes that much of the research is done by academics who must produce the research in a relatively short period of time, thus reducing complicated problems and situations to simplistic conclusions that can be easily challenged by practitioner intuition and experience.

The quality of research that can be applied to practice is also affected by the fact that many academic researchers work in university settings that view teaching as the primary responsibility of the professor, with scholarly research at best equal in weight. Many of these professors have been practitioners, and they tend to rely upon their pedagogical experience rather than theory in the preparation of their students. In many universities, a heavy teaching load with other service-oriented duties relegate scholarly research to the status of an add-on activity when time permits. Also, as will be discussed in more detail, funding for research on teaching and the preparation of teachers is seriously lacking (Cruickshank 1990).

With all this being the case, the most stringent new objectivist initiative to alter this current situation has been initiated by the George W. Bush administration. In a restructuring of the Elementary and Secondary Education Act (ESEA), often referred to as the leave no child behind act of 2001, an emphasis on scientifically based research has been mandated. Through this law, Congress and the Bush administration aim to focus school reform more on research-based findings than intuition and experience. In addition, "research-based" will be defined as scientifically based research. The following is the definition of scientifically based research from the act (U.S. Department of Education 2002):

(37) scientifically based research—the term scientifically based research:

(A) means research that involves the application of rigorous, systematic, and objective procedures to obtain reliable and valid knowledge relevant to education activities and programs; and

(B) includes research that—

i. employs systematic, empirical methods that draw on observation or experiment;

ii. involves rigorous data analyses that are adequate to test the stated hypotheses and justify the general conclusions drawn;

iii. relies on measurements or observational methods that provide reliable and valid data across evaluators and observers, across multiple measurements and observations, and across studies by the same or different investigators;

iv. is evaluated using experimental or quasi-experimental designs in which individuals, entities, programs, or activities are assigned to different conditions and with appropriate controls to evaluate the effects of the condition of interest, with a preference for random-assignment experiments, or other designs to the extent that those designs contain within-condition or across-condition controls;

v. ensures that experimental studies are presented in sufficient detail and clarity to allow for replication or, at a minimum, offer the opportunity to build systematically on their findings; and

vi. has been accepted by a peer-reviewed journal or approved by a panel of independent experts through a comparably rigorous, objective, and scientific review. (Title IX, SEC. 9101, paragraph 37)

This definition has caused a debate in the educational community where educators with differing methodological philosophies have interpreted this statement in different ways. Some argue that this definition will result in only strictly controlled scientific studies that will be narrowly experimental and quasi-experimental in nature. They fear that there will not be a degree of latitude that will allow a diversity of research that may range from qualitative studies to literary explorations of educational issues. Some critics of this definition argue that good research simply poses significant questions, grounds the study in relevant theory, and uses the appropriate research tools, which may be objectivist or subjectivist, that can answer the question. The problem that these critics have with the Bush definition is that it clearly does not recognize constructivist or subjectivist qualitative research as legitimate research methodology. Others see a reliance on purely positivistic research as a denial of the experience and intuition of the practitioner, and a further disempowerment of those practitioners in educational decision making. Their fear is that a scientific culture will be fostered that will fail to fully explore the complexity that is inherent in education.

Another fear of some critics is that qualitative research, which employs and promotes participatory research that significantly involves and empowers teachers and administrators in the research process, often referred to as action research, will be considered as inappropriate research. These critics further point out that the definition given in the act has significant implications for practitioners who conduct action research to improve their schools and their teaching. One consequence of a devaluation of participatory research is that the highly contextual local knowledge of the individual practitioners will be supplanted by the formal objectivist knowledge of experts external to school environments. An additional problem that some qualitative researchers have with the Bush plan is the reductionist tendency of empirical research. This fear is supported by SERP's intent to select a few important problems at a time and devote their research focus and resources to the scientific resolution of these problems. This opens the door to a focus on whatever issues are politically hot at any given time, which means overlooking the myriad of other and perhaps more important issues deemed problematic by educational scholars and practitioners.

Creating and Implementing Quality Research Standards

The important question is whether the federal government or state governments can enforce a mandated definition of quality research. Some experts claim that most state departments of education, for various reasons, do not have the expertise to draw up or enforce research standards that would align with the intent of the act of 2001.

Since most dissemination of educational research occurs in professional journals, the organizations and associations that sponsor these journals would have to align their purpose, mission, and manuscript guidelines with the federal definition. This would be indeed problematic for many journals. Those that serve practitioners and tend to have larger subscription bases do not rely on rigid research-based criteria for what they include in their issues. Also, any journal, no matter how currently respected in the profession, that does not conform to the definition imposed by the federal government would have to change its basic purpose and philosophy to conform. Some scholars feel that this change should not occur, because these autonomous journals support a diversity of research methodologies that provide the multiple lenses needed to understand the complexity of education. They are also skeptical that this research diversity can be replaced by a standard definition. Also, the fact that there are numerous writing formats for scholarly research becomes a problem. Since the format provided by the American Psychological Association (APA 2001) is the most scientific, does that mean that APA format will become the only acceptable format?

One additional factor in the implementation of a standard definition is that there is a scarcity of federally funded research organizations that can further define the Bush administration's intent. The regional research laboratories established during the Johnson administration of the 1960s no longer exert influence on educational research, having been absorbed into the National Institute of Education (NIE). One problem that has always plagued education is the lack of an organization like the National Institutes of Health that can provide a well-funded focus on research. The creation of NIE in 1972 failed to provide this focus due to consistently poor funding and the specific instructions attached to the funding by Congress. In 1985, the NIE was absorbed into the Office of Education Research and Improvement (OERI); however, the OERI has also been continuously underfunded and mostly focuses on statistics and program assessment.

Another impediment to the implementation of the act's definition of scientifically based research is the hierarchical organization of educational research. In the current system, university researchers have greater authority in defining and doing research than professors who train teachers and administrators. In relation to the universities and colleges, public school practitioners not only do little research but also are uninformed about research jargon and methodology. Merely establishing a scientific focus among university professors would do little to overcome the resistance of practitioners to the esoteric language used in research and to compensate for the lack of practitioner understanding of what constitutes good research.

Political Pressure on Educational Research

Unlike other fields, there is a continuously intense political pressure on educational research to support the mandate of the moment. On a state level, state departments of education are pressured to recognize the quality and effectiveness of programs mandated by the governor and legislature. In addition, the ranking of the educational achievement of the states and the pressure to conform to programs that are popular in many other states cause state educational agencies to focus more on the political context than on a research context.

On a national level, currently many educators and other experts are determining that the only way a scientific culture can be established is to insulate national and state educational agencies from political interference. In support of this conclusion, they cite examples of the contradictory and dual roles that educational agencies must perform. On one hand, these agencies are to be impartial evaluators of educational research, but on the other they must help the government successfully implement government-desired mandates. One outcome is that education agencies must always put the appropriate spin on the research they report, a spin that suits the political preferences of those who control the agencies—the president and Congress.

Educational research is also susceptible to the political pressure that arises from change in society. Carlson (1996) reports three cycles of organizational change in society that affect education: political, technical, and cultural. Each of these aspects of society experiences a natural occurrence of change. In other words, change is a constant factor in society. Carlson proposes that it is not so much that education fails to meet the needs of society, but rather that education must better manage these cycles of change. As this inevitable change occurs, those most immediately affected by the change charge that the change is due to the failure of education. They then demand that education immediately change to accommodate the needs of that sector of society. Their demands instantly translate into political pressure through the governments on education. This change scenario relates to educational research, in that how educational research is defined will affect how well education can proactively understand how societal change impacts the educational system, and how well education can respond to this continuing challenge. If research is narrowly defined, then numerous other ways of seeing and understanding this change phenomenon will not contribute to the understanding and successful management of how societal change impacts educational practice.

A final aspect of the politics of educational research is the assertion by some academic researchers that there actually is good research that never gets implemented. If research supports programs that are traditionally opposed by the political party in control of the government, that research will largely be ignored. Also, because of the lack of a common agreement on what constitutes good research and the lack of respect by many quantitative and qualitative researchers for each other's methodologies, good research generated by both methodologies is denigrated by the other side.

The Inadequate Funding of Educational Research

Educators, regardless of their position on research, agree with the assertion that funding of educational research is woefully lacking. Ironically, while federal support for education is rising, the funding for research is falling. A National Research Council committee recently reported that while the total funding for OERI increased from 1980 to 2000, the percentage of funding for actual research bottomed out at 15 percent (Olsen and Viadero 2002, paragraph 33). The rest of the money is service oriented, in that support is provided for schools to implement mandated programs and specific research projects deemed necessary by the government. Other educators point to the bigger picture, in which federal support for medical research runs into the billions of dollars per year, while a few hundred million are set aside to cover the entire spectrum of costs associated with educational research. In relation to federal budget allocations for national defense, 15 percent of the defense budget goes toward research, while only 0.1 percent of the education budget allocation goes toward research (Berliner and Biddle 1995, 347).

A significant trend in the allocation of funding for educational research and development started in 1973. At that time over $400 million was allocated for this purpose. Within a year, the funding was cut in half, and through the 1980s and early 1990s it remained below $100 million. The political views and economic events of those decades relegated educational research to a low national priority. Another factor in the low level of federal funding of educational research was the transfer of responsibility for curriculum development from the NSF to the newly created Department of Education. This brought to an end the influence and funding that the NSF had used to promote research in the field of curriculum. Obviously, such a low level of research and development funding has contributed to the current condition of educational re-search. Private organizations such as the Spencer Foundation have gen-erously provided research grants; without significant federal and state funding, however, many believe that educational research can never at-tain the status that research has attained in other fields.

THE QUANDARY OF QUANTITATIVE AND QUALITATIVE RESEARCH

A full understanding of the dilemma facing educational research now requires looking at greater length at the great divide between quantita-tive research and qualitative research. That division still seems valid, since the underlying philosophy of quantitative research is objectivism, and qualitative research has been more and more characterized by ei-ther constructivism or subjectivism.

Quantitative Research

The recent call by the Bush administration for a scientific research base to become the foundation for educational decision making is a call for one kind of research, scientific quantitative research, to become the ex-clusive source of educational information. Scientific research is per-ceived to be systematic, testable, and objective. In all scientific re-search, variables that affect an outcome are to be controlled so as to lead to valid and reliable results that can be generalized to other popu-lations and places, and that can be used to make cause-and-effect pre-dictions. Quantitative research is based on the belief that a degree of certainty can be derived from the discoveries obtained through a disci-plined scientific inquiry. Validity (based on whether the research actu-ally measured what it was supposed to measure) and reliability (based on the ability to consistently replicate the findings) are obtained through the control of unanticipated variables that might affect the outcome of the research. This control is achieved through the use of proper procedures by the researcher and by the use of statistical meas-ures designed to quantify the influence of the unanticipated variables on the research findings. Statistics are also used to determine the sig-nificance of the research. Significance is defined in relation to the de-gree of probability that the result obtained by the researcher was caused by the treatment applied to the subject by the researcher, and not by other variables or chance. Probability statements, or P-values, which give a number to the level of probability that the result was caused by the treatment being researched, represent the ultimate statistical abstraction of reality.

The basic design of scientific research is represented by the format used by researchers to report their findings. The basic format used to report research findings consists of the following parts: introduction, review of the literature, description of methodology used, results, discussion of results, and a reference list for the prior research used to provide a theoretical basis for the study. These parts of a research paper approximate the sequential nature of quantitative research. Generally, in quantitative research a research question or hypothesis is developed in relation to a problem, a methodology or strategy is developed that will allow the proper collection and analysis of data, and results are obtained and analyzed. At the end of this process, to some degree the question is answered or the hypothesis is proved or disproved.

In reporting research, the introduction provides background on the problem or question, a problem statement, a discussion of the significance of the problem, a statement of the research question or hypothesis, and a declaration of the purpose of the research. The introduction is followed by a review of the literature, that is, prior studies related to the research question. The purposes of the literature review are varied. In the literature review, the researcher can refine the research problem, develop significance for the research, identify methodological techniques, identify contradictory findings, and develop the research hypothesis. A basic literature review may include a summary and an analysis of previous research, and provide a link between previous research and the purpose of the study under investigation (McMillan 2000). The construction and nature of the literature review emphasizes the importance of grounding current research in previous research and of following the research protocols established by the scholarly scientific community.

These protocols are restrictive, in that only sources that used an acceptable quantitative design, were published in peer-reviewed scholarly journals, and conformed to the publication formats provided by professional organizations such as the American Psychological Association are considered appropriate sources to ground a research study. The purpose of the blind peer review process is to inject a degree of objectivity in the inevitably subjective assignment of merit to research projects. Generally, when research is submitted to a scholarly journal, the editor of the journal sends an anonymous copy of the research to three other scholars in that field. Their job is to critique every aspect of the research and to recommend rejection, revisions, or acceptance. This process is the last check on the scholarly rigor of the design, theoretical grounding, methodology, and findings of the research. Even though the purpose of this process is to ensure an objective evaluation of the research through the anonymity of the researcher and the reviewers, the research bias of the reviewers, the journal editor, and the journal philosophy is a palpable subjective presence in the process.

Nonscientific research by a nonscientist in an unapproved journal is not acceptable as a source to be included in a review of literature. In fact, distinctions are made between scholarly journals and practitioner journals, as well as between scholarly journals. Practitioner journals are not considered purveyors of acceptable research because invariably they do not contain peer-reviewed articles and do not conform to the other research protocols for conducting and reporting research. Within the world of scholarly journals, there is a recognized hierarchy of scholarly journals based upon subscription rate, acceptance rate of submitted manuscripts, the prestige of the scholars on the journals' editorial boards, journal prestige, and how often authors who were published in the journal were cited in other scholarly publications. This structure is maintained because of the promotion and tenure system in higher education. All universities use scholarly publication as a significant determinant of the promotion and granting of tenure to professors. Some top research universities even designate a few specific journals as the only ones that can be used to attain promotion and tenure.

In the accepted design of research, the methodology section follows the review of the literature. The purpose of the methodology is to disclose the data gathering and analysis strategy by describing in detail the data collection and analysis methods. This section normally includes a detailed description of the data collection methods, the instrument that was used to collect the data or used to apply the treatment (the independent variable) to the subjects, the sample or subjects of the study, the data collection procedure, and the data analysis techniques. As the significance of the review of the literature is to ground the present study in prior theory, so the significance of the methodology is to establish that the current research is valid and reliable. The researcher accomplishes this through the anticipation and control of any variables or procedures that could diminish the validity and reliability of the researcher's conclusions. The essence of this process is to prove to the reader that the research was conducted in an objective, value-neutral, and unbiased manner; and that the research measured what it was supposed to measure, thus providing a degree of confidence that if the study were replicated, the same results would occur.

Methodology is followed by an identification of the results. In this section, there is no discussion of the results. Findings gotten from the statistical analysis are presented in the form of charts and tables. A section called the discussion of results, in which the researcher has the latitude to analyze and critique the findings, follows the results section. Here the researcher can discuss the data in light of the previously disclosed theory, or the researcher can discuss any weaknesses in the methodology.

As stated, the essence of this type of research design is the employment of systematic objectivity in the discovery of meanings that can be generalized to other populations and places. Central to this design is the imperative to reduce human activity to its individual parts, making each part a variable that can be controlled. In this reductionist process, at least one independent variable is isolated that will affect a dependent variable identified by the researcher. Any other variables in the situation are called extraneous or confounding variables, which need to be controlled because they may affect the results.

For instance, if a researcher wanted to find out the effects of homework on student achievement on a standardized test, the test results would be the dependent variable because they constitute the variable the researcher is focusing on, trying to discover whether they "depend" on the performance of homework. The test results are of course dependent on or influenced by many other factors, many independent variables. This particular dependent variable could be influenced not only by homework but by independent variables such as the age of the students, the reliability of the test, student characteristics (i.e., race, gender, and socioeconomic status), the time of day the test is administered, the time of the school year the test is given, situations involving the student the night before the test, state funding provided for the school, student test anxiety, procedures used to administer the test, and as many other variables as can be identified.

The challenge to the researcher is, having selected the one independent variable on which the study focuses, in this example homework, to control all of the other variables, now defined as extraneous or confounding variables, so that they do not have any influence over the dependent variable, or at least so that any influence they might have can be quantified and taken into account. If the researcher can prove that the extraneous variables were controlled, then the findings are viewed as valid and reliable because only the isolated independent variable affected the dependent variable. The standard way to control for extraneous variables is to set up a control group. In this case, the idea would be to choose two groups of students alike in every way and give one group homework and the other not. The test administered at the end of the period would be exactly the same for both groups, and so on. The only thing that would be different, in theory, would be the homework, and so the researcher would be entitled to conclude that any difference between the two groups in achievement on the test was the result of the homework.

In the case of the example, if the research is valid, then the results will only indicate the way the independent variable, homework, is acting on the dependent variable, student achievement on a standardized test. The researcher can then say with some degree of scientific confidence, the level of which is indicated by a P-value, that the use of homework does or does not contribute to higher student achievement on a standardized test. The important point of this example is that a complex human situation has been reduced to its individual components, and through this reduction a conclusion has been derived that is now presented as a fact that can be used to support an educational decision. One criticism of this research process is that a complex, highly contextual human situation has been transformed into an abstraction devoid of the concrete context that is essential to any broad and deep understanding of human activity.

There are variations on this basic scientific research design. Experimental research involves the use of control groups along with experimental groups; however, there are nonexperimental quantitative research designs. These include descriptive studies, comparative studies, and correlational studies. Whether experimental or quasi-experimental in design, all quantitative studies start with the researcher's hypothesis, or educated guess, grounded in prior theory, theory that is supposed to itself be based on research conducted in an objective, unbiased, and systematic manner, research that, it is hoped, has resulted in valid and reliable findings. Whether quantitative or qualitative, all research has its own distinctive way of seeing the world, the role of the researcher, the nature of the subjects, and the nature of reality. These distinctions have profound implications for educational reform.

Qualitative Research

Norman K. Denzin and Yvonna S. Lincoln (1994) point out that qualitative research is a complex interconnected family of terms. They state that qualitative research is a field that includes interdisciplinary, transdisciplinary, and counterdisciplinary perspectives on inquiry. In other words, within the boundary of qualitative research reside research traditions that cross the boundaries between separate disciplines such as sociology, anthropology, education, political science, and science in an attempt to increase the understanding of a phenomenon. Because of this diversity of research inquiry, it is not surprising that the field of qualitative research contains elements of objectivism, constructivism, and subjectivism. Some qualitative researchers are objectivist; they utilize the essential understandings of the nature of research and research methodology that is found in quantitative research. This objectivist type of qualitative researcher is often described as postpositivist. In contrast, those qualitative researchers who are at the subjectivist end of the continuum believe that it is not possible to discern an objective reality through the use of any methodology. They also do not believe that research findings have sufficient authority to enable researchers to make cause-and-effect declarations. Instead of valuing explanation and prediction, they value the interpretations of reality that are made by researchers and the participants in the research.

Constructivist qualitative researchers, in the tradition of Egon Guba and Yvonna Lincoln (1989), see reality as pluralistic and relativistic, in the sense that there are multiple and possibly conflicting constructions of meaning about a specific phenomenon. According to Thomas Schwandt (1994), "truth is a matter of the best-informed and most sophisticated construction on which there is consensus at a given time" (128). This constructivist view differs from the postpositivist view that an objective reality can be approximated because it promotes the idea that there are many constructions of reality and the "correct one" is that which is consensually agreed upon at the time. The constructivist view differs from the subjectivist view of qualitative research in that subjectivist researchers are narrowly focused on the individual's interpretations or constructions as the most important understanding of reality. Collective constructions of reality or collective agreement about reality is subordinate to the focus on the individual's constructions.

Postpositivist qualitative researchers employ the same research design used by quantitative researchers, except in a less rigorous manner. Concerns about validity and reliability are central considerations in their research design and inquiry. In addition, a similar emphasis is placed on the need and ability to discover and verify theories that may lead to the prediction of reality. One distinction between postpositivist qualitative researchers and quantitative researchers is that the latter believe that an objective reality can be discovered and quantified, whereas the former tend to occupy something closer to the constructivist middle ground, believing that, due to the inherent complexity of human activity, an objective reality cannot be fully discovered but only approximated.

All qualitative researchers assume that multiple methods lead to a better understanding of reality. These methods may include case studies, interviews, questionnaires, observations, and other ways to capture and interpret human experience. However, some postpositivist qualitative researchers tend to limit themselves to methods that allow statistical analysis, or that can lead to more valid and reliable conclusions within an objectivist context. Constructivist and subjectivist qualitative researchers utilize a wider range of methods, including such nonscientific and value-laden methods as autobiography, life histories, historical narratives, phenomenology, hermeneutics, semiotics, psychoanalysis, cultural studies, and participant observation.

The distinction between these two types of qualitative researchers can be more fully understood when both are placed in a historical context. When qualitative methods were employed in the early 1900s, to be even remotely considered respectable in academic circles required an adherence to the established and dominant objectivist philosophy and definition of research preeminently manifested in quantitative research. Objectivist definitions of validity and reliability influenced the methods employed by qualitative researchers. However, as the assault on the primacy of objectivist thought grew through the mid to late 1900s, other qualitative methodologies and new definitions of validity gained credence. Professional journals and organizations were established that created a sense of legitimacy for the constructivist and subjectivist methodologies. The result of this assault on the sole legitimacy of objectivist research and of the establishment of professional networks that supported the development of qualitative research was the development of significant bodies of literature supporting both constructivist and subjectivist forms of qualitative research. In the first chapter of their *Handbook of Qualitative Research,* Denzin and Lincoln detail the historical progression of non-positivistic qualitative research. For the sake of clarifying the issues, the rest of this discussion will simply use the term "qualitative research" for nonobjectivist qualitative research, even though some qualitative researchers are still influenced by objectivist thinking.

The diversity of qualitative research is especially found in the various ways to conduct qualitative research. Basic types of qualitative research used to gain knowledge and understand situations are ethnography (a focus on society or culture), phenomenology (a focus on the essence or structure of a phenomenon), grounded theory (a focus on the development of theory), and case study (a focus on the intensive study of a bounded and specific system) (Merriam 1998). Besides these basic types of qualitative research, there are a multitude of nontraditional types of qualitative research, syntheses of different types, and other variations on the qualitative theme. Essentially, in designing a qualitative research project the researcher sharply diverges from the quantitative formula.

In most cases, qualitative researchers approach the research without formulating a hypothesis that is grounded in prior formal research. Generally, the methodology is designed, and information collection and information analysis then begin. As the collection and analysis process occur simultaneously, the researcher attempts to discern emergent patterns and themes. These patterns and themes are critically scrutinized and in some cases inform and mediate the evolution of research design. What this means is that as the context of the subject under study broadens and deepens through the accumulation and analysis of increasing amounts of information, the research may go in directions that were unanticipated by the researcher. Much of what constitutes qualitative research is actually a dynamic process that uncovers aspects of the phenomenon that could not be predicted but are essential in the understanding of the phenomenon. One essential goal of qualitative research is to uncover as much information as possible so that the whole picture can be seen as well as possible.

During a qualitative study, certain essential strategies are employed. One is constant critical self-reflection by the researcher to uncover researcher and participant bias that can mask or filter the reality of a phenomenon. Another is the inclusion of the participant in the research process. The idea is that the more the participant participates, the more it will be possible to uncover deeper and broader understandings, and the more the research approaches a closer approximation of reality. Also, a variety of information collection methods may be employed, such as observation, interviews, questionnaires, focus groups, textual analysis, collection and analysis of cultural artifacts, analysis of researcher involvement and interpretation, and analysis of symbolic representations. It becomes quickly evident that information collection and analysis are inherently interpretive, not only on the part of the researcher, but also in the way the participants interpret the phenomenon. The difference between quantitative and qualitative research methodology is also evident in the terminology used in the research. In qualitative research, objectivist language is replaced with more personal terminology. Data becomes information, and the sample and the subjects become the participants. These and other differences in terminology represent a distinctly different view of the research process and the role played by individuals.

This difference is also evident in the way the research is reported. Although some postpositivistic types of qualitative research closely mimic the formal presentation structure of quantitative research, nonpositivistic qualitative research takes a different approach. Instead of statistical presentations in tabular and graphic form, descriptive statistics (such as percentages and frequency distributions) may be used to help establish the context, but the bulk of the information is in narrative form, with researcher findings supported by segments of transcribed participant commentary and coded information. References to other research may be made throughout the entire document as deemed relevant to the analysis and understanding of the findings instead of being concentrated in a review of literature. Qualitative reports can range from information presented within a quantitative structure with the parts of the research process separated by traditional titles, to flowing narratives more reminiscent of literary work. One such literary representation is called portraiture, in which the researcher and the participant write literary portraits of their investigation of a phenomenon. Some qualitative reports are even fictive narratives, fictional stories used to represent the real experiences of the researcher and participant.

One recent subjectivist presentation is *Troubling the Angels,* by Patti Lather and Chris Smithies (1997). In this report on women living with HIV/AIDS, the authors employ a split text format in which the researcher commentary flows at the bottom of the page in tandem with the participants' stories and interpretations at the top. This split text is periodically punctuated by interludes consisting of a diversity of information about angels and the AIDS epidemic. This split text format with its interludes of angel lore challenges the different readers (meant to include both academics and laypeople) to engage the more scholarly commentary of the researchers, the common speech of the participants, and the abstract and personal understandings of the angel material. In this format, the authors attempt to bring together two disparate groups, academics and the general public, and facilitate their crossing boundaries created by language.

Qualitative research of this kind is thus in opposition to the basic premises of quantitative research. Qualitative researchers maintain that certainty and predictability are not possible in any research design. They argue that, due to the complexity of human activity and the ongoing change inherent in reality, the whole of a human experience cannot be understood through a reductionist research method. All of the variables that are a part of human activity cannot possibly be identified, much less controlled. They further argue that any attempt to control the parts of an experience actually creates an artificial abstraction of the experience by stripping it of the full context that gives meaning to the experience. They maintain that any attempt to control for bias additionally removes important, if not essential, characteristics of the research experience. These qualitative researchers believe that values and bias are a natural and inherent part of any experience and need to be identified and disclosed, since it is useless to attempt to control them.

There are distinctive differences between quantitative and qualitative research. Sharan B. Merriam (1998) identifies these distinguishing marks of qualitative research:

- ⇨ The focus of the research is on the participant, not the researcher.
- ⇨ The primary instrument for data collection and analysis is the researcher, not an object such as a questionnaire or a computer that performs statistical analysis.
- ⇨ The research is usually fieldwork: The researcher goes into the natural setting to observe the behavior of people in their natural and fully contextualized environment.
- ⇨ Qualitative research is inductive: Theory is developed from the information that emerges from the observations gotten in the field. Quantitative research is deductive: The research starts with a theory, which must be proved or disproved.
- ⇨ Qualitative research is richly descriptive in order to capture as much of the context of the phenomenon as possible. Quantitative research is tightly contained within the boundaries established by the hypothesis or the operational definition of the research question.

Other significant differences involve the role of the researcher, the role of the participants, the definition of validity and reliability, and the issue of the degree of authority claimed by the finished research. In quantitative research, the ideal researcher is viewed as the expert, who is knowledgeable in theory and method and who uses this expertise to create an unbiased and tightly controlled research environment. The ability to control the environment is essential if appropriate degrees of validity and reliability are to be maintained. The researcher is seen as a value-neutral participant in the research, in that the researcher's planning and possible presence are believed to have no effect on the outcome of the research. This quantitative view of the researcher is sharply contrasted by the role of the qualitative researcher.

In qualitative research, ideal researchers are also seen as knowledgeable in theory and method; however, the mere fact that they have engaged in the act of research makes their own biases part of the research. Qualitative researchers are viewed as participants in the research process, and therefore they give an account of their own biases. A familiar term used to describe the role of the qualitative researcher is "participant-observer." Because of the researcher's participation, the methodology and reporting of the findings must take into account the biases brought to the research experience by the researcher. Qualitative researchers must critically reflect upon the effects of their involvement during the whole course of the research. Sometimes techniques such as member checking or utilizing a critical friend are used to uncover and disclose the effects of the researcher's bias on the research. Generally, these techniques will include another individual who is not involved in the research as an external source of reflection and critique (as in the use of a critical friend), or allow participant review and critique of the researcher's information (as in member checking).

One distinctive difference in the role of the researcher between the two research methodologies is the methods that they employ. As previously explained, quantitative researchers are restricted to the scientific method and statistical analysis. On the other hand, some scholars argue that the quintessential qualitative researcher must become a *bricoleur* (from the French term for someone who putters about, using whatever comes to hand) (Crotty 1998; Denzin and Lincoln 1994; Kincheloe 1998; Lévi-Strauss 1966). The basic understanding of the researcher-as-bricoleur is that the researcher employs a wide range of methodological tools in the attempt to understand a phenomenon. This definition is broadened by some to see the researcher not merely as an artisan who is skilled in the use of different methods of inquiry, but also as an individual who creatively and reflectively utilizes a diversity of data collection methods and epistemological philosophies in an attempt to discern the deeper and well-hidden aspects of a phenomenon.

Those researchers who employ bricolage do not restrict themselves to the narrow confines of one category of research methodology or one research philosophy. Kincheloe (1991) argues that this bricolage is a necessary component of critical research. In order to better engage the deep and hidden complexities of human experience, Kincheloe proposes that it is necessary for the researcher to reject the positivist claims of rationality, objectivity, and truth that are fostered by the reliance on a few narrow research methodologies. To go beyond the technical understanding of a phenomenon toward a grasp of the political and ethical nature of the phenomenon requires bricolage.

How the role of the qualitative researcher is defined is directly linked to the issue of validity, reliability, and representation and authority. Qualitative research does not seek to generalize findings to other individuals, cultures, or locations. The rich description that is generated by qualitative research is solely a description of the uniqueness of the one phenomenon, culture, or individual that is the subject of the research. Qualitative research is presented as an approximation of that subject within the boundaries established by the research, the time of the research, and the place. As subject, time, and place change, so the possibility lessens that the same findings can be replicated.

What then is the value of qualitative research to others if it is context specific? Qualitative researchers maintain that the sharing of this kind of research creates the potential for others to better understand the same phenomenon within their own unique context. Some qualitative researchers argue for the use of a "working hypothesis" instead of claims of generalizability (Merriam 1998). A working hypothesis can be used by others to better understand their own situation, which may be similar to the situation that is the basis for the working hypothesis. For example, a story about one teacher's attempt to raise student achievement scores on a standardized test may not be generalizable in the quantitative sense but may still provide important pedagogical techniques, analysis of teacher and student attitudes, and a similar analysis of the emotions in the classroom. Since there is a difference between the situation of the teacher in the narrative and that of the teacher reading the narrative, it is the reader's responsibility to make decisions about what aspects of the narrative are appropriate for the reader's educational situation. Thus, the ever-changing context of human activity necessitates a critical examination by the reader of the working hypothesis supported by the narrative description of another teacher's experience.

Concerns about validity also are different between the two views of research. In actuality, concerns about validity supersede concerns about reliability. For instance, if research doesn't accurately describe the reality of the subject under investigation, how can it be accurately applied in any form to other populations and places? Constructivist qualitative researchers attempt to legitimate their findings through the use of techniques such as triangulation, member checks, long-term observation, peer evaluation, increasing participant involvement in all aspects of the research, identifying the nature and effects of researcher bias, the use of audit trails, and providing rich thick description (Merriam 1998). The purpose of these techniques is not to arrive at an objective determination of validity as proposed by objectivist research philosophy, but to establish the authority of the research in relation to the research's accuracy, truth, and completeness. However, the more subjectivist researchers assert that even these techniques are a postpositivistic attempt by the researcher to impose the researcher's meanings on the reader. This imposition of researcher authority is challenged by the subjectivist belief that the reader creates meaning and that only the reader has the power to determine the authority of a text. In other words, the reader determines how closely the research findings approximate reality as the reader knows it. In contrast, an objectivist view of research would consider validity to be proved by adherence to a predetermined research method. Also, in the case of the constructivist view, the trustworthiness and authority of the research would be enhanced if the researcher's findings agreed with a collective or consensual opinion fostered by similar research findings of other researchers.

One subjectivist view of validity is that its nature changes with different audiences and different purposes of the research. In this perspective, a definition of validity would be relative to the intent of the researcher and to those who would read the research. For example, research intended for an academic audience and research intended to reach classroom teachers in a specific school would have distinctly different purposes and audiences. In the case of the academic audience, the legitimacy of the research would more than likely be determined by professional standards shared by the academic community. If the research did not conform to these protocols, then the authority of the research would be diminished. However, if teachers are engaging in action research to solve a problem specific to their school, their efforts to establish the validity or authority of the research may be less stringent and formal because of their intimate knowledge of and experience with the research environment. The question is, is one way better than the other? Objectivists would insist that authority and legitimacy can only be established through the practice of precise measures and procedures of validity and reliability; however, constructivists and subjectivists would insist that the meaning constructed (or created) by the practitioners has an equal level of authority.

To further complicate or to enrich the issue of validity, legitimacy, and authority, different groups with different intents have reconceptualized the understanding of research authority (Altheide and Johnson 1994). For instance, in the social sciences, ethnographic researchers pose validity-as-culture as the determinant of validity. From this point of view, the researcher and the participants may decrease the validity of the research because of their bias. Therefore, validity and research authority are enhanced by including as many points of view from the culture in which the research is occurring as possible. Along the same lines are validity-as-ideology and validity-as-gender, in which the effects of power from ideology and gender relationships found in the study and in the researcher need to be disclosed.

Lather (1991) poses another type of validity, called catalytic validity. Lather proposes that the legitimacy of research can be judged by how well it moves the participants toward a greater understanding of themselves and of the world. This concept is diametrically opposed to the objectivist concept of validity, in which the legitimacy of the research is based upon how well the research conforms to empirical protocols. In contrast, the degree of emancipation or empowerment that occurs in the participant is the indicator of legitimacy. Notice that one essential difference between the two views of legitimacy is in the direction of the research intent. In the objectivist view, the intent is to produce a valid assessment of an abstract theory. In the subjectivist view of Lather, the research is focused on the emancipation, critical growth, and empowerment of the participant.

As all researchers understand, validity is always about whether or not a researcher can speak with authority about the subject of the research. This is not only a central issue between objectivists and others, but also a highly political issue. The problem is that any attempt to claim that one type of research is more authoritative than another leads to the establishment of a rigid hierarchy of power and control. Those whose research is deemed authoritative can establish the definitions, standards, and protocols that result in the empowerment of some and the marginalization of others. As the Bush administration attempts to establish an objectivist research base for education, the ensuing debate is actually not about what information is valid, but is about the imposition on education of one way of seeing the world.

The distinction between quantitative and qualitative research is significant to educational reform. How research is defined and what research is accepted define educational reform. If only objectivist research is deemed appropriate, than only reforms that comply with the objectivist findings will be considered appropriate and will be implemented. The important point is that if only one type of research is mandated as legitimate, then there will be only one way of seeing the world, and the direction of educational reform will be determined by that one type of research. The debate between quantitative and qualitative research can also be seen as a debate about whether the world can best be understood by seeing it as only consisting of the sum of its parts, or by taking a holistic view and attempting to see the big picture, in which the whole is more than the sum of its parts. Also, how one sees the world affects the way one deals with other stakeholders in an educational system on a personal level. On this personal level, significant issues of power, respect, and values affect all stakeholders, individually and collectively.

THE CONTENTIOUS RELATIONSHIP
OF THEORY AND PRACTICE

Another great divide in education that problematizes reform is the contentious relationship of theory and practice. The relationship appears to be a simple one: Theory, as proposed by scholars, has more authority than the knowledge and skill of practitioners. In many instances, however, the attempt to implement theory that is incompatible with practitioner intuition and experience is successfully resisted by administrators and teachers.

The separation of educators into theorists and practitioners has resulted in the creation of two disparate educational cultures. This development of two subcultures within the same field is similar to the distinction between doctors and nurses in medicine and between lawyers and paralegal aids in law. In these two instances as well as in education, there are distinct power differences between the two groups. Also, in all three cases, there is a historical gender component, in that traditionally, nurses, legal aids, and teachers have tended to be women. In the 1800s through the middle of the 1900s, teaching, especially in the elementary grades, was largely considered women's work. In education, at least until the latter part of the 1900s, the university became the abode of the scholar, dominated by males. In the public schools, the high schools reflected the university structure, being organized by disciplines and employing mostly male teachers, while the elementary grades represented a softer, more holistic curriculum and were generally staffed by women because of their alleged innate ability to nurture. However, the most important fact for the separation of theory and practice is that universities were staffed with scholarly experts who generated theory, and the schools were populated with practitioners who implemented the theory. Location, credentials, power, and cultural tradition defined the sharp boundaries between the two groups.

Defining the Relationship between
Theory and Practice: Dewey and Thorndike

The relationship between theory and practice could be quite different today if the ideas of John Dewey instead of those of Edward Thorndike guided education. Ellen Lagemann (2000) provides a detailed analysis of the pivotal point in the history of education that shaped the current situation. Lagemann's premise is that Thorndike's "win" and Dewey's "loss" in the early part of the twentieth century set the tone and direction of educational research because of what it meant for the relationship between theory and practice, and the relationship between scholars and practitioners. Lagemann states that the "win" by Thorndike was the pivotal factor in the move by education away from close interactions between policy, theory, and practice, and toward excessive quantification, scientism, and the resultant separation of theory and practice (xi).

Coming from a pragmatic and critical foundation, Dewey proposed that education should be about helping children develop the skills and knowledge necessary to be effective democratic citizens. To accomplish this goal, children's learning should take place in educational environments that would be creative communities, in that opportunities would be provided for children to learn not only necessary skills and knowledge but also how to freely participate in a democratic society. To Dewey, education was more than learning the "material"; it was also about promoting the development of an effective and efficient democratic society through the concomitant development of a free and critical citizenry.

To achieve this goal, Dewey proposed that schools should mirror the kind of society that they wanted to achieve. In Dewey's experimental school at the University of Chicago, the artificial dichotomies of theory and practice, scholars and practitioners, and male theorists and female practitioners were collapsed, in an egalitarian community in which all professionals were both scholars and practitioners, both thinkers and doers. Instead of promoting a hierarchical separation of teachers and researchers, a separation of the disciplines, and a separation of professional roles, Dewey envisioned teachers-as-researchers, an interdisciplinary curriculum, and a sharing of the professional responsibilities for teaching and administration. This view put Dewey clearly at odds with those who saw education as hierarchical, specialized, professionalized, and gendered.

The significance of Dewey's position is that it put him squarely at odds with the structure of education at that time. As in our current structure of education, during Dewey's professional life the university represented the scholarly male-dominated generation of scientific research intended to lead to empirically based theory, and the public schools represented the practitioner female-centered implementation of the university-generated theory. Lagemann captures this distinction in her statement that "for Dewey, the study of education necessitated a partnership between and among many different people—a wide range of scholars and citizens as well as teachers, administrators, and parents; it could not be advanced through a hierarchy that differentiated among scholars, practitioners, and parents" (50).

Dewey proposed that the generation of theory to make education more effective in the promotion of student learning and democratic society would be a natural outcome of direct experimentation by the teachers in the school in the natural setting of the school. Pursuing the development, implementation, and subsequent evaluation of theory within the naturalistic setting of the school would not only foster the development of effective learning but also provide a concrete model for the school's students as they grew to become critical student-researchers.

In contrast, Thorndike, a behavioral psychologist, represented the empirical tradition of experimental science. Thorndike believed that all human experience could be quantified through statistical analysis. Of course, this view of research required a controlled environment and the development of professional experts in scientific research methods and statistical analysis. These requirements meant that research needed to be contained in the laboratory, that a strict adherence to scientific and scholarly procedures was essential, and that professionals needed to be developed who were specialists in these procedures. Thorndike's view fit nicely with the established organization of education. Universities were staffed with mostly male specialists with Ph.D.'s who developed theory, while schools were staffed mostly with women who implemented the university-generated theory.

The separation of theory and practice fostered by Thorndike's view reinforced the concurrent movement to manage the schools scientifically and to move toward greater differentiation of educational roles. Professionalism came to mean that university professors were trained to specialize in the generation of theory, school administrators would be trained to provide school leadership, and teachers would be trained to implement the theory and follow the dictates of the administrators. Distinct professional boundaries, defined by advanced degrees and certifications, were established to maintain the hierarchical structure. Lagemann summarizes the distinction between these two views thus: "Whereas Dewey's approach to educational study favored synthesis across disciplines and open communication and collaboration across roles and was therefore in opposition to advancing professionalization, Thorndike's approach advocated reliance on specialized expertise and fostered efforts to promote educational study as a professional science" (62).

This kind of professional hierarchy led eventually to the specialization of all educational stakeholders and the isolation of teachers by discipline and by grade level in the schools. Dewey's view of education as interdisciplinary, with blurred boundaries between teachers and administrators as they actively created, implemented, and critiqued theory, was not only the opposite of the professionalism proposed by

Thorndike but also was in direct opposition to the organization of education at that time. Thorndike's influence reinforced the establishment of a hierarchical organization and the division of educational experience into the separate areas of theory and practice.

As Lagemann suggests, education and schooling would be quite different if Dewey had won. Coming from a pragmatic view of life, his focus on the consequences of theory and practice would have fostered a tighter relationship between theory and practice, and therefore a tighter relationship between scholars and practitioners. Also, Dewey's emphasis on promoting a democratic citizenry through education would have added a substantial critical factor in the creation, implementation, and critique of theory and practice. For instance, a critical view of the consequences of standardized testing would not be focused only on student achievement on the test, but also on how well the test measures the rest of the non-content knowledge and skills that are necessary to be an informed and active democratic citizen. Also, Dewey's emphasis on student participation in learning would have promoted a constructivist view of learning and worked against the narrow reliance on memorization, repetition, and low-level critical thinking that currently characterizes public school education that is tightly standards based and test driven. Giroux's (1988) view of teachers as transformative intellectuals would reflect normal reality, rather than seeming an idealistic notion, quite different from the limited, technicist, and uncritical role that teachers currently perform.

Some individuals disagree with Lagemann's conclusion that Thorndike won and Dewey lost. Jeanne S. Chall (2000), a leading conservative educator, maintains that "Thorndike did win in moving education toward greater use of quantitative research, surveys, scientific experiments, and objective assessments" (47). However, Chall sees Thorndike's win as incomplete. She describes the progressive movement and the few current progressive tendencies of education as proof that more work needs to be done to permanently establish the objectivism of Thorndike as the foundation for an effective educational system. Chall points out that "the current questioning of quantitative research methods and the growing interest in case studies, portfolios, and other qualitative assessments indicates that Dewey's methods of analysis are back today, perhaps stronger than ever" (47). Chall claims that "many of the dilemmas we face today stem from the differences between these two traditions in psychology and education, that is, the scientific approach of Thorndike and the search for social change of Dewey" (47). As described earlier in this chapter, the efforts of the Bush administration to legally mandate Thorndike's empirical view is an attempt to answer the conservative fears reflected in Chall's comments.

Attempts to Recombine Theory and Practice

Besides the philosophical debate over the effects of the separation of theory and practice, the real-life negative aspects of this separation have historically surfaced in the mutual criticisms of scholars and practitioners. Practitioners argue that university classes are too theoretical and deny them the prescriptive practical information necessary to have success in the classroom. Scholarly professors view the curricular focus on practice by some of their peers as less than rigorous and as a "workshop mentality" that has no place in higher education. By the same token, the many teachers and administrators who want "practical information" instead of theory are strengthening the dichotomy between theory and relevance, seeing considerations of theory in college courses or in professional development activities as irrelevant to their professional needs. Practitioner demands for nuts-and-bolts information and recipes for success, along with the attitude by scholarly professors that the practitioner-students who voice these demands are lazy and unprofessional, are all indicative of the divide within education fostered by the separation of theory and practice, and by the differentiation between scholars and practitioners.

In the last two decades, there have been numerous attempts to reintegrate theory and practice. One ongoing strategy to reintegrate the two is the professional development school (PDS). The idea of a PDS is that a university can work in partnership with a local public school district to better train prospective teachers, to deliver relevant and efficient professional development for teachers, to bring theory into the practice of teachers and administrators, and to bring the concerns of practitioners into the university classroom. A basic PDS format is one in which student teachers from a teacher certification program are placed in a school district. A professor is assigned, not only to supervise their preservice teaching but also to teach university courses in the school district environment. Since the professor is now an intimate presence within the school, the professor and the university can offer professional development workshops and graduate degree programs to practicing teachers on site. Ideally, the professors will inform their curriculum and personal research with the issues and concerns of the practitioners.

One problem that can occur to derail this attempt to balance theory and practice is the adoption of an excessively client-centered relationship by a university. If the university is overly focused on meeting practitioner needs and increasing enrollment in their graduate programs, a tendency to de-emphasize theory and research in favor of practitioner needs may develop. In this case, the program simply pan-ders to practitioner needs and devalues theory and research, with the result being an imbalance between theory and practice. The same prob-lem can arise when the university participating in the PDS is primarily a teaching university. In universities like these, many of the professors are former teachers and administrators who remain atheoretical, untrained in formal research, and overly sensitive to the concerns of the practi-tioners. The development of interpersonal relationships through fre-quent contact with practitioners also becomes a significant influence on the professor to lessen the importance of theory. This interpersonal situation contributes to an overemphasis on practical relevance at the expense of theoretical and scholarly work.

Both of these problems are exacerbated when a state mandates a standards-based, standardized test–driven educational system. With the inordinate pressure on the schools to have their students perform on a mandated level, PDS universities are more prone to also feel this per-formance urgency and allocate more time to very real practitioner con-cerns rather than to the creation, presentation, and critique of theory.

In a related way, some graduate programs are not directly in-volved in PDS situations but attempt to meet practitioner needs by cre-ating graduate programs that are marketed as practitioner-friendly. The very nature of this marketing strategy creates a programmatic bias to-ward practice and away from theory. These programs generally empha-size what is known as action research. Action research is focused on the knowledge that can be uncovered by a practitioner within the practi-tioner's environment by utilizing less rigorous research techniques than those proposed by objectivist and constructivist formal researchers. The "softness" and user-friendly appeal of action research is evident in these representations of teacher action research that appear in a popular ac-tion research text. The authors distinguish between the big "R" of formal research versus the little "r" of action research. They introduce the book by citing this statement by Charles Kettering (quoted in Hubbard and Power 1999): "research is a high-hat word that scares a lot of people, it needn't. It's rather simple. Essentially research is nothing but a state of mind . . . a friendly, welcoming attitude toward change . . . going out to look for change instead of waiting for it to come" (1).

Many traditionalists in the field of research decry this attempt to "water down" the essential rigor of research. However, over the last two decades, a significant body of literature has been constructed that deals with action research, teacher knowledge, and teachers-as-leaders. This knowledge base attempts to promote the value of the knowledge gained through practitioner research and to establish a bridge between theory and practice, and scholars and practitioners. The proponents of action research send the clear message that teachers are no longer merely the object of study but also can be empowered to be researchers. Opponents of action research base their opposition not only on what they see as unscientific and less than rigorous knowledge production, but also on the threat that teacher empowerment poses to the established hierarchical order of power arrangement and decision making. Action research opposes the idea that teachers should work in isolation, be excluded from knowledge production, and be subjugated to external quality control (Sagor 1997).

Action research has shown potential to recombine theory and practice. However, the emphasis on theory is in most cases narrowly defined. The theory that emerges from the teacher's own research has little or no linkage to prior formal research and is constrained by the limited theoretical knowledge of the teacher and the theory that emerges from the research. One objection to action research is that the very nature of action research creates the potential for either a very narrow focus on a teacher's practice, or the generation of "bad" research through the use of poor research techniques. Also, if teachers only focus on incremental parts of their practice or only on the parts of their practice that administrators identify as important, then the goal of teacher empowerment is subverted. Also, whether quantitative or qualitative action research, the validity, reliability, and trustworthiness of teacher research is suspect because of the lack of external review and the lack of a teacher's own knowledge of the processes of legitimation.

In line with the action research movement, the Educational Resources Information Center (ERIC) was established by the Office of Education to provide a convenient database of educational research that would be accessible to practitioners. ERIC appeared to be a logical step in the connection of practitioners with research-based knowledge. However, as Lagemann sums it up, "Practitioners tended not to be interested in education research. Whether this was a result of weaknesses in their training—either a lack of exposure to research or poor teaching in research courses—or a reflection of problems of quality and general public indifference, practitioners' lack of interest meant that there was very slight demand for the goods that ERIC had to offer" (Lagemann 2000, 187).

A recent attempt to overcome this practitioner reluctance to engage theory is the attempt to train educators as scholar-practitioners. In this training the focus is directly on the blurring of the boundaries between theory and practice, and the roles of scholar and practitioner. Whether teachers or administrators, educators would be critically grounded in theory related to their specialization and also related to a foundational knowledge of the history and pedagogy of education. This scholarly knowledge base would be used to inform and mediate their experience as practicing educators. In a reciprocal manner, they would also use their experience as a basis for a critique of the theory. The essential ingredient in the development of scholar-practitioners is their ability to develop the skill of critical reflection. A reliance on only theory or only experience gained through practice as the basis for decision making leads to a reductionist and narrow perspective on understanding educational situations. This limited perspective leads to less-than-accurate decisions with at best a short-term effectiveness.

Another essential ingredient in the development of scholar-practitioners is the expansion of the practitioners' perception of knowledge and the acquisition of knowledge through inquiry into their practice. Jenlink (1999) identified three levels of knowledge and inquiry in relation to practice that are critical components of the scholar-practitioner concept. Knowledge and inquiry-*for*-practice involve acquiring and understanding formal knowledge and research in a scholarly manner. Knowledge and inquiry-*in*-practice relate to the knowledge embedded in practice that emerges from critical reflection in and on practice. Finally, knowledge and inquiry-*of*-practice pose knowledge and inquiry as material for interpretation and examination, and as the place where knowledge is individually and collectively constructed in communities of inquiry, such as universities and schools. In Jenlink's view, schools and universities are communities that in some manner collectively inquire into knowledge and in turn construct a shared definition of knowledge.

Critical reflection into the nature of knowledge and into the nature of inquiry is essential in achieving a deep and broad understanding of what theory and practices are appropriate for each specific place. Of course, scholar-practitioners who are skilled in the arts of inquiry and reflection, have a well-developed theoretical knowledge base, and intimately understand practice are the individuals who can lead their communities in a critical inquiry into their contextual uniqueness, into relevant knowledge, and into any externally imposed mandates or influences. Once again, the term "critical" implies not only the use of higher-order thinking skills but also an awareness of the implications of theory and practice for the power arrangements within the community. Scholar-practitioners who engage in critical reflection of this kind are concerned about issues of social justice, caring, and democracy.

As seen in all of the attempts to recombine theory and practice, the reconciliation of theory and practice is a challenging task. The development of scholar-practitioners faces the same myriad of challenges.

The great divide in educational research, which was fostered by the inability of the field of education to coherently deal with the diverse positions of Dewey and Thorndike, continues to impact education in many ways. The recent position of the Bush administration is only the latest manifestation of the divisiveness within the field. The larger societal and cultural battles to install one ideological view as the dominant view further complicate this educational dilemma. Because education does not have the respect afforded by public perceptions of certainty, validity, and expertise that other fields have been able to achieve, ideological interests are able to appropriate educational research as a site in their battle.

REFERENCES

Altheide, David L., and John M. Johnson. 1994. Criteria for assessing interpretive validity in qualitative research. In *Handbook of qualitative research,* edited by Norman K. Denzin and Yvonna S. Lincoln. Thousand Oaks, CA: Sage Publications.

American Psychological Association. 2001. *Publication manual of the American Psychological Association.* 5th ed. Washington, DC: American Psychological Association.

Bentz, Valerie M., and Jeremy J. Shapiro. 1998. *Mindful inquiry in social research.* Thousand Oaks, CA: Sage Publications.

Berliner, David C., and Bruce J. Biddle. 1995. *The manufactured crisis: Myths, fraud, and the attack on America's public schools.* Cambridge, MA: Perseus Books.

Carlson, Robert V. 1996. *Reframing and reforming: Perspectives on organization, leadership, and school change.* White Plains, NY: Longman Publishers.

Chall, Jeanne S. 2000. *The academic achievement challenge: What really works in the classroom?* New York: Guilford Press.

Connelly, F. Michael, and D. Jean Clandinin. 1999. *Shaping a professional identity: Stories of educational practice.* New York: Teachers College Press.

Cooperrider, David L., Peter F. Sorensen, Jr., Diana Whitney, and Therese F. Yaeger, eds. 2000. *Appreciative inquiry: Rethinking human organization toward a positive theory of change.* Champaign, IL: Stipes Publishing.

Crotty, Michael. 1998. *The foundations of social research: Meaning and perspective in the research process.* Thousand Oaks, CA: Sage Publications.

Denzin, Norman K., and Yvonna S. Lincoln. 1994. Introduction: Entering the field of qualitative research. In *Handbook of qualitative research,* edited by Norman K. Denzin and Yvonna S. Lincoln. Thousand Oaks, CA: Sage Publications.

Giroux, Henry A. 1988. *Teachers as intellectuals: Toward a critical pedagogy of learning.* Westport, CT: Bergin and Garvey.

Guba, Egon G., and Yvonna S. Lincoln. 1989. *Fourth generation evaluation.* Thousand Oaks, CA: Sage Publications.

Hubbard, Ruth S., and Brenda M. Power. 1999. *Living the question: A guide for teacher-researchers.* York, MA: Stenhouse Publishers.

Jenlink, Patrick M. 1999. *Educational leaders as scholarly practitioners: Considerations for preparation and practice.* Paper presented at the National Council of Professors of Educational Administration annual conference, Jackson Hole, Wyoming.

Kincheloe, Joe L. 1993. *Toward a critical politics of teacher thinking: Mapping the postmodern.* Westport, CT: Bergin and Garvey.

———. 1998. Critical research in science education. In *International handbook of science education,* edited by B. J. Fraser and K. G. Tobin. New York and London: Kluwer Academic Publishers.

Lagemann, Ellen C. 2000. *An elusive science: The troubling history of education research.* Chicago: University of Chicago Press.

Lather, Patti. 1991. *Getting smart: Feminist research and pedagogy with/in the postmodern.* New York: Routledge.

———. 1999. Ideology and methodological attitude. In *Contemporary curriculum discourses: Twenty years of JCT,* edited by W. F. Pinar. New York: Peter Lang.

Lather, Patti, and Chris Smithies. 1997. *Troubling the angels: Women living with HIV/AIDS.* Boulder, CO: Westview Press.

Lévi-Strauss, C. 1966. *The savage mind.* Chicago: University of Chicago Press.

Lincoln, Yvonna S., and Egon Guba. 1985. *Naturalistic inquiry.* Beverly Hills, CA: Sage Publications.

McMillan, James H. 2000. *Educational research: Fundamentals for the consumer.* 3d ed. New York: Longman.

Merriam, Sharan B. 1998. *Qualitative research and case study applications in education.* San Francisco: Jossey-Bass Publishers.

Olsen, Lynn, and Debra Viadero. 2002. Law mandates scientific base for research. *Education Week,* January 30.

Polkinghorne, Donald E. 1995. *Narrative configuration in qualitative analysis.* Edited by J. Amos Hatch and Richard Wisniewski. London: Falmer Press.

Sagor, Richard. 1997. Collaborative action research for educational change. In *ASCD yearbook: Rethinking educational change with heart and mind,* edited by A. Hargreaves. Alexandria, VA: Association for Supervision and Curriculum Development.

Schwandt, Thomas A. 1994. *Constructivist, interpretivist approaches to human inquiry.* Edited by Norman K. Denzin and Yvonna S. Lincoln. Thousand Oaks, CA: Sage Publications.

Sederberg, P. C. 1984. *The politics of meaning: Power and explanation in the construction of social reality.* Tucson, AZ: University of Arizona Press.

United States Department of Education. No Child Left Behind Act of 2001. Public Law print of PL 107–110, Title IX. Available online: *http://www.ed. gov/legislation/ESEA02/pg107.html.*

Viadero, Debra. 2001. Panel to detail national strategy for research. *Education Week,* August 8.

Witherell, Carol, and Nel Noddings. 1991. *Stories lives tell: Narrative and dialogue in education.* New York: Teachers College Press.

Chapter Seven

❧ Reform in Curriculum, Instruction, and Assessment

The ultimate target of all reform is the student. Fulfilling the purpose of any reform requires the reform to be translated into actions that will impact the knowledge, values, and beliefs of the student. The means used to move the reform from a state of intent to that of an active agent with the potential to impact students are curriculum, instruction, and assessment. If a reform doesn't become part of the school curriculum, the teachers' instructional methods, and the manner in which students are assessed, then the reform has little chance of success. Curriculum, instruction, and assessment are not mere way stations in a reform's journey, but essential areas that need to not only reflect the purpose of the reform but also to function as the active structures that implement the reform. In a military analogy, school classrooms are the front lines in the battle to realize the theoretical and philosophical intent of a reform. The initial planning and theoretical foundation for a reform mean little if the reform cannot become a part of the curriculum, instruction, and assessment that structure the classroom experience.

Because of the position of curriculum, instruction, and assessment in the reform process, how these three are constructed and presented reflects the political nature of reform as much as the political activity that is evident in the creation of the reform. Because this political context of reform is extended into curriculum, instruction, and assessment, how these three aspects of the learning environment are defined reflects the political conflicts identified in previous chapters. Curriculum, instruction, and assessment can be constructed to promote any position on the political spectrum. Traditional, progressive, and radical curriculum, instruction, and assessment are inherently different from one another because of their inherently different views of the way society should be structured and the way it should function. These different views are reflected in the various definitions of curriculum that have been constructed by those in the field of curriculum.

It may be helpful to make the connection explicit between the terms used for curriculum above and the terms used earlier. The term "progressive curriculum" refers to the liberal curriculum movement started during the Progressive Era of the early 1900s. Current liberal and radical curriculum theorists trace their origins to the progressive curriculum developed by John Dewey and other progressives of that time. "Traditional curriculum" can refer to essentialist, disciplinary, humanist, or scientifically managed curriculum, all of which also started during the first half of the twentieth century. Traditional curriculum may also be referred to as conservative curriculum within the context of the political spectrum.

Curriculum as a field was born in the early to mid 1900s. Depending on the historian, curriculum as a field of study may have started with the publication of Franklin Bobbitt's *Curriculum* in 1918 or earlier, with the published reports of the Committee of Ten in 1893 and the Committee of Fifteen in 1895 (Pinar, Reynolds, Slattery, and Taubman 1995, 70–71). Regardless of when the field started, since at least the beginning of the twentieth century curriculum has been the object of intense scrutiny and debate. As times have changed and new challenges have been presented to education, curriculum has been the focus of different interests, each of which vies to have its view be the one to meet the challenges and solve the problems. In order to clarify the role of curriculum in educational reform, this chapter will describe the many definitions of curriculum; give an account of the various historical representations and manifestations of curriculum, instruction, and assessment; and place these definitions and representations in the context of the current standards and accountability reform movement. In educational reform, each of the aspects of curriculum focused on by the various definitions can become the object of a reform initiative, or a comprehensive reform may attempt to redefine all these aspects of curriculum.

DEFINING CURRICULUM

One result of the study of curriculum has been that curriculum has been defined in many ways. The term "curriculum" can simply refer to the written action plan that teachers use as the basis for their lessons. In this case, curriculum deals with the sequence of content, instructional methods, and assessment techniques. In this definition, the focus of curricular study and development is on the actual curriculum document. Such a document is often called a program of studies (which focuses on the curriculum of a whole school), or a course of studies (which focuses on the content, instruction, and assessment found in a specific course). Curriculum also can be defined in terms of the experiences of the learner. Here the focus of the study is on the learner's engagement with the various presentations of content, instructional techniques, and types of assessment. Another definition of curriculum is confined to the study of content, instruction, and assessment, and their effects on the learner within a subject matter area (e.g., science, math, language, social studies) or within a grade level (whether the larger divisions of primary, intermediate, middle school, junior high school, and senior high school, or by grade level). In the context of this definition, a curriculum reform would be directed at the math curriculum or the fourth grade curriculum.

Other definitions attempt to understand the broader contexts of learning. One such definition is a systems definition. Here the focus is not on one part of the school, such as a document, learners, or organized levels, but on the way all aspects of curriculum interact and the effects of these interactions. Another broader definition of curriculum deals with the field of curriculum. Here the foundations of the field and the domains of knowledge represented within the field are studied. The focus of this definition is generally on the theory that attempts to guide the more narrow definitions of curriculum, instruction, and assessment. A model of curriculum that attempts to broadly explain the organization of the field distinguishes between curriculum (as a system that creates an instructional plan), instruction (the system of teaching and learning the curriculum), teaching (teacher activity to implement the curriculum), and learning (the student involvement in the curriculum and instruction) (Macdonald and Leeper 1965). A final definition expands the study of curriculum to include the hidden curriculum that pervades all curriculum, instruction, and assessment within and outside of the school.

A study of curriculum that includes the hidden curriculum investigates the values, beliefs, and opinions that are attached to curriculum documents, the presentation of content, the instructional methods, and the types of assessment. It also explores how values, beliefs, and opinions inform and mediate educational systems and the field of curriculum. This definition further broadens the study of curriculum to include the knowledge, values, and beliefs that are attached to other sources of information that are external to the classroom and the school. These sources include the messages that are conveyed through the media, the marketing of products, and any other aspect of the general society that affects the knowledge, values, and beliefs of students, educators, and the general public.

Those who study the hidden curriculum believe that when a child enters a classroom, the child brings knowledge, values, and beliefs to the classroom experience. Even though these are not easily evident as variables in the classroom learning process, they greatly affect what and how the child learns in school. Some proponents of this view argue that the most significant learnings of children occur not in school but in their contact with the organizations and institutions external to the school. These learnings are then brought into the school and the classroom, and affect what goes on in the classroom and the school without the knowledge of the educators and the students. Therefore, a study of the hidden curriculum deals with what is not openly disclosed in the formal curriculum within the school, as well as with the knowledge, values, and beliefs that are generated by individuals and organizations outside of the school.

Those who study the hidden curriculum (see, e.g., Dalton 1999; Giroux 1991; Giroux and Purpel 1983; hooks 1994, 1996; Steinberg and Kincheloe 1997) are extending their research beyond the boundaries of the formal school system to include the curricular context added by the teachings of the larger society. They see the school, classroom, and educational stakeholders as the targets of attempts to instill knowledge, values, and beliefs by ideological groups, communities, media, the business sector, family, governments, and any other special interests. They maintain that to understand education and the attempts to reform education requires this broader and more highly contextualized view. These individuals are actually expanding their study of education to include the activities of the larger culture in which the schools are nested. This is undoubtedly a more critical and radical definition of curriculum. In this definition, all curriculum is assumed to contain social values that are not easily seen, values that actually limit the choices that individuals make (Popkewitz 1991). Simply, they see all curriculum as value-laden and political, in that issues of power driven by the special interests of individuals and organizations are always part of the intent in any reform of curriculum, instruction, and assessment.

Proponents of this broad critical view of curriculum believe that the idea of curriculum was created to provide discipline in teaching through the creation of structures that determine the appropriate options and the permissible actions of teachers and students (Popkewitz 1991). The intended outcome of this curricular structure is order, regularity, and a predetermined and defined coherence. In this view, curriculum represents definitional structures that control teachers, teaching, and student learning. Because of this controlling characteristic of curriculum, curriculum is as much about the management of power arrangements as it is about the content that is taught and tested. This view of the relationship between curriculum and power is supported by the often used phrase "knowledge is power." Curriculum is about the selection of knowledge and the approved structure that transmits knowledge to students, or, in the case of progressive curriculum, it is about facilitating the discovery of knowledge by students. The phrase "knowledge is power" can be seen as implying that individuals can gain power through the acquisition of knowledge, in which case curriculum can be viewed as an empowering phenomenon. However, if the focus is on the power arrangements that govern what students learn, then the focus may be on the way curriculum can be disempowering for students.

Popkewitz states that Foucault (an influential French postmodern philosopher) "defines power as embodied in the manner in which people gain knowledge and use the knowledge to intervene in social affairs" (1991, 30). In this case, the structures of curriculum that function to selectively disseminate different types of knowledge to different individuals empower some and disempower others, depending on the type of knowledge that is disseminated. Here, curriculum is actually functioning as a ranking and sorting mechanism. This ranking and sorting activity functions to support social class, gender, and racial distinctions among individuals.

The broader significance of this Foucauldian perspective is that regardless of how curriculum is defined, there is a political or power component. This significance extends to the attempts to reform curriculum. Popkewitz and others argue that the establishment of curriculum is an attempt to establish the authority and legitimacy of one point of view. The nature of the curriculum that is established actually defines what knowledge and whose views of knowledge will become authoritatively the norm. The school- and teacher-sanctioned curriculum that students then learn is unquestionably viewed by the students as legitimate. Consequently, any other knowledge is inferred to be illegitimate. This assumption of legitimacy by teachers and students is reinforced by the common perception that the school-sanctioned curriculum is neutral, or value-free.

Those who take a broader and more critical view of curriculum, who focus on the hidden curriculum, consider the belief that the knowledge contained in curriculum is value-free to be a false assumption. They point out that when curriculum is defined as purveying knowledge, the disciplines vie with each other to establish their own version of knowledge as objective, stable, and true. In fact, however, the different versions are being debated and are actually in a state of flux (Popkewitz 1991). The individuals who must teach and learn the knowledge are not aware of this debate or the social and historical contexts in which the disciplinary knowledge is nested. Consequently, these teachers and students merely follow the dictates of the discipline and uncritically promote the assumptions and truth statements of the disciplines. For example, if any disciplinary knowledge is assessed by a standardized test to which educators and students are held accountable, the educators will uncritically use their expertise and creativity to ensure the uncritical student learning of the knowledge.

Obviously, the broadening of the definition of curriculum to include the hidden curriculum has important implications for reform of curriculum. Another way in which the study of curriculum has been broadened is by focusing on the curriculum that students experience as a factor in the formation of their personal and social identity (Kincheloe 1999; Popkewitz 1991). When students are tracked into vocational curriculum, college prep curriculum, or a general curriculum, the students' identities are affected by what some argue is an inherently political process. The same is true concerning the effects of assessment on the students' identities. The philosophy of assessment, whether it is manifested as standardized tests or portfolios, has strong effects on the formation of the students' identities. When used as the sole requirement for admission to higher education, SAT or GRE scores perform the political function of ranking and sorting students according to the values of those who mandated the assessment. In turn, their scores on these tests affect students' assessment of their own capabilities and personal efficacy. The scores of individuals on these tests affect not only their placement in higher education, but also the way they see and define themselves.

Some scholars argue that the more narrow the focus and definition of curriculum, the more overtly political is the intent of the curriculum. They claim that more empowering forms of curriculum are those that contain curricular structures that promote flexibility in enhancing the learning of all students. Regardless of the differing views on the definition of curriculum, any educational reform that attempts to rewrite curriculum will have significant effects on what the students know, how they know it, and how they see themselves fitting into society.

THE DIFFERING MANIFESTATIONS
OF CURRICULUM, INSTRUCTION, AND ASSESSMENT

In the broad-ranging discussion of the previous section, the term "curriculum" has been used, as it often is, as an umbrella term that includes content, instructional methods, and types of assessment. However, to acquire a full understanding of how educational reform seeks to achieve its goals through the targeting of curriculum, each of these aspects of the umbrella term needs to be explored. In this section, the term "curriculum" will refer to content, reflecting the narrower definitions previously identified.

Curriculum

School curriculum that is defined as content, instruction, and assessment is often called the written, taught, and tested curriculum. Larry Cuban (1993) differentiates between the official curriculum (i.e., the content, skills, and values that authorities expect teachers to teach) and the taught curriculum (i.e., what teachers actually teach, as shaped by teacher beliefs about what they are expected to teach). Curriculum can be further defined in four ways (Powell, Farrar, and Cohen 1985). Horizontal curriculum refers to the different subjects such as math and science. Vertical curriculum refers to the same course, such as math, offered at different levels of difficulty to accommodate sections of college prep, vocational, and general students. Also, there is the extracurricular area of sports and other nonacademic activities. In addition, the extensive service curriculum attempts to meet the social, emotional, and safety needs of the students.

All of these different types of curriculum become the target of reform at one time or another. For instance, the current standards and accountability movement targets the written and the tested curriculum. Mandated standards or benchmarks designate the required content and skills, which are then tested with a standardized test. Although not a direct target of mandated instructional techniques, the accountability measures attached to the results of the test indirectly affect the taught curriculum. This is evident in the strategy of teachers when they alter their instruction in order to teach directly to the test, in the hope that test scores will be higher. Also, the recent school violence, intensely profiled in the media, spurred reform directed at the service curriculum that deals with the social, emotional, and safety needs of the students.

Probably the type of curriculum that is the least susceptible to change is the basic organization and position of the extracurricular curriculum. Because of the deeply engrained support for most extracurricular activities within the school community, little changes beyond occasional coaching or advisor changes. Some reforms have attempted to alter the vertical curriculum. A sustained move to group students heterogeneously (i.e., to group them randomly in classes rather than by ability or achievement) always falls short because of the course scheduling processes. For example, in most schools, math classes are homogeneously grouped (students of similar achievement levels are placed in the same class) because of the sequential nature of the math curriculum. Therefore, administrators who create the school schedule usually schedule these courses first, which, in turn, influences the grouping of the other content area courses. The result is only a limited possibility of heterogeneous grouping for the other courses.

How the written curriculum is organized also has been the target of reform. The current and pervasive structure of written curriculum includes documents that serve as organizational maps for the curriculum. In many schools, these include a program of studies, which contains the entire written curriculum in a school; a course of study or curriculum guide, which contains the curriculum for individual courses; units, which organize sections of a course; and lesson plans, which detail incremental parts of the curriculum to be taught within a daily instructional schedule. Written curriculum is further defined by "Carnegie units," credits, or credit-hours. In this organizational context, courses are assigned credits, which indicate the number of hours in which the courses will be taught. Written curriculum is further organized into content, skills, and attitudes or values. Most school systems attempt to align the scope and sequence of the curriculum from kindergarten through the twelfth grade. The purpose of this alignment is to eliminate duplication of curriculum, to eliminate the potential for untaught or missed curriculum, and to promote the efficient management of curriculum.

The traditional and current organization of most public school curriculum is the result of the scientific management movement of the early 1900s. In the view promoted by this movement, curriculum is a phenomenon that can be quantified, organized, and objectively measured. Behavioral psychology has contributed to this view of curriculum with its influence on the development of behavioral objectives. More precision was added to the organization of written curriculum when a group of experts led by Benjamin Bloom developed a classification system or taxonomy of educational objectives. Now known as Bloom's Taxonomy, it organizes student engagement with the curriculum into domains, which include thinking or cognitive goals and affective or feeling goals (Bloom, Engelhart, Frust, Hill, and Krathwohl 1956). Curriculum organized around cognitive or thinking objectives requires students to know, comprehend, apply, analyze, synthesize, and evaluate information. Curriculum organized around affective or feeling objectives requires students to receive, respond to, value, and organize the information, as well as characterize it by value (i.e., consistently act out or display the value of the information).

As in most taxonomies, there is a linear progression in complexity of these activities. In other words, Bloom's Taxonomy implies that in order for a student to engage in more complex or higher-order cognitive activity, such as synthesis and evaluation, the student first needs to learn how to gather, comprehend, and apply knowledge. Following the model of Bloom's Taxonomy, other researchers created objectives for physical activity that added a psychomotor domain. The explicit wording of educational objectives greatly facilitates the management and evaluation of a teacher's delivery of the written curriculum, as well as the assessment of how well students master the objective.

Some scholars argue that behavioral objectives eliminate the differences in students and in how they learn, and therefore create an artificial and inauthentic learning experience. This criticism is expanded to include the wider use of behavioral objectives in relation to school goals and program goals, as well as course and classroom goals. Despite this criticism, the use of educational objectives is common practice because of their value in concisely describing an activity that leads to a measurable outcome. To become a viable part of the practice of schools, educational reforms need to eventually become part of this organizational structure found in the written curriculum.

How curriculum is organized reflects the philosophies and purposes of education reformers discussed earlier. The curricular organization of a school is an excellent indicator of the current educational philosophies of those in charge of the school, and of the philosophical antecedents that led to the current curriculum. Also, how the curriculum is evaluated indicates a specific philosophy. If objectivist assessment is used to measure student achievement and teacher effectiveness, then objectivist and positivist philosophies are the basis for curriculum decisions within that school district. Conversely, if more subjectivist assessments are used, then the pragmatic and progressive philosophies hold sway.

Besides being influenced by philosophy, school curriculum is significantly influenced by government agencies, the business sector, university disciplines, and public opinion. As seen in the history of educational reform, government influence on curriculum increases when there is a perceived threat to national security, a desire on the part of the government to promote special interests, a perceived need to assimilate newcomers and people who are different, and a perceived need to promote social equality. Also, in an attempt to promote their economic interests, businesses attempt to influence school curriculum through the funding of special curriculum projects in the schools, through lobbying efforts supporting government reform of curriculum, and through direct involvement of businesspeople on school boards and school commissions. Universities attempt to influence school curriculum through their own teacher preparation curriculum, and also through university involvement in establishing curriculum standards within each discipline. Also, with the establishment of the field of curriculum, university and private-sector professional organizations were formed that greatly impact school curriculum through the development of curricular standards and professional development related to curriculum.

One of the greatest influences on curriculum has been the field of psychology. As discussed in Chapter 6, the "victory" of the behaviorist Edward Thorndike over the pragmatist John Dewey in the first half of the twentieth century ensured a major presence for psychology, especially behavioral psychology, with its emphasis on experiment, in the determination of curriculum, instruction, and education. The history of the development of educational curriculum reads like a who's who of the field of psychology. One educator states, "All agree that teaching the curriculum and learning the curriculum are interrelated, and psychology cements the relationship" (Ornstein and Hunkins 1998, 100). Another scholar writes that as education moved into the twentieth century, psychology "provided the dominant discipline around which a school discourse about pedagogy evolved" (Popkewitz 1991, 102).

The obligatory educational psychology course that is taken in some form by all prospective teachers not only "cements" the influence of psychology but also promotes the psychological interpretation of education that is most popular at that moment. A study of curriculum finds that when behavioral psychology was dominant, the names of Thorndike, John Watson, B. F. Skinner, and Alfred Bandura were prominent in the determination of proper curriculum. Cognitive psychologists such as Piaget, Sternberg, Gardner, and Bruner also had their time of influence. During the 1960s, the humanistic psychologists such as Abraham Maslow and Carl Rogers also significantly influenced curriculum. Current curriculum, instruction, and assessment primarily reflect behavioral, cognitive, and humanistic psychology. A detailed history of the involvement of psychology in education can be found in Ellen C. Lagemann's *An Elusive Science: The Troubling History of Education Research* (2000). Joe L. Kincheloe, Shirley R. Steinberg, and Patricia H. Hinchey provide a critique of the influence of traditional psychology in *The Post-Formal Reader: Cognition and Education* (1999).

Herbert Kliebard (1995) has identified four broad groups that have attempted to influence curriculum: the humanists, the developmentalists, the social efficiency movement, and the social meliorists. The humanists had nothing to do with the later humanistic psychology;

rather, they were those individuals who desired to base curriculum on the academic disciplines of Western civilization. The developmentalists, influenced by behavioral psychology, attempted to create a scientific foundation for curriculum dealing with the developmental stages of children. Promoters of the social efficiency movement, also influenced by behavioral psychology, desired to apply the principles of scientific management to curriculum, and the social meliorists saw curriculum as an opportunity to improve society. Each of these groups has influenced American curriculum to some extent. Another way of looking at curriculum movements is to categorize the development of curriculum according to the technical-rational movement, the reconceptualist movement, and the neo-technical movement.

The technical movement focused on the scientific management of curriculum. In this view, curriculum is viewed as a phenomenon that can be organized into objectives by curriculum specialists, allowing the success of their implementation to be measured. This approach to curriculum essentially started with the ideas of Franklin Bobbitt (1918). Bobbitt's idea that objectives should be stated and then measured was expanded by Ralph Tyler's four-part rationale (1949). Tyler agreed that the educational purposes or objectives of the school must be identified but stated that the educational experiences related to these purposes also needed to be identified. These first two steps were to be followed by the organization of the necessary educational experiences, and then students were to be evaluated to see if the purposes were attained. Others contributed to this technical movement by specifying the importance of training individuals in this process. These curriculum specialists would then be able to provide the curriculum expertise needed by practitioners.

Some individuals who believed in the technical model altered this basic technical design. Hilda Taba (1962) added the idea that it was essential for teachers to be trained to engage in this curriculum development process. Taba's grassroots model was in opposition to the traditional top-down concept that had curriculum specialists developing the objectives and measurements, and administrators supervising the implementation of the curriculum by the teachers. Taba's model was criticized as being unworkable because of its reliance on the democratic participation of the teachers. Unlike Taba's idea, in which teachers would be equitable participants in the creation, implementation, and evaluation of curriculum, the technicist view saw teachers as technicians who would solely function as implementers of curriculum designed by experts. This technical model of curriculum development was strictly empirical in nature, in that scientifically trained specialists would apply the methods of science to the study of curriculum.

In the 1970s, the reconceptualist movement challenged the technical movement. One main distinction between the two is that the technical movement focused on curriculum development and the reconceptualists focused on curriculum understanding. Reconceptual thinking is oriented toward the theoretical, in that reconceptualists are more concerned about the "why" problems of curriculum than about the "how to" problems (Pinar, Reynolds, Slattery, and Taubman 1995). Reconceptualists are concerned about the implications of the foundations of curriculum in relation to research methods employed in curriculum work, the status of the field of curriculum, the function of curriculum in relation to all of education, and the effects of curriculum on all educational stakeholders.

Another significant difference between the two movements is that reconceptualists are concerned about the critical implications of curriculum in relation to social justice, caring, and democratic participation. Reconceptual curriculum is inherently emancipatory, in that a greater degree of freedom for all educational stakeholders is a priority. To accomplish this emancipatory goal, reconceptualists deconstruct the symbols and representations inherent in all curriculum. Whereas the technical view embraces the value-neutrality proposed by science, reconceptualists try to identify hidden values and analyze them for their critical implications. To accomplish this goal, reconceptualists avoid the technical practice of reducing the complexity of teaching and learning to its manageable parts and instead attempt to increase the complexity of teaching and learning by adding to the contextual understanding of the curriculum and of the learning process.

Some reconceptualists attempt to expand their understanding of curriculum by engaging in post-formal inquiry (Kincheloe, Steinberg, and Hinchey 1999). Post-formal inquiry explores the origins, context, and emergent patterns of understanding through the use of a diversity of research methods and philosophies. Through this post-formal process, deep and hidden curriculum patterns within and outside of schools emerge. One main outcome of post-formal inquiry into curriculum is the disclosure of the complex connections between school curriculum and the curriculum generated by individuals and organizations outside of the school.

Reconceptualists see curriculum as a text to be read. In using the term "text," reconceptualists make the point that curriculum, like language, has multiple meanings that involve symbols and language systems, traditions, histories, political legacies, and generally social realities (Pinar et al. 1995). Reconceptualists argue that to understand curriculum requires the reading of all of these aspects of the text. Reconceptual understanding of curriculum requires the reading of curriculum as political text, racial text, gender text, phenomenological text, post-structural and postmodern text, autobiographical and biographical text, aesthetic text, and theological text (Pinar et al. 1995; Slattery 1995). Coinciding with the reconceptualist view of curriculum as text is the development of critical pedagogy.

In opposition to the technical curriculum development view that identified the primary function of curriculum as the transmission or delivery of expert-identified knowledge, skills, and values to students, critical pedagogy is an essential element of the reconceptualist view of curriculum understanding. "Pedagogy" is a general term that refers to all aspects of education, including the science and art of teaching and learning. Referring to a teacher's pedagogy would be a reference to all aspects of the teacher's practice, and referring to the pedagogical implications of a reform refers to the impact of the reform on teaching and learning. Adding the term "critical" as an additional descriptor brings into play the additional political dimension of the use and effects of power on teaching and learning. Proponents of critical pedagogy wish to do more than identify the ways power arrangements within American culture, schools, and society mediate and inform teaching, learning, and all aspects of the educational environment. They strive to fulfill their emancipatory intent by facilitating the development of critical knowledge, skills, and attitudes in students and teachers.

One of the most important critical skills and critical attitudes is what Freire (1996; see also Leistyna, Woodrum, and Sherblom 1996) describes as praxis. Individuals who engage in praxis are committed to a cycle of critical action, critical reflection on that action, and new action. Critical pedagogues believe that individuals can be freer in the determination of their own identities and life experiences if they gain a critical awareness of the cultural and political forces that attempt to influence their identity and life experiences.

To critical pedagogues, critical awareness is achieved through the development of a critical literacy. In fact, most proponents of this curriculum view see critical literacy as a precondition for engaging in and understanding the power struggles that occur in education (Giroux 1988a). The purpose of critical literacy is to connect the relationship of power and knowledge not only to what teachers teach and how they teach, but also to the cultural and social meanings that students bring to the classroom (Giroux 1988a). This critical investigation into power and knowledge requires teachers to facilitate the development of skills that enable students and teachers to critically engage and problematize the political dimension of the institutional structures and everyday practices of schools that affect student and teacher identity and life experience. This is accomplished by creating safe spaces in the educational environment where students can affirm and interrogate the complexity of their own personal and social experience (Giroux 1988a, 1988b).

Teachers who employ a critical pedagogy are compelled to value student knowledge, without either endorsing or delegitimizing that knowledge (Giroux 1988b). Allowing student voices to be heard facilitates the development of a critical literacy and the subsequent empowerment of the students. Simply, the target of a critical literacy is to foster the students' understanding of how power, language, culture, and history affect who they are, why they are who they currently are, and what the future holds for them. By allowing students to participate in a dialogue about these matters, teachers encourage students to think about themselves and others in relation to how power is arranged in their society and the effects of that arrangement on all individuals.

Critical pedagogy involves an understanding of curriculum quite different from the standard view that curriculum is to be developed by experts to ensure the transmission of knowledge and culture. Critical pedagogy envisions teachers as empowered transformative intellectuals who in turn empower their students through the development of student critical awareness and student critical action. In this view, teachers are critical agents who are actively engaged in the development, implementation, and critique of curriculum. This view is directly opposed to the view of teachers as skilled technicians who merely carry out the curriculum devised by others. Also, knowledge takes on a new definition. All sources of knowledge are valued and at the same time critically scrutinized. Knowledge is seen as a phenomenon that is socially constructed and reproduced by those who dominate society. Therefore, knowledge must be critiqued to determine the hidden curriculum with its political implications that is attached to the knowledge. Knowledge is seen, not as something to be discovered by experts and learned by nonexperts, but as something that must be rigorously interrogated to uncover the hidden meanings in its language, history, and cultural context.

In a critical pedagogy, values are openly disclosed and evaluated for their effect on individuals. Instead of students being passive receptors of values transmitted by those in power, critical pedagogues teach students to identify and interrogate the values inherent in school curriculum and those that the students encounter in the larger society and culture. Students are viewed as active and critical participants in the construction of an equitable and just democracy, not passive recipients of citizenship education that merely reproduces the power arrangements of a dominant culture.

A final difference lies in the role of the student in education. By allowing for student voice, by encouraging student critique of curriculum and culture, and by providing safe public spaces for students to engage and critique their differences and the effects of the ways these differences are dealt with by individuals and society, critical pedagogues use the understanding of curriculum as a means of promoting student participation in their understanding of their own education. In this view, students must be active participants in their own education. This includes student involvement in the construction, implementation, and critique of school curriculum. Detailed discussions of the theory and practice of critical pedagogy can be found in the works of Michael Apple, Stanley Aronowitz, Landon Beyer, C. A. Bowers, Dennis Carlson, Paulo Freire, Jesse Goodman, Henry Giroux, Joe Kincheloe, Peter McLaren, William Pinar, and Lois Weis.

Aronowitz, Giroux, Kincheloe, McLaren, and others have extended the principles of critical pedagogy to the study of the hidden curriculum in popular culture, with the intent of facilitating teacher and student understanding of the curriculum contained in popular culture. These scholars argue that the critical issues concerning knowledge, power, and values found in formal schooling pervade all of the structures of society and culture. The discipline that reflects this view is known as cultural studies, and it applies the same critical tools to understand the larger curriculum represented in media, business practices, and any aspect of or influence on popular culture.

This larger critical view of curriculum allows connections to be made between the curriculum of schools and the cultural curriculum of society. This expansion of the definition of curriculum has facilitated the identification and interrogation of related curricular patterns that surface in schools and in society. Issues involving race, gender, social class, sexual preference, lifestyle preference, age, and body image are only some of the issues that are now seen as manifested in both school curriculum and societal curriculum. This definition of curriculum understanding dissolves the boundaries between schools and other societal institutions in its understanding of the critical context of these issues. Numerous scholars work in this area of curriculum understanding; typical examples of this type of pedagogy are found in the work of Aristides Gazetas (2000), Giroux, bell hooks, and Kincheloe.

As a response to the reconceptualist movement in the field of curriculum, a neo-technical movement has developed that promotes the view of curriculum development. In addition, some neo-technicists claim that the reconceptual movement is moving the focus of the field away from public schools and the needs of society to a study of symbolic individual and theoretical concerns (Hlebowitsh 1993, 1999). Those who hold this position see the theoretical and historical analysis of the reconceptualists as mere politicized cultural criticism that leads to an enervating relativism concerning school curriculum. Instead, these individuals argue that there is a need for a highly focused and concentrated effort to design solutions to educational problems through the development of curriculum that can move quickly into classroom practice. Some neo-technicists have been identified as part of a liberal technocratic movement that attempts to refocus the study of curriculum on the development and implementation of incremental educational reform guided by the curriculum specialist. Attention is once again given to curriculum specialists who provide the technical expertise that is supposedly needed by practitioners to implement mandated curriculum.

Neo-technicists also argue that the reconceptualists' emphasis on the theoretical analysis of curriculum has separated the reconceptualists from practicing teachers. They see this separation as a disabling of the field. In this argument the clear distinction between curriculum *understanding* and curriculum *doing* becomes evident when some neo-technicists argue that reconceptualists are more inclined to write about the work of the field rather than to actually do the work of the field (Hlebowitsh 1999). Pinar (1999) contests this assumption by pointing out that the reconceptualist *doing* lies in the struggle with the theory that guides everyday educational life and in facilitating practitioner understanding of the dynamic relationship between theory and practice that guides their professional lives. Pinar further argues that reconceptualist thinking has expanded the field of curriculum from its reliance on the narrow implementation and evaluation procedures of the Tyler Rationale to a broader and deeper understanding of not only knowledge, instruction, and assessment, but also the ideologies and theories that drive the practice of educators.

Another difference between the two groups of curriculum theorists lies in their understanding of their mission. Reconceptualists want to develop practitioners who will take a critical approach to the values of society, the construction of knowledge, and the instruction of that knowledge; neo-technicists believe that curriculum developers have an obligation to respect the values held by society, the knowledge deemed valuable by society, and the way society wants that knowledge taught. These are two very different positions concerning the issue of individual autonomy and societal control, and both are highly political.

Proponents of the neo-technical movement have returned to the function of curriculum as proposed by Tyler, Bloom, and the educational psychologists. Those in this movement who are more liberal advocate a degree of empowerment for teachers and students, but they stop short of the radical interpretations of teacher and student roles in education. The neo-technical movement is more influential in the practice of education, due to the promotion of curriculum development techniques by large market-oriented professional organizations such as the Association for Supervision and Curriculum Development. In addition, the pervasive standards and accountability movement and the position of the Bush administration, as seen in the Leave No Child Behind Act, have strengthened the neo-technical position.

Also, the field of curriculum experiences an ongoing tension between those who promote a specialist view of curriculum and those who promote a generalist view. This tension is clearly evident in the social studies curriculum, where one group advocates that the focus of social studies curriculum should be on the specific knowledge of content areas such as history, geography, political science, and economics. Another group focuses on a broader conceptual understanding of society in which curriculum is not separated into disciplines but instead is based on activities that combine the disciplines. E. D. Hirsch's (1988) insistence on the teaching of disciplinary facts is representative of the specialist view. In contrast, the conceptual view of curriculum is promoted by curriculum proposals like those advanced by the National Council for the Social Studies (NCSS). The NCSS standards (NCSS 1994) are organized into ten strands, representing conceptual areas such as culture, global connections, civic ideals and practice, and individuals, groups and institutions. These strands require the students not to study a specific discipline but to utilize all disciplinary knowledge and skills in the understanding of the conceptual areas that represent human social experience.

The distinction between these two views deals with context. The disciplinary view reduces human social experience to compartments such as history, economics, and so on. The interdisciplinary view attempts to promote a more authentic and holistic view of human social experience. This contextual difference is evident not only in social studies curriculum but also in how school curriculum is organized.

Schools that organize their curriculum into disciplinary areas such as math, language arts, science, social studies, art, and music represent the decontextualized and compartmentalized view of curriculum. Math is taught in math class and science is taught in science class. The other view hearkens back to John Dewey, in that curriculum would be organized to provide authentic and practical learning activities, such as a project in which students would construct a building or repair an automobile. These activities are inherently authentic because to achieve the curricular outcome students would have to use knowledge from all of the disciplines in an authentic setting to complete the task. Physics, math, language, aesthetics, and the political, economic, cultural, and social implications of the house or car could all become realistic components in the learning activity. The teaching of curriculum in the form of a holistic project versus the teaching of isolated disciplines is just one manifestation of the tension between the philosophies behind curriculum development and curriculum understanding. These distinctive philosophies are also evident in instruction.

Instruction

The philosophies that provide the foundation for instructional methodology can be identified as teacher centered, or teacher directed and student centered, or student directed. Teacher-centered methodologies derive their theoretical support from the objectivist view of education, and student-centered from the constructivist or subjectivist view. As documented by Larry Cuban (1993), teacher-centered instruction has been the dominant type of instruction in elementary and secondary schools. Freire (1996) has described teacher-centered instruction as the banking method of education. In this analogy, students are seen as empty containers, and the teacher as depositing information into their minds. Students are treated as objects that are acted upon instead of as active and knowledgeable participants in the educational process (Leistyna et al. 1996).

This transfer of knowledge is accomplished through traditional methods such as teacher lecture, teacher-directed student recitation, worksheets, and video presentations. Students generally take notes, refer to textbooks, engage in structured research activities, memorize portions of the content, and apply the content in appropriate ways as determined by the teacher. In teacher-centered instruction, teachers rely heavily on the textbook and supplemental materials provided by the textbook publisher or other providers of instructional materials. Units and lesson plans are generally aligned with the textbook. Student activities allowing student choice and student-to-student interaction (e.g., small group activities, debates, role playing, simulation gaming) are also structured by the teacher and closely aligned with the course and unit objectives.

Teacher-centered instruction became even more formal and structured when teacher effectiveness instructional formats were promoted. Madeline Hunter (1982) provided one of the more notable direct-instruction formats. In her model, teachers would follow a prearranged lesson plan format that consisted of an opening activity that would briefly review the previous lesson followed by an introduction to the new lesson that would identify what was to be learned, the purpose of the lesson, the linkage between the old and the new information, and the accountability procedure that would motivate the student to learn the information. This introduction to the lesson would be followed by a teaching segment, in which the teacher would present the lesson's information and model it for the student. The teaching would be followed by an activity guided by the teacher, in which the student would work with the lesson content and skills. Finally, the teacher would provide closure, which could consist of a review or a check on the students' acquisition of the lesson content. Follow-up homework relating to the lesson would then be assigned. Some variations of the Hunter model included provisions for a pretest and posttest to better assess student attainment of the content.

This direct instruction model became popular with school administrators because of the ease with which the elements of the model could become evaluative criteria of a teacher's pedagogical effectiveness. In most schools that adopted a direct instruction model, supervision of teacher effectiveness was based entirely on their ability to follow this model. One result was strict adherence to this model by teachers.

Cuban (1993) also provides evidence that a hybrid model of student-centered instruction took hold and was utilized, though to a smaller extent. Proponents of this type of instruction believed that children needed to be active learners in the construction or discovery of knowledge. With roots in the progressive view of curriculum, student-centered instruction was more popular in the 1960s and 1970s than it has been since. In the 1960s and 1970s, students were provided with more choice in course selection and lesson activities than in a traditional teacher-directed classroom. Curriculum that focused on student inquiry and discovery was readily available for teacher use. This student-centered curriculum was supported by progressive initiatives such as the work done by Jerome Bruner through the National Science Foundation. Other curriculum theorists like Hilda Taba also promoted instruction that would support this philosophy of learning.

The conservative restoration of the 1980s and the subsequent outpouring of criticism of education convinced many schools to return to a more structured type of instruction. It is true that in the 1980s education witnessed the rise of the constructivist philosophy of education. However, in the 1990s, even as many educators and professional organizations were promoting constructivism, the move toward constructivist-oriented instruction was blunted by the rise of standardized testing to assess student achievement. The emphasis on the use of one assessment instrument, a standardized test, encouraged educators to teach to the test; a process that is best done with teacher-centered instructional techniques. In many cases, teachers modified other student-centered instructional techniques, such as cooperative learning, individualized learning, and discovery learning, to fit the teacher-centered instructional philosophy.

There is a relationship between the arrangement of the learning environment and the type of instruction employed in that environment. In many schools, the arrangement of the learning environment still mirrors that of classrooms in the early to mid 1900s. Student desks are arranged in rows facing blackboards and the teacher desk or some sort of teacher station. This arrangement accommodates the teacher-centered instruction that is used. Shaped by the movement toward scientific management of education, classrooms are invariably self-contained, with teachers and students moving to different areas defined by the discipline that is taught in that area. In the progressive environment of the 1960s and 1970s, some learning environments were organized to support student-centered instruction. In the open space schools that attempted to implement student-centered learning in the open classroom environment, large areas that would normally contain up to six self-contained classrooms were open or without walls. Student seating was arranged in various combinations that included tables for student interaction and other arrangements for other student-centered activities. Libraries became media centers, open and accessible to allow for easy access by the teachers and students.

Many schools that went to the open classroom concept experienced problems with student noise and student discipline. One reason for these problems was the incompatibility between the configuration of the learning environment and the type of instruction employed by the teachers. Teacher-centered instruction in an open space environment became a recipe for disaster. As teachers continued to lecture and use teacher-centered questioning techniques, teachers would erect makeshift walls in an attempt to restructure the environment into one that was compatible with their instructional methodology.

The type of instruction used in schools is also related to the type of instructional materials that are available. As mentioned, teacher-centered instruction heavily relies on prepackaged instructional materials such as textbooks. Proponents of student-centered instruction rely on instructional materials that are constructed by the teachers and the students. This activity is viewed as an essential activity if the purpose of the instruction is for students to engage the course content and skills in a meaningful, relevant, and authentic manner. Also, in a student-centered instructional environment, the direction of the students' inquiry may deviate to a degree from the original unit or lesson plan. This necessitates a degree of flexibility and expertise in the teacher to accommodate student inquiry and still maintain the curricular intent of the course. In order to cultivate the flexibility and expertise that this type of instruction requires, certain kinds of support need to be provided for teachers. This support includes adequate teacher planning time, teacher professional development in the skills required to create instructional materials, and additional instructional equipment and resources. Due to these requirements, many school districts determined that student-centered instruction was not cost-effective.

Another important variable that affects instruction is the school schedule. Many schools still organize their school day around some version of the traditional 45-minute class period. This organization of time best accommodates a teacher-centered, direct-instruction philosophy. The promotion of student activity in the learning process requires more time. When students are asked to research, construct, or discover, all too often the bell to pass to the next class cuts short their learning activity. In the student-centered climate of the 1960s and 1970s, some schools experimented with flexible and modular schedules. In this format, students would schedule appointments with teachers as their need for contact arose. A modification of this more radical school schedule divided the school day into blocks or modules of 15 or 20 minutes, which would be flexibly allocated between the various disciplines based on their instructional need. These types of school schedules were considered experimental and were infrequently used.

In the 1990s, a move toward block scheduling attempted to resolve the problem of providing for an adequate amount of time for student activity. In this case, the school day is subdivided into larger blocks ranging anywhere from 80 to 90 minutes. To offset student boredom due to the instructional repetition and inactivity of the students in teacher-centered pedagogy, teachers had to adapt their instructional methods to this longer period of time. The ideal solution was to move teacher instruction from the traditional teacher-centered activities to a more student-centered activity-oriented type of instruction. Teacher resistance to this change in instruction often resulted in the retention of teacher-centered instruction with the inclusion of more variety in the activities required of the students. One instructional model of block scheduling proclaimed that every 10 minutes students should be doing something different, regardless of the flow of learning. An additional complication for block schedules is the need to more directly teach to the tests required by the current standards

and accountability movement. Pressure to increase student achievement on the tests is met by teaching to the test, which makes the use of
student-centered activities during the instructional block problematic.

One direction of reform in instruction has been greatly affected
by psychology, in a way that has made shifting to student-centered instruction even more difficult. With the growing influence of cognitive
psychology on educational practice, teachers are increasingly required
to accommodate individual student learning needs. Brain-based learning principles, diverse learning styles, and multiple intelligences have
become the catchwords in teacher instruction. Besides dealing with
content, skills, attitudes, and classroom discipline, teachers now must
factor these psychological variables into their instructional methods.
Many teachers will attest to the fact that in the nonintensive academic
classes that are somewhat heterogeneously grouped, with students in
one class that range from special education to gifted, taking into account these psychological components of instruction becomes very
challenging. Accommodating learning styles and multiple intelligences
becomes an even more significant challenge when the teacher is attempting to meet the additional challenge of ensuring acceptable student achievement on a standardized test. A further complication arises
when teachers are asked or required to meet the multicultural challenge
presented by the diversity of their students.

All of these challenges to instruction are further intensified, depending on whether the classroom is in an urban, suburban, or rural
environment. Each of these distinctively different environments poses
its own challenges to a teacher's instruction. Each environment has
the potential to contain different student demographics, different degrees of parental involvement, and different levels of funding. There
are large bodies of literature concerning the different instructional
strategies and student needs for each type of instruction and each type
of environment. However, funding is the critical variable, in that the
funding provided for the school often dictates the availability of instructional resources, the number of teachers and teacher aides, the
salaries and financial benefits for teachers, and the availability of support services. In most states, funding is not equitably provided for different schools, due to the way the funding is generated and the funding philosophy of the state legislatures. In addition, the move to
redirect public school funding, through vouchers, cyber schools, and
other privatization initiatives, further limits the money available for
public schools.

Assessment

As in the case of curriculum and instruction, objectivist, constructivist, and subjectivist philosophies influence views on assessment, creating a range from a scientific/positivistic/quantitative approach to a humanist/subjective/qualitative approach. Another perspective on this continuum would involve classifying types of assessment, with their purposes ranging from the intent to only rank and sort students to the intent to assess the progress of individual students only in relation to themselves. Numerous terms are used in educational assessment to describe each type of assessment and its purpose.

Some scholars distinguish between measurement and evaluation. In this distinction, measurement involves assigning numbers to student behavior instead of words and recording the number of times a designated behavior occurs. Evaluation implies the making of value judgments concerning the numerically coded data that have been collected. For example, a teacher can count the number of correct answers made by a student on a test. A raw score or an average can be calculated to describe the student's effort. This would constitute a measurement of the student's effort. An evaluation would be when the teacher determines how many correct answers constitute an excellent, good, average, or bad effort. In this evaluation process, the teacher then assigns a value to the student's score. The evaluation of the measurement of a student's effort allows the teacher to make a value judgment on the student, either only in relation to the student's score on previous tests, or also in relation to the scores of other students.

A distinction is also made between an assessment and an evaluation. Some educators see assessment as a formative process that is used in a diagnostic context. In this process, the performance of the student is assessed and used to determine future instruction and curriculum strategies. The intent of formative assessment is diagnostic, to help the teacher understand what instructional procedures need to be revised to better meet the student's learning needs. Formative assessment usually takes place at established intervals to ensure appropriate and effective student learning. Evaluation is often referred to as summative assessment. Summative assessment or evaluation generally occurs at the end of an educational activity with the sole purpose of drawing conclusions or making value judgments about a student's progress. In essence, the teacher uses a measurement of some sort to sum up the student's progress.

Two other terms reflect two different approaches to assessment—norm-referenced and criterion-referenced assessment. Norm-referenced assessment compares a student's performance to the performance of other students. In this type of assessment, a student's grade is affected by the student's performance in relation to the performance of the other students. Grading on the curve is a statistical procedure that calculates the average performance of all students and then compares each student's performance to the average. Grading by a curve assures that there will always be students in each grading category (for example, A, B, C, D, F) regardless of their raw score. The most common types of norm-referenced tests are standardized tests. Another way to assess student performance is through criterion-referenced assessment. Here the teacher sets a list of performance criteria and assesses student achievement in relation to how well the students meet the criteria. Students are not compared to each other but to the criteria. Instead of determining student success in relation to other students, this kind of assessment determines student success by how well the student meets the criteria. The terms "mastery learning" and "performance assessment" indicate criterion-referenced assessment.

Another dichotomy used to distinguish between types of assessment philosophies is the distinction between authentic assessment and high-stakes assessment. Authentic learning is also known as performance and alternative assessment. Authentic assessment attempts to assess student performance in relation to real-life situations instead of the artificial assessment contexts of paper-and-pencil tests. In these assessments, students apply the content, skills, and attitudes they have learned just as they would in related real-life situations. By approximating real-life performance, the assessment gains a degree of relevance for the student and the curriculum and increases student motivation to perform the activity on a higher level.

Authentic assessment may use different means of evaluation. Rubrics, which specify the criteria for different performance levels, are commonly used, as are portfolios and exhibitions of student performances. Portfolios may be collection folders that showcase the best work of the student. They also can perform both a formative and summative function by including a series of performances by the student of the same kind over a period of time. In this way, periodic diagnostic assessments are possible, and at any time an evaluation of the student's progress can be made.

Authentic assessment is idiosyncratic in that it is only an assessment of that one student. It allows the teacher to develop a larger picture or story of the student's performance in relation to the attainment of skills, content, and attitudes. Authentic assessments are often linked to a mastery-learning continuous-progress system. In this type of system, students progress from one level of achievement to another after mastering the performance objectives at their individual rate of progress.

On the other hand, high-stakes testing is most frequently a norm-referenced assessment in the form of a standardized test that requires multiple-choice or true-and-false questions. Some high-stakes tests include writing samples, which are graded on the student's ability to follow a specific writing format or to meet certain criteria. The student performance is converted into a numerical assessment that can be statistically measured. These tests are called high-stakes because they have an accountability consequence attached. In some states, such as Texas, regardless of any other measure of a student's performance, the student may not receive a diploma unless the test is passed. Also, student performance on tests such as the SAT and GRE carry high stakes for the student's entry into higher education programs.

A primary purpose of high-stakes testing is to guarantee an easily measured degree of accountability for student performance. The high degree of context provided by portfolios and exhibitions provides a more detailed and authentic assessment of student performance, but such means are cumbersome when used to rank and sort students, teachers, and schools according to student achievement. In addition, high-stakes testing is by far the least costly method of ranking student achievement and the effectiveness of teachers and schools. The additional cost of portfolios and other authentic assessments is in the time that is needed to develop teacher, student, and parent expertise in using and understanding the assessment, in the time needed to do portfolios in the classroom, and in the time needed to confer with students and parents about the student performance levels indicated by the portfolio. High-stakes tests have acquired a greater profile and use simply because they are easier and cheaper in the generation of evaluative data on student achievement and teacher effectiveness.

Over the years education has developed a rich diversity of assessment methods and contexts to fit objectivist, constructivist, and subjectivist philosophies. A list, not intended to be inclusive, would include standardized tests, teacher-made tests, final exams, mid-term exams, written test questions, objective test questions, worksheets, student reflections (such as journals, autobiographies, activity records, diaries, logs), charts, checklists, anecdotal records, surveys, debates, role-playing, observations, projects, term papers, writing projects, experiments, research projects, simulation games, model construction, problem solving, and discussions. This diversity of assessment enhances assessment flexibility and student and teacher creativity.

One consideration that informs the need for diversity is that of the validity and reliability of student assessment. Some, though not all, standardized tests provide validity and reliability statistics that prove their effectiveness in measuring what they intend to measure, based on the use of the test with the general student population. However, this is only one level of validity, in that the test only measures specific content, skills, and attitudes in one place at one time. Some educators argue that this type of validity only provides a highly decontextualized snapshot of student performance. These same educators also argue that only a comprehensive assessment that utilizes a number of assessment methods over a longer period of time can capture the true performance of students and therefore can be truly valid.

Besides the rich diversity of assessment methods, there is a concomitant diversity in assessment contexts. Assessment can take place individually, in pairs, in small groups, or as a whole class. Each of these contexts has its own diverse variations. Also, assessment can occur in the context of peer or self-assessment. Assessment can be included as an ongoing daily function of a class, or occur only at predetermined times. Assessment can be written or oral. Individual or group assessment can involve projects or exhibitions, in which students demonstrate a broad collection of interrelated skills, knowledge, or attitudes within the context of a complex task.

Whether norm-referenced or criterion-referenced, whether involving measurement or evaluation, all assessment has specific targets in mind. Generally, all forms act to determine the effectiveness of a school's curriculum and instruction. Specifically, they target the content, skills, and attitudes identified in the curriculum. Also, in relation to some types of assessments, instruction itself becomes a target. In a standards and accountability system, the curriculum is determined by the mandated standards, assessment is defined as the test, but what about instruction? Instruction does not have to be mandated because instruction is steered by the assessment. In essence, a Darwinian situation develops, in that those instructional techniques that allow a school to survive a test become the accepted instructional techniques. In this case, the type of assessment in a sense determines the instructional philosophy of a school or a university. More significantly, assessments are employed to determine the effectiveness of educational reform initiatives. If the assessments used indicate that a reform is not successful, then it is concluded that the purposes of those who initiated the reform have not been realized.

The reporting of assessment outcomes completes the assessment process. Traditionally, schools have reported student achievement in terms of grade point average (GPA), class rank, or the results of standardized tests. Interim reports and report cards traditionally communicate individual student achievement to students and parents. Some report cards reflect an objectivist orientation, in that percentages and other statistics are coded as letter grades. A few schools utilize a simple pass or fail, supported by anecdotal comments based on documented evidence of student performance.

The value-laden and political aspect of assessment is seen in the rituals of reporting student achievement. Honor rolls are posted in local newspapers, and some parents proudly display their student's achievement in bumper stickers that proclaim the child's attainment of honor roll status. Many schools have a national honor society that selectively includes students who attain a certain degree of academic achievement. Back-to-school nights and regularly scheduled opportunities for parent conferences are used to provide opportunities to discuss student achievement. Some schools and teachers employ token economies, in which students are motivated to be successful and showcased as successful by receiving stickers, stars, treats, and other motivational incentives. Awards assemblies occur at least on a yearly basis, with trophies, plaques, and money being disbursed to the highly successful. The standardized test scores of a school are printed in local newspapers so the community can become aware of the level of performance of the school. Some schools go so far as to have community celebrations of their students' achievement on a standardized test, especially if the school has been rewarded with a monetary prize from the state. In some communities, the standardized test scores or school ratings mediate even the real estate decisions of prospective buyers. In some states, diplomas are differentiated according to student performance. For instance, in Pennsylvania, the state legislature mandated that a seal be attached to a student's diploma indicating a certain level of performance on the state's standardized tests.

Actual student performance and how that performance is assessed and reported have a great impact on the school, the students, and the teachers. Within the school, students are tracked and grouped according to their performance levels. The direction of career counseling is strongly influenced by student performance. How schools handle lower levels of student performance affects student retention or dropout rates. There is significant research that indicates that students who are retained in a grade due to their low performance learn less the following years, develop negative self-concepts, are more likely to drop out of school, and are more likely to get into trouble with the law (Brown 1992, 33). Also, in some instances, some students who perform below level are reclassified in some category of special education or with a learning disability primarily due to their academic performance.

In some states, schools can be taken over by the state government if their student performance does not meet state requirements. The effect of this action is the loss of local control of the schools. Teachers and administrators are also affected by student performance. The job security of administrators is an issue in states that classify schools according to their student achievement. School districts that do poorly are apt to fire the administrators in the schools that are low performing. Teachers in nonunionized states are at risk if their students perform poorly, since they can be summarily dismissed. Some groups and individuals lobby for the salaries of teachers to be related to the performance of their students on standardized tests. Some states have established elaborate computerized systems to track student achievement to individual schools and teachers. Even measures that pronounce student success are a two-edged sword. If a large percentage of a school's students achieve honor roll status, some individuals in the community decry this as grade inflation. In this case, the assumption is that if too many students are achieving at a high level, it must be because the teachers are too easy in their assessment.

The Standards and Accountability Movement

The current and pervasive standards and accountability movement is a nationwide educational reform that is manifested in some form in most states; it directly focuses on curriculum and assessment. Even though there is no national curriculum and no national accountability test, there are some commonalities within this movement. In all standards and accountability initiatives there are established standards or benchmarks that are directly tied to a specific assessment—a standardized test. All of these tests are paper-and-pencil tests. Alternative assessments are secondary to the mandated test, and if they are used they function as add-on assessments in a school's assessment plan. Also, there is some form of accountability for student performance for students, teachers, and schools. These accountability measures range from the ranking of schools with positive or negative outcomes to simply publishing a ranking of school performance on the test. In some states, students must pass the test to graduate; in others they suffer no direct consequence for their test performance. Tests target the core disciplines of math, science, language arts, and in some cases social studies. The tests are focused on student achievement in disciplinary content and skills. Disciplines that are considered secondary or second-tier disciplines are not included in the test content. Also, the growing trend is to have the tests function as high-stakes exit-level tests.

One unintended consequence for curriculum, instruction, and assessment due to the reliance on a single assessment—a standardized test—is the growing disconnection between the best practices proposed by educational psychology and the perceived need by educators to teach to the test. Even though professional development activity for teachers promotes strategies geared to the accommodation of constructivism, learning styles, multiple intelligences, brain-based learning techniques, and other instructional strategies that are currently viewed as best practice, the actual implementation of these strategies in the classroom is negated by administrator and teacher conclusions that teaching to the test is the most efficient means of assuring mandated student achievement levels. Also, even though the best practices are taught to prospective teachers in certification programs, many of these individuals abandon these practices and return to traditional teacher-centered instruction when as teachers they are faced with the pressure to ensure certain levels of student performance on a state-mandated test.

Another outcome is the use of technical standards instead of complex standards (Kincheloe 2001). Technical standards focus on a narrow view of knowledge, skill, and attitudes. They also tend to reduce curriculum to isolated facts and decontextualized skills, instead of positioning these facts and skills in an authentic real-world context. This view of curriculum tends to promote memorization, rote learning, and lower-order thinking by the students. In the context of Bloom's Taxonomy, some educators argue that the measurement of higher levels of thinking, such as analysis, synthesis, and evaluation, can be accomplished on a standardized test. However, others contest this assertion by pointing out that the context of these activities is sharply limited to an inauthentic testing situation that restricts the students' use of the thinking skill to a defined process with the purpose of merely arriving at a predetermined correct answer.

For example, in a social studies question, students may be asked to analyze and evaluate strategies used by the federal government in dealing with civil rights. However, the makers of the test assume that there is a correct answer and a correct way for the thinking process to unfold, and students who may logically arrive at a different but accurate conclusion would be marked wrong. In this case, students are asked to be able to retrieve information, organize it according to the way they learned it, and arrive at the intended conclusion. Some educators criticize this scenario as a de-emphasis of the complexity of a historical situation, and the disregard for the broader relationships that entered into the historical situation. This type of testing scenario also leaves no room for student insight and creativity in dealing with complex situations of this type. Other educators more harshly describe this type of assessment as a dumbing down of what is expected of the students.

More complex standards require students to ask questions, explore the inherently more complex context of situations, and become aware of the origins of the knowledge that they engage. Kincheloe (2001) maintains that when students engage standards of complexity, they "not only possess knowledge but they know where it came from, the conditions of its production, the ways it can be used to bring desired states into being, the problems its unexamined use may create, and alternative information that may exist about similar topics produced by differing logics of inquiry" (360). The problem with the type of standards proposed by Kincheloe and others is that they are difficult to measure with a single assessment, especially with a standardized test. Therefore, even though state standards may call for the development of thinking skills and creativity by the students, the use of a standardized test negates the learning of these admirable qualities. In addition, some argue that the use of a single standardized test promotes a less-than-rigorous understanding of knowledge. They also argue that the use of skills in highly restricted assessment situations creates a disconnection between the student's learning of the skill and the student's subsequent use of the skill in real-life situations.

Some critics of the use of technical standards and a standardized test as the basis for a standards and accountability system view those as a means of control by those who desire to reproduce their own view of society. This reproduction of values occurs through the control of the knowledge, skills, and values in the curriculum standards, and through the control of student responses in the test by designating the "correct" answers and the correct methods of arriving at the correct answer. Complex standards and multiple assessments are inherently less controlling because of their emphasis on divergent and creative thinking, which through multiple assessments has a greater potential to be reinforced. Both of these views of standards and accountability are highly political in their intent. Through their different interactions with teachers and students through curriculum and assessment, each strives to create a society that aligns with its view of how society should be.

The basic question that should arise from this discussion of standards and accountability is not whether we should or should not have standards and accountability procedures. Instead, the question is what kind of standards and accountability procedures will achieve what we want to see happen. There are very different types of standards and very different methods to assess them. All types of standards and accountability systems have consequences and significant implications for society. The challenge is to understand these differences, to determine what types of curriculum, instruction, and assessment are appropriate for the type of student that is to be produced, and to act to implement the standards and assessment methods that will guarantee the desired outcome.

REFERENCES

Bloom, Benjamin, Max D. Engelhart, Edward J. Frust, Walter H. Hill, and David R. Krathwohl. 1956. *Taxonomy of educational objectives.* New York: David McKay.

Bobbitt, Franklin. 1918. *The curriculum.* New York: Houghton Mifflin.

Brown, Frank. 1992. *The reform of elementary school education: A report on elementary schools in America and how they can change to improve teaching and learning.* Malabar, FL: Krieger Publishing.

Cuban, Larry. 1993. *How teachers taught: Constancy and change in American classrooms, 1880–1990.* 2d ed. New York: Teachers College Press.

Dalton, Mary M. 1999. *The Hollywood curriculum: Teachers and teaching in the movies.* New York: Peter Lang.

Freire, Paulo. 1996. *Pedagogy of the oppressed.* New York: Continuum.

Gazetas, Aristides. 2000. *Imagining selves: The politics of representation, film narratives, and adult education.* New York: Peter Lang.

Giroux, Henry A. 1988a. *Schooling and the struggle for public life: Critical pedagogy in the modern age.* Minneapolis: University of Minnesota Press.

———. 1988b. *Teachers as intellectuals: Toward a critical pedagogy of learning.* Westport, CT: Bergin and Garvey.

Giroux, Henry, ed. 1991. *Postmodernism, feminism, and cultural politics: Redrawing educational boundaries.* New York: State University of New York Press.

Giroux, Henry, and David Purpel, eds. 1983. *The hidden curriculum and moral education: Deception or discovery?* California: McCutchan Publishing.

Hirsch, E. D., Jr. 1988. *Cultural literacy: What every American needs to know.* New York: Vintage Books.

Hlebowitsh, Peter S. 1993. *Radical curriculum theory reconsidered.* New York: Teachers College Press.

———. 1999. The burdens of the new curricularist. *Curriculum Inquiry* 29 (3): 343–354.

hooks, bell. 1994. *Outlaw culture: Resisting representations.* New York: Routledge.

———. 1996. *Reel to reel: Race, sex, and class at the movies.* New York: Routledge.

Hunter, Madeline. 1982. *Mastery teaching.* El Segundo, CA: TIP Publications.

Kincheloe, Joe L. 1999. Schools where Ronnie and Brandon would have excelled:

A curriculum theory of academic and vocational integration. In *Contemporary curriculum discourses: Twenty years of JCT,* edited by William F. Pinar. New York: Peter Lang.

———. 2001. See your standards and raise you: Standards of complexity and the new rigor in education. In *American standards: Quality education in a complex world—The Texas case,* edited by Raymond A. Horn, Jr., and Joe L. Kincheloe. New York: Peter Lang.

Kincheloe, Joe L., Shirley R. Steinberg, and Patricia H. Hinchey, eds. 1999. *The Post-formal reader: Cognition and education.* New York: Falmer Press.

Kliebard, Herbert M. 1995. *The struggle for the American curriculum: 1893–1958.* 2d ed. New York: Routledge.

Lagemann, Ellen C. 2000. *An elusive science: The troubling history of education research.* Chicago: University of Chicago Press.

Leistyna, Pepi, Arlie Woodrum, and Stephen A. Sherblom. 1996. *Breaking free: The transformative power of critical pedagogy.* Cambridge, MA: Harvard Educational Review.

Macdonald, James B., and Robert R. Leeper, eds. 1965. *Theories of instruction.* Washington, DC: Association for Supervision and Curriculum Development.

National Council for the Social Studies. 1994. *Curriculum standards for social studies: Expectations of excellence.* Washington, DC: National Council for the Social Studies.

Ornstein, Allan C., and Francis P. Hunkins. 1998. *Curriculum: Foundations, principles, and issues.* 3d ed. Needham Heights, MA: Allyn and Bacon.

Pinar, William F. 1999. Not burdens—Breakthroughs. *Curriculum Inquiry* 29 (3): 365–367.

Pinar, William F., William M. Reynolds, Patrick Slattery, and Peter M. Taubman. 1995. *Understanding curriculum.* New York: Peter Lang.

Popkewitz, Thomas S. 1991. *A political sociology of educational reform: Power/knowledge in teaching, teacher education, and research.* New York: Teachers College Press.

Powell, Arthur G., Eleanor Farrar, and David K. Cohen. 1985. *The shopping mall high school: Winners and losers in the educational marketplace.* Boston, MA: Houghton Mifflin.

Slattery, Patrick. 1995. *Curriculum development in the postmodern era.* New York: Garland.

Steinberg, Shirley R., and Joe L. Kincheloe, eds. 1997. *Kinderculture: The corporate construction of childhood.* Boulder, CO: Westview Press.

Taba, Hilda. 1962. *Curriculum development: Theory and practice.* New York: Harcourt Brace.

Tyler, Ralph. 1949. *Basic principles of curriculum and instruction.* Chicago, IL: University of Chicago Press.

Chapter Eight

●◆ The Role of the Public in Education Reform

The process of educational reform is assumed to be the responsibility of professional educational organizations, governments, and related groups of professional individuals. Traditionally, educators, government officials, and business leaders have been responsible for the initiation, implementation, and evaluation of reform. However, the clarion call for educational reform in the 1980s invited another participant into the reform process—parents and community. Nested within the restructuring movement was a move toward parent and community involvement known as site-based or school-based management. Proponents of this view argued that significant and effective reform can only occur with the direct involvement of parents and the larger community in educational decision making. From the 1980s to the present, a recurrent theme in educational reform literature is the need to either involve the larger community or to create community in our schools. In either case, the call for community is a call for the involvement of the public in educational reform.

This chapter will examine the role of the public in educational reform. Like all aspects of education and educational reform, this is a complex issue. The first level of complexity lies in the multiple ways in which community and community involvement in education can be defined. Then there is the issue of how well the public understands education and its reform. Of course, there is the fact that the public has always been involved to some degree at various times in educational reform, and thus understanding public involvement involves understanding the historical and evolving relationship between the school and the community. The site-based and school-based initiatives form part of this history. Finally, the school choice initiative cannot be overlooked as a way to include the public in decisions about education.

DEFINING COMMUNITY

Many times when the term "community" is used in a public forum, those who use the term assume that there is a common understanding of this term. The reality is that quite the opposite is true. In fact, the term "community" has many different meanings, and consequences are attached to each way of defining it. Dictionary definitions provide a beginning in the attempt to resolve this definitional issue. Such definitions usually include terms and phrases alluding to communities as groups of people with common interests or characteristics, people living in close proximity, or people in some sort of interactive relationship. Dictionary definitions are sufficient to begin a discussion of the definition of community, but they quickly lose their definitional power when one is faced with the multiple purposes of schools, the multiple agendas of special interests concerning the schools and the general public, and the multiple value systems that are reflected in how community is defined. In a discussion of the definition of community, questions raised by the multiple purposes of schools (i.e., academic, service, extracurricular, social) and the special interest agendas (i.e., ideological, economic, cultural, political) are subsumed by the larger questions raised by differing values about how people should live together.

Communitarian thought (i.e., thought about how people should live together) can be essentialized, as Joseph Kahne does, into traditional ideas about community, ideas about community in the modern world, and democratic community (1996). Kahne uses the Old Order Amish communities as examples of the traditional view of community. In Amish society the school, like the community, is shaped by the Christian values that dominate and organize all Amish institutions. In this case, the purpose of schools is to reproduce these religious beliefs. Reform in an Amish school community means guarding against secular or anti-Amish beliefs that would conflict with Amish beliefs. Here, school and community are indistinguishable.

In a modern society, problems arise with this tight and restrictive continuity between community and school. Modern societies are by definition societies pervaded by difference—political, cultural, economic, social, racial, gendered, and individual differences. One set of values, whether religious or secular, cannot be effective in meeting the needs of this pervasive difference. One group's values may conflict with another group's values. How then do these different groups arrive at some workable covenant that mediates this difference? Democratic views of community attempt to mitigate this difference in values. Traditionally, within a democratic or representative community structure, public schools have been organized as secular bureaucracies that attempt to maintain a neutral political correctness in relation to the diverse values within the communities served by the schools. To maintain this neutrality, community involvement had to be formalized and tightly regulated by school boards and school administrators in accordance with federal mandates and federal scrutiny concerning issues such as civil rights and separation of church and state; otherwise, one set of values might unduly influence the purpose and functioning of the school. However, because of the turmoil created by a society in transition, a postmodern society, the ability of this traditional formula for neutrality to meet the needs of society became suspect.

In the 1980s and 1990s, the waves of restructuring attempted to deal not only with the alleged academic shortcomings of schools but also with the values dilemma created by a society in transition from an industrial age to an information age. One component of this restructuring was a strategy to move from a centralized educational system to a decentralized system. Instead of having education solely controlled by a professional group of educators, the idea was to promote involvement of traditionally less powerful stakeholders, such as parents and other members of the community. Three general strategies emerged to promote community involvement. The site-based movement represented one strategy; another was the move toward schools or schools-within-schools that shared common values, and yet another was the idea of developing egalitarian and gemeinschaft communities.

In relation to the third option, many scholars and practitioners have proposed the development of communities with shared visions mutually created by either all members of the community or at least by representatives of the different groups in a community. However, the ideas of Thomas Sergiovanni (1994) best exemplify this movement. Sergiovanni proposes that effective schools are those that can become instrumental agents in the creation of gemeinschaft communities. Sergiovanni's idea is based on the distinction made by Ferdinand Tönnies between gesellschaft and gemeinschaft communities. (See the glossary for an explanation of each term.) The difference lies in the ability of a gemeinschaft community to form a trusting relationship that is centered on the development of common values and beliefs. Sergiovanni's proposal is built on the assumption that it is possible for a community to somehow subordinate its differences and achieve a workable degree of homogeneity in its values.

Sergiovanni's view was and still is echoed by other educators who see the establishment of community as the panacea to the problems of education. In a review of the educational literature relating to community, Joel Westheimer (1999) identifies five common features of community. The first is the creation of shared beliefs or community bonds made possible by a common language, ideology, or purpose. Another is participation by all members of the community, which functions to create a common identity that is compatible with the different identities of the various groups and individuals within the community. Third is interdependence, based on the ability to recognize a mutual need that can be better accommodated by collective action than by individual or factional action. Another feature is the recognition and concern for individual and minority views that are typically marginalized or left out of the community decisions. A final feature is the recognition of the need for the development of meaningful relationships among all stakeholders in the community.

Other individuals propose that, unlike the view represented by Sergiovanni and reported by Westheimer, which necessitates the development of a "collective we," communities can be organized around difference, or otherness (Shields 1999). Proponents of this view argue that a community of difference can be just as effective in providing direction and purpose for educational reform. In this case, an emphasis would be placed on creating an awareness of how different individuals and groups are represented in the community, and how their identities are affected by the interactions of people within the community. One striking difference between this view and that based on the desire for commonality is the valuing of difference. In this case, the accommodation of difference is more important in binding people together than any trying to homogenize different values and the identities attached to those values into one common culture.

These differences may involve race, gender, social class, and age. For instance, a consideration of age would entail understanding the unique needs and situations of the youth of the community, as well as those of retirees living on a fixed income. Proponents of this view argue that the rationale for the valuation of difference is that to attain a commitment by all toward an effective school and community requires recognition and the valuing of the cultural and personal differences of individuals within the community. Of course, the bottom line for personal commitment is the recognition that solutions to these personal issues become part of the reform plan.

A critical component in this view of community building is the avoidance of stereotyping and the recognition of and response to individual differences (Shields 1999). Shields reports that the difficult task is to develop accurate and realistic images of these different individuals through a dialogue that does not privilege one form of knowledge and values over another. A major difference between this view and that represented by Sergiovanni's proposition is in the process of community building. In the latter, it is assumed that differences will be suppressed by or subordinated to a neutral common vision, whereas in the former, the bonds that will sustain the community lie in the equitable interactions between those holding different views and in their certainty that their knowledge and values will not be subordinated but enhanced by the resultant vision. Both of these views attempt to deal with the dilemma of individual values in relation to the need for effective and equitable community action within the realm of educational reform in distinctively different ways.

Lynn Beck (1999) offers another perspective on how community is defined. Beck analyzed the literature on community to see how community is defined in a metaphorical sense. The metaphors that people use to describe a phenomenon can be used to discern patterns in how community is represented. Through her metaphorical analysis, Beck found that the concept of community is a rich and multifaceted concept that is not limited by scholarly definitions. Beck found that metaphors used to describe community consisted of references to family, village, music, psychology, behavior, structures, political activity, and ethics. In her analysis, individuals defined community in terms of the way families and villages function, as well as in terms of the way the individual and collective activities unfold in jazz and orchestral performances. Psychological metaphors included references to interpersonal interactions involving issues of personal identity, need fulfillment, emotional relationships, self-efficacy, and self-esteem. Behavioral metaphors described community in terms of acts, skills, assessment, monitoring, feedback, interaction, and conversation. Other metaphors took a structural view, describing communities as shopping malls, factories, bureaucracies, compartmentalized organizations, and bounded human systems.

Other structural considerations of community were concerned about whether the boundaries within and between communities were rigid or permeable. Political metaphors focused on power arrangements, conflict, struggle, influence, governance, and caring within the community. Some political considerations were focused on the challenging or maintenance of traditional power structures, and the idea of communities as learning organizations. Ethical metaphors described communities in terms of spirituality, caring, values, justice, and critical consciousness versus constructed consciousness (see glossary).

Beck concluded that community means many things at the same time, and is invariably a complex concept. One suggestion that she provides is that "researchers interested in the idea of community might do well to focus less on evaluating or measuring its impact and more on understanding it from a range of perspectives" (Beck 1999, 37). She also concluded that "attempts to identify core values or goals or to create communal structures are unlikely to work if they are not accompanied by some basic fundamental sense of relatedness among people at a site" (37). In relation to educational reform, Beck points out that discussions of community represent a complex and dynamic phenomenon that resists simple or linear definitions, and attempts to institute effective and equitable communities are challenged by the definitional complexity found in the metaphors that people use to understand their communities.

PUBLIC UNDERSTANDING OF
AND PARTICIPATION IN EDUCATIONAL REFORM

The understanding of education that the public brings to the process of educational reform affects the nature and degree of their participation, as well as the way professional educators perceive their participation. The public's understanding of education is mediated by a number of factors. A primary factor is their own experience with public education. Individuals' past interactions with schools as students, parents, and citizens are their first consideration when evaluating educational reform. Unfortunately, many individuals only look back on education with fondness in relation to a few influential teachers and in relation to their athletic and extracurricular experiences, and fail to critically reflect on their broader experience with the schools. Another factor is the political and cultural attitudes of their community toward the schools. If the school is perceived to be a separate entity, disconnected from the larger community, this will reinforce any negative memories of the school. If the school is perceived to be an integral part of the community in a positive way, other memories will gain ascendance when new reforms must be evaluated. A larger context of the effect of community attitudes about a school and a proposed reform will be additionally mediated by the attitudes gotten from the larger society in which the local community is nested. For instance, if messages from the larger society indicate that schools are ineffective, then this will affect the public's perceptions of their own schools.

Another factor is the anti-intellectualism that is a pervasive theme throughout American history. Messages that devalue intellectual work appeal to some blue-collar segments of a community. This factor is also related to the economic conditions and cultural norms in a community. Persistent and systemic poverty often provides a basis for a negative perception of the effectiveness of schools, even though the schools have no control over conditions of public employment and income level. A transgenerational resistance to the knowledge and values fostered by schools in a community becomes the basis for a critique of school effectiveness and the merits of a specific reform. These factors that affect public perceptions of schools and educational reform are not easily offset by the public relations efforts of schools. Even when the benefits of the noneducational services provided by schools are used in public relations efforts, their effectiveness in fostering a positive attitude about the schools or a reform may be diluted by the cultural, economic, and political characteristics of the community.

However, a more basic factor in the public's understanding of education and educational reform is the public's lack of critical awareness, and their lack of skill in effectively participating in their schools and in debates about educational reform. As described in the discussion about the reconceptualist goal of promoting curricular understanding, critical awareness is a complex phenomenon. Critical awareness requires all the skills involved in moving from a superficial understanding of an issue to an understanding that allows the discernment of the hidden agendas behind a reform effort and its likely outcomes. The ability to analyze, synthesize, and evaluate programs and actions is not innate but a learned process. If individuals have not acquired these skills, if they have not been given the opportunity to learn them in an authentic way that has allowed these skills to be transferred to their adult lives, then they will not be able to use them to uncover the complexity of an educational issue. Effective and constructive participation in debating educational issues and reforms also depends on the ability to listen, respond, and engage in problem solving. Again, these are not innate abilities but abilities that need to be learned.

Another factor in the public's understanding of educational reform is the intent and ability of those promoting the reform to divert the public's attention from the hidden implications and related conditions of the reform. Westheimer (1999) reports that the term "community," and the related values imposed by reformers on a community, are often misused as a way to avoid dealing with more fundamental issues that are causing the problems experienced by the community. For instance, Westheimer points out that many educational problems are directly related to the issue of school funding. If funding is inadequate, the chances are good that no reform that doesn't address the issue of funding will solve the underlying causes of an educational problem. Since funding is a controversial issue that is difficult to resolve to the satisfaction of all citizens, some government-mandated reforms redirect the focus from funding to other proposed solutions such as student achievement, public participation in education, or public choice in schools. Also, Westheimer adds that some reforms are initiated to obviate having to deal with issues of power, race, gender, and social class that are the fundamental ingredients in a community's problems.

Individuals and groups do participate in educational reform. Their participation has been manifested in various kinds of activism. Some parents, students, and other citizens take an activist role in educational issues. This may be in the guise of forming community action groups to promote their interests, or of seeking satisfaction by taking legal action. Also, as recently seen in public opposition to the takeover of the Philadelphia school system by the state of Pennsylvania, community groups and individuals can engage in organized civil protest demonstrations. Also, individuals and groups participate in a less activist manner by participating in parent-teacher organizations, by participating in site-based councils, or by basing their votes in an election on the candidates' positions on educational issues. The more typical forms of public participation in education involve parents meeting with teachers, administrators, and school boards concerning specific issues related to their own children. It is this level of participation that most concerns individual schools and educators.

THE RELATIONSHIP BETWEEN THE SCHOOL AND THE PUBLIC

Understanding the role that the public plays in educational reform requires a concomitant understanding of the relationship between the school and the general public or community. Community can be identified as the larger social systems such as the nation and the state, or simply as the local community in which the school is nested. The most direct interaction between the public and the school occurs on this local level.

An important aspect of this relationship is that each school has and strives to maintain an identity as a professional organization. Every profession (medicine, law, business, law enforcement, the military) has established conventions and protocols that seek to foster a sense of legitimacy and proficiency through the creation of a professional identity that sets it apart from other professions and sets its members apart from the general public. The legitimacy of the professional identity is maintained through the general educational requirements and the legal certifications and degrees needed for entry into the profession. In addition, each profession has a field or fields of knowledge, specific skills, and attitudes and values that are necessary for maintaining the professional identity of the organization and individuals. Everything that identifies a profession also acts to define the boundaries between the profession and other societal organizations and individuals. Just as there is a difference between a doctor, nurse, lawyer, or real estate agent and individuals who are not members of these professions, there also is a professional difference between educators and non-educators. Within and outside of the school, the authority of administrators and teachers is directly based on their individual and collective professional identity.

This condition of professionalism is a central component in the relationship between the school and the community. As in all professions, to function effectively educators and schools need to establish orderly and stable work environments that facilitate their professional effectiveness. Because education is a profession, certain language, knowledge, skill, values, and attitudes are required on a daily basis for the orderly and effective functioning of the profession. As with all professions, because the public is either not aware or only partially aware of these professional elements, an element of trust is required between the profession and the public. This trust between the school and the community is almost contractual in nature and definitely reciprocal. The profession assumes that the public will show its trust by supporting the activities of the profession, and the public assumes that the profession will demonstrate that it is worthy of trust by effectively performing and fulfilling its social purpose.

In the case of education, in many communities and states this relationship of trust has been voided, and new arrangements have been legislated in an attempt to guarantee the effectiveness of the profession. Mayoral takeovers of schools, state takeovers of schools, highly restrictive state control of curriculum and assessment, federal mandates, public schools being run by businesses, educational decision making conducted by non-educators, and school choice initiatives all indicate an erosion of public confidence in the professionalism of education. What happened to the relationship between the schools and the community? And what is the role that educational professionalism plays in this deteriorating relationship?

One part of the answer to the first question lies in the traditional bridging and buffering activities used by schools to mediate their contact with the community. The organizational structures and professional systems of a school can be referred to as the core technologies of a school. Schools realize that the external environment, consisting of parents, other individuals, and community organizations, provides support and needed resources for the school. Because of their need for this support, schools attempt to build bridges with the community. On the other hand, since the external environment can also pose threats to the professional routines of the school, schools create buffers between themselves and the community. As Rodney Ogawa simply states, schools "bridge between their core technologies and the environment and they buffer their core technologies from the environment" (1998, 8–9).

All parents have experienced the bridging phenomenon in various ways, ranging from back-to-school nights, newsletters, and parent-teacher conferences to the inclusion of community individuals on school committees. In addition, many of the nonacademic services, including extracurricular activities and sports, serve important bridging functions. Community members also commonly experience buffering activity, when their attempt to interact with teachers or the school is controlled by school regulations and procedures. In his study of bridging and buffering in schools, Ogawa describes the traditional expectation of teachers that their principals will shield them from unwanted interactions with the public. However, he also points out that all members of the school engage in bridging and buffering in both formal and informal ways. In relation to the question concerning the deteriorating relationship between schools and their communities, is the answer merely improper bridging and buffering, or is the professionalism of schools truly lacking?

A more detailed look at community involvement in schools suggests that most schools have the potential for a diversity of effective bridges with the community. Joyce L. Epstein (1995) describes six types of school and community involvement. First, schools can provide programs that aid parents in providing supportive home environments for their children. Also, communication between the school and community can foster a high degree of involvement. In addition, significant involvement can occur when parents and other individuals volunteer in schools. Another bridge that promotes community involvement is when home study, most frequently in the form of traditional homework, is required by the school. As mentioned, parents can be involved in educational decision making; the community also becomes involved in the school when educators solicit collaborative help from community organizations and individuals in meeting the needs of the school. Another type of community involvement in schools is the interagency collaboration of which many schools are a part. Obviously, each type of involvement has great potential in fostering positive community involvement in the schools, but each also carries its own challenges for the educators. Undoubtedly in some schools part of the problem with the school and community relationship is due to either a lack of sufficient bridging, or too much buffering.

Concerning the issue of professionalism, the nature of the community in which the school is nested is an important consideration in understanding the relationship between the school and the public. Some scholars have shown that communities that are economically and culturally stable have positive relationships with their schools. If the schools are adequately funded and are perceived to adequately serve the needs of the community, the public is generally satisfied with the performance of their schools, and their involvement with the schools. However, in communities that are economically stressed, some studies have shown that schools often become the targets of public criticism. In many cases, this criticism is realistic; however, the schools argue that if they are underfunded, there is no way that they can meet the needs and demands of the public. This scenario is frequently observed in poorly funded urban schools that are situated in economically distressed cities. As these urban areas engage in urban regeneration and renewal, the role of the schools in this renewal becomes critical.

Robert Crowson (1998) points out that in situations such as this, schools need to readapt their definition and practice of professionalism to meet the community-development orientation of the urban place. Crowson describes the way many urban schools have attempted to engage in a coordinated services movement. In this movement, schools participate in the coordination of disconnected services that are important to families within the community. In some urban areas, the coordinated services movement has been subsumed by community development. In community development, urban communities attempt to deal with the larger community issues in a coordinated manner. One characteristic of community development is the establishment of grassroots activism, which attempts to galvanize public participation in the resolution of these larger issues. Since the schools are seen as vital components in the regeneration of the community through the resolution of these larger issues, public activists see their involvement in school decisions as a natural extension of their community activism. This demand for additional public participation in school decisions can pose problems for schools that maintain their traditional bridging and buffering strategies. Also, this more intensive public activism may become a threat to the established professional structures and procedures of the schools. In this case, schools are faced with deciding whether to change the way they define their professionalism or to increase their buffering functions.

Crowson reviews a related problem for schools in urban areas that are designated as enterprise zones. Enterprise zones seek "economic improvement of poor neighborhoods though a strengthening of indigenous community institutions, investment incentives and the encouragement of public-private partnerships, and a preference for market forces above governmental intervention" (Crowson 1998, 62). The enterprise zone movement is driven by the belief that market forces can succeed in remedying the problems of the community. This belief creates problems for the professionalism of schools. Many community members come to believe that if they can become empowered through market forces to solve the larger community problems, then the same strategies can work in solving school problems. Crowson points out that one result is the school's perception that it is losing control to the politics of the community. If the school's answer is an increase in buffering strategies, or if the school cannot adapt its professional technologies to accommodate the community, the natural assumption of the public in a market-driven movement is to see an increased viability in the privatization of educational services. Crowson identifies the dilemma that faces schools as that of moving from seeing themselves as "supplying and servicing" organizations to taking the approach of "meeting and responding" (65). There is a distinctive difference in autonomous authority between a school that supplies and services and one that meets and responds.

In another study involving the relationship between schools and the community, Hanne Mawhinney (1998) defines this dilemma about the professional nature of the schools in terms of the difference between cognitive and normative professionalism. Cognitive professionalism defines the professionalism of schools as activity that deals with increasing the expert knowledge, skills, and training of the schools' professionals. In the case of school improvement, cognitive professionalism sees school improvement as activity relating to professional improvement as previously defined. Normative professionalism sees school improvement as improving the ability of schools to serve the needs of the community. In relation to the dilemma identified by Crowson, community development projects demand an increase in normative professionalism, in the ability of the schools to serve the needs of the community. An argument can be made that perhaps both can occur; however, the problem for schools lies in the danger of loss of their autonomy. Simply, the dilemma is about control over the educational system.

Some individuals argue that resolution of community problems is not the responsibility of schools, but rather falls under the responsibility of national, state, and local governments. One view often promoted is that if schools are to become participants in the solution of community problems, then they will not be able to perform their specific function of facilitating the learning, personal growth, and professional preparation of their students. Proponents of this view argue that the changing relationship between the schools and their communities is not the result of the failure of the schools, but the failure of governments and the general public to adequately address both the problems of the communities and the problems of the schools. Of course, a primary focus of this view is the inadequate funding of both the school and the community in poorer areas.

As the relationships between schools and their communities change, the professional identity of the schools, the authority of the schools, and the degree of trust between the school and the public also changes. In some cases, schools attempt to maintain their professional identity and authority by resisting the new needs and demands of a changed community. The result of this resistance to change is mistrust between the schools and the community. A change in the cultural and social class demographics of a community requires a comparable change in the attitude of the school toward the essentially new community. The new community, whether in an urban area or a suburban area that has experienced a pronounced growth in population, represents values and needs quite different from those of the old community. The result is an added challenge to school and community relationships. To further complicate the situation, this change takes place within the context of the current educational reform, whatever that is. For example, many schools and communities struggle to deal with the change in their relationship while attempting to meet external educational mandates imposed by the state and the nation. Community politics, national politics, state politics, the politics of reform, and the way the purpose of education and the nature of school professionalism are defined—all affect the relationship between the school and the public.

Public Involvement through Site-Based Reforms

One reform theme from the 1960s to the present that directly relates to the role of the public in education deals with the issue of centralization versus decentralization of education. Traditionally, the control of education is centered on those furthest away from the student. Governments, universities, and educational administrators traditionally make all of the educational decisions. As part of the restructuring movement of the 1980s, a reform trend developed aimed at decentralizing education, at moving some educational decision making to those who are closest to the students—teachers and parents. This restructuring effort to decentralize education became known as site-based or school-based reform. The impetus for this educational reform came from the business sector, which found that productivity could be enhanced if those closest to the work were empowered beyond the traditional limits of their ability to make work-related decisions. The assumption is that if individuals are involved in decision making, then they will have a heightened sense of ownership and a greater degree of commitment to the completion of their assigned task.

The term "school-based management" (SBM) came to indicate a decentralized management structure that included individuals in educational decision making who previously only functioned to carry out the decisions of others. Schools that employ SBM strategies empower, to varying degrees, principals, teachers, and parents in decisions concerning school curriculum, budget, personnel, strategic planning, and school change. To accommodate this restructuring of educational decision making, school-based councils are established in participating schools. These councils usually comprise the building administrators, teachers, and parents. Councils may be formed for districtwide decision making, or each individual school may have its own council.

School-based management is about governance, or who has the power to make the decisions that will affect a district or a school. SBM initiatives are an attempt to redistribute power within a school. Theoretically, they present an alternative to the traditional top-down administrative structure found in modern schools that are organized in accordance with the factory model of schooling. In SBM, instead of an administrative structure dominated by career administrators, the administrative decision-making structure includes teachers and parents. Some researchers report, however, that instead of achieving its ideal of shifting power through the establishment of new forms of school governance, SBM allows the traditional hierarchy to be maintained. Within the traditional hierarchical structure, power can simply be shifted to other individuals who are not administrators but either hold the same values as the administrators or can be easily influenced by the professional opinions of the administrators. In either case, governance remains an administrative function, and professionals continue to make the decisions, even when they act through community members. This sort of buffering technique blunts the idealistic intent of community involvement through SBM.

There are two basic reasons why this buffering can occur. One is the simple fact that professional knowledge and skill are required in educational decision making, and that community members may not have access to this knowledge and may not have developed the necessary skills. Another reason is that in its ideal form, SBM requires all of the participants to have the necessary collaborative skills required for this type of decision making process. Without these skills, an SBM council can quickly acquire the attributes of a traditional expert-driven hierarchy.

Public Involvement through School Choice

Another type of school reform that can also be classified under the heading of public involvement in educational reform is school choice. In school choice initiatives, the public has the ability to evaluate the public schools and follow up their evaluation with the decision to send their children elsewhere. Here, the public performs the role of school critic and has the potential to support the public school or to withdraw support by sending their children to other schools. There are many options provided under the school choice umbrella. School choice can occur within the pubic school system with the establishment of charter schools, magnet schools, and schools-within-schools (see glossary). In all school choice initiatives, the parents are able to choose schools that are different in some way from the regular schools in the school district. School choice may also involve private, or nonpublic, schools. In this case, parents are reimbursed to some extent for the costs they incur when they send their children to nonpublic schools. These schools can include parochial schools and secular private schools. Another form of school choice is involved in home schooling. Home schooling allows the parent to keep the child at home and personally supervise the child's education. In home schooling, the ability of the public school to affect the child is minimal or nonexistent.

Reimbursement to parents who send their children to nonpublic schools usually comes in the form of vouchers. The idea of vouchers is not new, but can be traced at least to the voucher proposal made by the economists Milton Friedman and Rose D. Friedman in the 1960s. Proponents of school choice have proposed different forms of vouchers. Vouchers may be in the form of a tax credit, a cash stipend paid to the parents, or a shifting of school funds from the public school to the nonpublic school. There are many different views on how to implement vouchers, and the difference between them usually involves how much free choice parents would have in the use of the money. Proponents of vouchers usually represent the market philosophy of education. This philosophy maintains that education will be more effective and efficient if driven by the market forces of competition and supply and demand. Proponents of the move to privatize education support the idea of vouchers. In this view, schools would become additional institutions in the free enterprise marketplace.

The parents' choice to transfer their child from a public school to a nonpublic school is a significant decision. Some individuals argue that school choice is a threat to the traditional idea of a guaranteed free public education for all American children. They further argue that school choice involving nonpublic schools will further deplete the current level of funding for public schools. Both critical multicultural and cultural assimilationist arguments against school choice are centered on the possibility that it might lead to the inequitable segregation of students along racial and social class lines. One outcome would be the inability of society to develop an inclusive culture that could accommodate the diversity inherent in American society. However, the reality of the school choice issue is that for parents to engage this option requires some level of dissatisfaction with the public schools. There is also the possibility that these parents either do not feel a part of the community, or perceive the public school as not meeting the needs of the local community.

CONCLUSION

Traditionally, the public has played an indirect role in educational reform. Historically, their participation has been constrained by the authority and control of educational experts, and by their own willingness to defer to the reform leadership provided by educational professionals, the government, and other public leaders. Even with the limited invitation provided by some of the restructuring initiatives started in the 1980s, generally the public chooses to be restrained in their participation in educational reform. Research and common sense both indicate that public participation in reform is a stronger presence on the local and, to some degree, the state levels. State funding of education in the form of taxation usually provokes some public response. However, that which is closest to the public, the actions of their local school districts, most significantly prompts public response to educational reform. On the local level in the local school, the public can see the concrete effects of educational reform on their children, themselves, and their community. These concrete effects represent the tangible evidence of the efficiency and effectiveness of educational reform initiatives.

One downside of the public's delay in becoming involved in educational reform until it is concretely manifested on the local level is that their understanding and concerns would be more effectively and appropriately expressed when the reform is being originally debated and planned. Because of this delay in public involvement, reformers who have been unable to anticipate public reaction have promoted flawed reforms. This inability to factor in the concerns of the general public, sometimes resulting in the vociferous opposition of the public to a reform, has crippled many reform efforts. The result has been inefficient, costly, and failed reform, and a lessening of the public respect for educators in general and reformers in particular.

REFERENCES

Beck, Lynn G. 1999. Metaphors of educational community: An analysis of the images that reflect and influence scholarship and practice. *Educational Administration Quarterly* 35 (1): 13–45.

Crowson, Robert L. 1998. Community empowerment and the public schools: Can educational professionalism survive? *Peabody Journal of Education* 73 (1): 56–68.

Epstein, Joyce L. 1995. School/family/community partnerships: Caring for the children we share. *Phi Delta Kappan* 76: 701–712.

Kahne, Joseph. 1996. *Reframing educational policy: Democracy, community, and the individual.* New York: Teachers College Press.

Mawhinney, Hanne B. 1998. School wars or school transformation: Professionalizing teaching and involving communities. *Peabody Journal of Education* 73 (1): 36–55.

Ogawa, Rodney. 1998. Organizing parent-teacher relations around the work of teaching. *Peabody Journal of Education* 73 (1): 6–14.

Sergiovanni, Thomas J. 1994. *Building community in schools.* San Francisco: Jossey-Bass.

Shields, Carolyn M. 1999. Learning from students about representation, identity, and community. *Educational Administration Quarterly* 35 (1): 106–129.

Westheimer, Joel. 1999. Communities and consequences: An inquiry into ideology and practice in teachers' professional work. *Educational Administration Quarterly* 35 (1): 71–105.

Chapter Nine

❧ Resistance to Reform

As discussed in Chapter 1, there is always the concern about the sustainability of educational reform. Like all aspects of educational reform, sustaining a reform is a complex challenge. The most important variable in this situation is the extent to which those who must implement the reform cooperate with the reformers. In other words, the most important individuals in the implementation and sustainability of a reform are the teachers and administrators. Their decision to comply or resist is the critical factor. Institutions, special interests, school boards, professional organizations and unions, parents, and community members all matter in the success of a reform, but the administrators and teachers are the professionals closest to the students, and the ultimate success of the reform depends on the effect the reform has on the students.

The centrality of these professionals, especially the teachers, is supported by the ubiquitous call for teacher participation and teacher empowerment in the reform literature over the last two decades. It is also supported by the current intensive effort by the standards and accountability initiatives to create accountability measures for teachers, with the purpose of forcing teacher compliance in effectively implementing and sustaining this reform. The irony lies in the fact that both attempts to control or empower teachers create reasons for teacher resistance to a reform. In addition, resistance can be active or passive, with both forms of resistance presenting equally challenging problems.

Resistance to reform can be found on an institutional level, in that educational bureaucracies may have more of an investment in the current practice and organization of schools than in the new practice and organization proposed by the reform. Proponents of the restructuring reforms that were initiated in the 1980s recognized this institutional potential for resistance. In an analysis of the restructuring reforms of the 1980s, Joseph Murphy (1990) summarized the attitude of the reformers toward institutional resistance by reporting their belief that "bureaucracies can evolve into organizations that displace system and client goals with strategies designed to enhance the welfare of the work force. Since the monopoly nature of schools provides few incentives to change, reform initiatives (such as full-year school programs) that clash with the operant goals—maintaining self-serving routines of employees—are rejected out of hand with little consideration of their potential impact on official organizational goals" (33). Essentially, as Murphy continues to point out, "results are sacrificed for bureaucratic convenience" (33).

This harsh condemnation of institutional resistance, voiced by Murphy and many others, has been followed by the creation of a link between student achievement, as measured by a standardized test, and evaluation of institutional effectiveness in fostering predetermined and normative (i.e., involving a comparison of the test results of a school with the norm) definitions of acceptable student achievement. However, despite the punitive consequences for schools (if student performance is not acceptable), individual administrators, and individual teachers, other additional factors have perpetuated and created resistance to the reforms. The inadequate funding of some public schools has continued to prove to be a stronger force than accountability measures. Without adequate funding, inadequate resources, deteriorating infrastructure, and a lack of professional support services become sources of resistance to any reform and prove to be more powerful than curricular, instructional, assessment, and accountability mandates. Also, as previously discussed, educational institutions are still essentially organized around the factory system model. This model is oppositional to and problematizes reforms that rely on teacher collaboration and empowerment. As will be discussed later in this chapter, the factory system of education fosters individualistic and balkanized administrative and teacher cultures that essentially contain built-in resistance to reform. In addition, as institutions, schools desire and require stability and autonomy. Because of this need, schools are inherently cautious about if not resistant to reform efforts that are not directly compatible with their traditional organizational structure and operation.

However, institutions do consist of people, and to understand resistance to reform requires a look at the culture in which these individuals work and their individual reasons to resist. This chapter will focus on these two areas by discussing the cultural context and the personal context of resistance to educational reform. It will conclude with a discussion concerning resistance and accountability.

THE CULTURAL CONTEXT OF
RESISTANCE TO REFORM

Like all human systems, schools develop a culture. Actually, to be more precise, schools include several subcultures. Schools have been analyzed in relation to their student culture, teacher culture, administrative culture, and all of the subculture variations within these larger cultures. Each of these cultures is shaped by norms, values, laws, beliefs, and mores that regulate the individual's behavior. Language, dress, rituals, knowledge, and power arrangements are all affected by the dominant culture of that specific place. One primary goal of all cultures is to ensure stability and constancy by reproducing the culture that dominates the group. It is in terms of this need to reproduce itself that the dominant culture assesses attempts to change aspects of the school culture and accordingly accommodates or resists those attempts. Understanding the change potential of a reform requires a critical assessment of the type of culture that is dominant. Some scholars have attempted to understand educational reform by studying the various cultures found in schools. Keeping in mind that the teacher is the ultimate gatekeeper in relation to changes that will affect themselves and their students, an understanding of teacher culture is critical in the understanding of educational reform. In the following discussion of teacher culture, related aspects of administrative culture also will be discussed.

Michael Fullan and Andy Hargreaves (1996) identify six aspects of teacher culture that are problematic for educational reform: overload, isolation, groupthink, untapped competence and neglected incompetence, and the narrowness of the teacher's role in the process of educational reform. The problem of overload is a significant source of teacher resistance to reform. Simply, what teachers are expected to do in relation to the time that is available to do it in creates an obvious resistance to do more or to change what they do and how they do it. Teachers are expected to be experts in the content they teach and in the use of appropriate instructional techniques for all of their students, regardless of ability, socioeconomic status, and learning style. The increasing intellectual, racial, ethnic, and social class diversity of their classrooms compounds the problem of learning and implementing instructional techniques that attempt to address this diversity. In addition, many teachers struggle to meet the needs of their students when faced with large classes, limited instructional resources, and inadequate facilities. Also, teachers are increasingly faced with the requirement to provide noneducational services for their students.

One reason some schools have moved to block scheduling has been the realization of the decreasing amount of time during a school day actually spent on academic instruction. The academic service, nonacademic service, public relations, and administrative responsibilities all vie for an increasingly scarce amount of time. Miles Huberman (1983) talks about the "classroom press," in the sense that on a daily basis teachers are required to spontaneously interact with different individuals, simultaneously carry on multiple tasks, adapt to ever changing conditions that are not predictable, and develop and maintain personal relationships with their colleagues and students. Because of this overload, demands to implement reform often receive a low priority from the teachers.

As Fullan and Hargreaves point out, teaching has long been known as the lonely profession. Despite rare attempts at interdisciplinary team teaching, teachers essentially function in isolation. In fact, many attempts at interdisciplinary and parallel disciplinary teaching actually only occur on paper in the curriculum guides. The typical teacher is still isolated in a contained classroom for most of the school day. As all teachers know, accommodations are made by all teachers to create a stable and effective environment within the context of this isolation. This need for stability within the context of physical isolation leads to a natural resistance to attempts to foster collegial interaction. Fullan and Hargreaves characterize this condition of isolation as one maintained by architecture, or the physical layout of the school, and time.

Groupthink is not restricted to education, but it is certainly another source of resistance to educational reform. The pressure of the group on an individual teacher to think like the group inhibits some teachers who might otherwise be receptive to a reform. In a demanding work environment that is characterized by overload and isolation, the need to be accepted by the group and the need for personal support can be a deadly combination that becomes a source of resistance to a reform, if the determination of the group is that the reform is frivolous or wrong. In some cases, groupthink is an unwanted result of reforms that promote teacher collaboration and teaming. If individuals do not have the critical skills and awareness to maintain their own ability to evaluate a reform, the individual is left with deferring to the group opinion. Conversely, some individuals may oppose the dictates of the group and use their professional isolation to resist the group when the group supports the reform initiative.

Fullan and Hargreaves identify the related problems of untapped competence and neglected incompetence as problems facing reform. In many schools, both older teachers and younger teachers are underutilized in attempts to foster change. Older teachers may be viewed as too conservative, traditional, or set in their ways. Younger teachers may be viewed as too idealistic and inexperienced to contribute to a reform on a level beyond that of merely being a technician who implements the reform. In either case, the teacher may be personally offended and either actively resist or passively resist by simply not participating except in the most minimal way. In both cases, valuable human resources are wasted or alienated, to the detriment of the reform. Some school administrators neglect to tap the reservoir of competence in these teachers, while others alienate the competent by applying mandates and regulations to everyone in order to ferret out the few who are incompetent. Not only is this inefficient practice, but it also creates reasons for resistance. In some schools, the personal negative feelings generated by inefficient and inequitable administrative actions are transferred to a reform viewed by the alienated teachers as the administrator's reform. In this case, resistance occurs, not because of issues the teacher has with the reform but because of the personal issues between the teacher and the administrator.

Despite the previously described overload of responsibility, the leadership roles that teachers play are limited. Fullan and Hargreaves describe the teaching profession as a "flat" profession (1996, 11). By this they mean that there is little room for teachers to assume leadership roles or to expand their creative potential if they remain teachers. Some teachers avoid professional burnout by moving into administration, but except for this vertical career move, there are few other options. Some teachers report that they feel trapped. One response is to direct their creative energy and need for positive reinforcement into athletics and extracurricular activities. Another response is to create their own personal work environment in a way that meets the needs that others fulfill by moving up or out of the profession. The personal autonomy that they gain from the routines they develop become very valuable in defining and sustaining their professional identity. Because of this condition, they carefully scrutinize every reform for its potential to disrupt their stability (Horn 2000).

Fullan and Hargreaves note that there is a trend in some schools to offset this problem of role narrowness by expanding the professional roles of teachers. Induction programs for new teachers, mentoring by more experienced teachers, peer coaching, and teacher leader programs all attempt to provide more opportunity for teachers to expand their professional learning, creativity, and leadership. However, these programs can also become sites of resistance by promoting an administratively driven groupthink, or by empowering teachers to resist reforms that they think are ineffective and inequitable. These techniques also create the empowering potential for the creation of professional networks within a school, which can then quickly galvanize opposition to a reform. These techniques especially gain potential as a source of organized resistance if the teachers are not part of the creation of the reform and therefore have no investment in it.

In an attempt to address these six aspects of teacher culture that are problematic for educational reform, Fullan and Hargreaves suggest the following strategies: evoking personal images, professional reading, professional dialogue, teacher support groups, teacher research, reading autobiographies and life histories of other teachers, and taking courses and advanced qualifications. However, in a culture that is highly restrictive, controlling, and time intensive, these strategies have limited appeal for teachers, and can become sources of resistance to reform. For instance, if the reality of a teacher's existence is the necessity to teach to a test in order to ensure a specified level of student achievement, reforms that ask the teacher to give time for the kind of activities suggested by Fullan and Hargreaves could be construed by the teacher as irrelevant to the teacher's real needs. Time devoted to these reforms would be thought of as wasted time. Teacher resistance to the reforms would be the logical response in this scenario. Through professional reading and additional course work, teachers can develop the critical skills and knowledge that facilitate their critique of an intended reform. They might apply their new awareness in a critique of the reform and find the reform to be ineffectual, inequitable, or otherwise harmful to their students. Through professional dialogue, informed and activist teachers can attempt to galvanize other teachers in their resistance to the reform. If teachers become teachers-as-researchers (Kincheloe 1991), their research conclusions, which will be locally contextualized, may uncover problems with a standardized reform that neglects the local context. Also, if teachers work to develop a strong personal image, they may be empowered to resist the reforms that they find problematic.

However, the issue of teacher empowerment through critical professional development as proposed by scholars such as Joe Kincheloe is problematized by four distinctly different forms of teacher culture. These four forms of teacher culture, identified by Andy Hargreaves (1994), also can be viewed as sources of resistance to reform. According to Hargreaves's research, teacher culture may be characterized by individualism, contrived collaboration, collegiality, or balkanization. Individualism relates to the isolation that characterizes the professional situation of many teachers. Hargreaves identifies three kinds of individualism that reflect three reasons for the individualism that characterizes many teacher cultures. First, there is constrained individualism, reflecting the fact that teachers work alone because of administrative or other situational constraints. Strategic individualism, the second variant, occurs because of the overload that they experience. In this case, preparation time cannot be wasted because of the overload of daily tasks. Simply, even if encouraged to do so, some teachers don't have the time to collaborate.

Finally, elective individualism occurs when individual teachers prefer to work alone. This may be because of a personal preference or, once again, a behavior that is encouraged by isolation and overload. Many teachers are driven by their ethical desire to meet the needs of their students, and they find that in the typical school environment, they need to maximize their time by relying on their own ability to make professional judgments about their use of time. In this sense, individualism may be viewed as a positive condition by teachers, and any encroachment on their time and work routines by a reform becomes a reason to resist the reform. Once again, any reform that requires collaboration or collegiality without building in adequate time for these activities could be viewed as a threat.

Hargreaves and many other scholars report that some reforms require the development of collaborative and collegial cultures. This appears to be a reform situation that many teachers would find acceptable; however, those teachers who are well adapted to a culture of individualism might see collaboration and collegiality as a threat to the autonomy that they experience in their isolated state. Hargreaves (1994) identifies the basic characteristics of collaborative cultures as spontaneous, voluntary, development-oriented, pervasive across time and space, and unpredictable. To teachers who have learned to work by themselves and have established stable and regular professional routines, these characteristics may be unsettling. Also, teachers who are receptive to the empowerment inherent in collaborative culture may resist collaborative reforms if they are perceived to be contrived.

Hargreaves sees contrived collegiality as resulting when the collegial or collaborative aspect of the reform is administratively regulated, compulsory, implementation-oriented, fixed in time and space, and predictable. Essentially, the way individuals collaborate is tightly controlled and specifically directed toward the implementation of the goals of others, rather than the goals of the teachers. Many teachers who in theory value the flexibility and empowerment of collaboration and collegiality strongly resent the manipulation that is inherent in any form of contrived collegiality. This problem with the contrivance of collaboration and collegiality is an empowerment issue. Many teachers limit their investment in a reform, depending on how much input they have had in the development of the reform, or in the adaptation of the reform to their local environment. The less participation, the more reason there is to actively or passively resist, or to make only a short-term commitment to the reform. As often experienced by educators, there is no simple definition of collaboration and collegiality, and unless they spring from favorable initial conditions, they are certainly no guarantee of success in implementing a reform.

The teacher culture that is probably most resistant to change is what Hargreaves characterizes as the balkanized culture. In this type of culture smaller subgroups of teachers are isolated from other subgroups. In many balkanized schools, these subgroups may be defined by the subject departments, grade levels, special needs units, or areas of specialization in elementary schools. As Hargreaves points out, their existence is clearly delineated in space (i.e., classrooms and other areas of the school), with clear demarcations establishing what space belongs to which group. Hargreaves identifies four characteristics of these balkanized groups that greatly contribute to their ability to resist change. The first is low permeability, in the sense that the groups are strongly isolated from one another because they all work to maintain rigid boundaries between these groups. Because of this isolation, each group is able to develop its own knowledge, values, and beliefs. Another characteristic is high permanence over time. Few, if any, teachers move from one group to another. This leads to another characteristic involving personal identification. Because of the low permeability and high permanence, teachers' professional identities are greatly affected by the nature of their group. As Hargreaves suggests, instead of referring to themselves as teachers, they identify themselves as social studies, English, math, or science teachers.

Finally, Hargreaves identifies a political complexion component in the subgroups. By this, he is referring to the promotion of the self-interest of the groups. The interests of the group are more important than the interests of the general school. This aspect is often seen in the political maneuvering that takes place during budget time, as each department vies with the others for the scarce funding for needed resources. Additionally, balkanization can occur within departments as well as between departments. Within a department, individuals may split into groups around ideological or personal issues. In this situation, the department factions work in the same way as larger balkanized groups to maintain their own identities and interests by enforcing boundaries that isolate them from the others.

The strength of the resistance of balkanized schools to educational reform lies in the same area from which successful sports teams draw their strength. Each group is composed of individuals who have developed shared identity traits, who rely on each other to achieve their individual goals, who are bonded together because of their isolation, and who see sharp distinctions between themselves and others. Like sports teams, balkanized teachers develop bonds that transcend contractual obligations, and when working with other groups, they seldom develop ties that exceed temporary and contractual levels. As reforms invade their environment, they scrutinize the reform in relation to their collective group values and interests. As a group, they form a response to the reform and have the collective strength to accommodate or resist. Reformers can see balkanized cultures as positive or negative situations. In one way, gaining assistance in implementing a reform may be an easier political process when one has to negotiate with groups instead of individuals. However, if a group or groups within a school decide to resist, the organized strength of their resistance can pose significant problems for the reformers.

Hargreaves offers one solution to this cultural dilemma in what he characterizes as the moving mosaic. In this solution, a school culture would be developed that would exhibit blurred boundaries between groups, between individual teachers, and between teachers and administrators. Groups would have overlapping categories and membership. Individuals and groups would be encouraged to be flexible and responsive, and uncertainty and vulnerability would be recognized and viewed in a positive way. Hargreaves offers this perspective on school culture as a moving mosaic: "Warm human relationships of mutual respect and understanding combined with the toleration and even encouragement of debate, discussion and disagreement create flexibility, risk-taking and continuous improvement among the staff which in turn lead to positive results among the students, and positive attitudes among the staff to changes and innovations which might benefit those students" (1994, 239).

The question arises, however, whether a culture of this nature would be effective in facilitating the implementation of externally imposed reforms. The primary benefit of this type of culture is the empowered participation of teachers in the determination of the nature of their school environment. An imposition of the externally mandated reforms of others inherently limits the degree to which teachers and administrators are empowered. Another question concerning the effectiveness of this type of culture is to what degree restrictions can be placed on faculty in this type of culture, without diminishing all of the motivational aspects of a moving mosaic that teachers might find attractive. Depending on the answer to these questions, personal resistance to reform may still be the end result.

THE PERSONAL CONTEXT OF
RESISTANCE TO REFORM

Ultimately, to understand resistance to educational reform, one must go to the individual teacher. Every school or group within a school has a gatekeeper function that regulates what comes into that group's domain, how that input gets processed, and how those within the school or group communicate with others outside the school or group. This regulatory process promotes stability and regularity within the group's system, and functions to protect their system from unwanted influences that would threaten their system. This gatekeeper function is a site of resistance or accommodation to reform attempts. However, since schools, groups, and cultures within schools are open systems, the individuals in these groups can evade the control of this gatekeeper function. Teachers have the freedom to research and investigate reforms, and to work politically for or against a reform.

In addition, teachers function as the gatekeepers to their classes. What aspects of a math or science reform enter the teacher's math or science classroom depends to a large degree on the teacher. Therefore, if individual teachers decide to resist a reform, they have the power to filter or mask certain aspects of the reform so that the complete intent of the reform is not realized. This is one reason why teacherproof materials are sometimes utilized by reformers. Prescribed lesson formats, programmed instruction, or scripted lessons reduce the teacher to the status of a mere technician, whose job is simply to transmit the prescribed curriculum in the mandated instructional manner. These programmed lessons, which control the teachers' curricular and instructional freedom, also restrict the resistance that teachers may offer by reducing their classroom gatekeeper role.

In order to understand the personal context of teacher resistance to reform, it is important to examine the actual ways in which teachers can resist. Peter Senge (1990) offers a detailed discussion of the forms of resistance. Senge is essentially speaking from a business orientation concerning employee resistance to change; however, he infers that these forms are evident in any organization, including educational systems. Senge's analysis deals with the various attitudes encountered in the workplace regarding a reform. He distinguishes between different types of commitment to and compliance with the reform. Senge reports that commitment is when the individual wants the reform and will create whatever laws or structures are required to implement the reform (219). On the other hand, individuals may "enroll" in the reform because they want it, but their commitment may be limited to whatever can be done "within the spirit of the law" (219). At this point, Senge distinguishes between these more committed attitudes and compliance; genuine compliance implies that the individual "sees the benefits of the vision. Does everything expected and more. Follows the 'letter of the law,' 'Good soldiers'" (219).

Senge then considers a level of compliance that is less desirable from the reformer's point of view. On this level, individuals may be formally compliant, in that they will do what is expected, but they refuse to do anything more. They may be grudgingly compliant, in that they don't see the benefits of the reform but want to keep their job, so they do what is expected but let everyone know that they don't agree with the reform. The last level he considers is one of noncompliance, in that the individual does not agree with the reform and refuses to take part in the implementation. On the same level is apathy, the state in which the individual just doesn't care one way or the other, and makes no effort in the reform initiative. This last level would include active or passive resistance to the reform. Passive resistance may take the form of inaction or grudging compliance; active resistance might involve what Senge characterizes as malicious obedience. When maliciously obedient, the individual takes the attitude that she or he will do whatever is necessary to prove that the reform will not work.

Senge points out that there are obviously subtle gradations between these levels of commitment; he proposes, however, that there is a real difference between commitment and compliance. To Senge, the significant difference lies in the degree of energy, passion, and excitement engendered by the reform in the teacher. Many reforms fail because those who must implement them are only compliant; many also because those who resist the reform do so with energy and passion. The previously discussed types of school culture are sources of energy and passion that can feed both commitment and resistance. Also, another source of energy and passion that can drive resistance to reform is systemic alienation. Some educational systems, whether school districts or individual schools, are organized and operated in such a manner that most individuals feel alienated from the school and most other individuals in the school. In this case, when reforms are mandated, the reforms become the focus of the frustration and anger caused by the alienation. In essence, the reform becomes the object of displaced teacher anger. In addition, depending on the systemic nature and intensity of the alienation, a pervasive feeling of alienation can resist attempts to build collaborative and collegial community.

Warren Breed (1971) talks about alienation as resentment and inauthenticity. Breed writes: "Alienation is not only a subjective feeling of resentment but also an expression of the objective conditions which expose a person to forces beyond his understanding and control" (198). In an educational context, Breed's objective conditions could be the relationship between administration and teachers, between teachers and teachers, and between teachers and students. If the tenor of the interpersonal relationships is essentially adversarial and combative, the negative feelings and behaviors caused by this type of interpersonal relationship will influence the stakeholders' emotional responses in relation to the proposed reform. Negative feelings would arise, especially when teachers are faced with a reform that they don't understand, don't agree with, or have no control over. The outcome would not be commitment or a positive type of compliance, but resistance. Any aspect of inauthenticity and irrelevance to the local context would further intensify the negative feelings and the concomitant resistance to the reform. In understanding what is or is not authentic, Breed focuses on the idea of responsiveness. Alienated and resisting teachers may find a reform inauthentic, if it is not responsive to the real or perceived needs of the students, themselves, or their place.

Breed suggests that the most alienating type of reform would be one that is proposed as a response to the needs of the local place and its stakeholders, but doesn't meet that promise. The worst-case scenario would be when the teachers can easily detect that the real intent of the reform is to meet the needs of individuals, groups, or organized special interests external to the local context, rather than to meet the needs of their students and themselves. Reform attempts that rely on deception and manipulation create a greater potential for resistance, especially if they are implemented in a school where feelings of alienation are systemic. Resistance and alienation can result in the kind of "anti-work" so humorously presented in the Dilbert cartoon strip. Those who engage in anti-work are aware of their resistance and alienation, and given any chance actively pursue their anti-work agenda. In essence, this activity becomes part of their identity.

What are the conditions that can lead to alienation and resistance? First, teachers generally have little knowledge and skill concerning the process of change. In their certification process, few teachers encounter courses that focus on the methods of change. Those teachers who may enroll in a graduate program might only encounter change in the narrow context of action research. Few teachers actually study the process of change as it unfolds across a whole educational system, whether that system is a statewide educational system, a school district, or an individual school. Because of their lack of knowledge and skill in dealing with the big picture of change, teachers can quickly find being part of attempts at educational change an incredibly frustrating experience. Adding to the complexity of change is the simple fact that many teachers know little about the systemic context and origins of their current system, the one that is to be changed. Because of the isolation, specialization, and deskilling of teachers, teachers are rarely focused on the origins, context, and patterns of their school environment. Teachers' lack of knowledge concerning the various philosophies and methodologies of change, together with their isolation and, often, alienation, becomes their reason to resist reform.

Second, the negative effects of their lack of knowledge concerning change are compounded by teachers' experience with change. Teachers who have been teaching for a number of years soon realize that educational change is a cyclic phenomenon. In other words, reforms come and go, and years later some are recycled. Most more experienced teachers have personally experienced the ephemeral nature of educational reform. Because of this they view educational reform as a phenomenon characterized by one-shot, quick-fix, and faddish solutions that are here today and gone tomorrow. When asked to approach a new reform with heightened energy and passion, they think back to all of the past failed reforms, to which their own commitment and that of the school district was short-lived. Their conclusion may well be that this too shall pass.

The aspects of teachers' experience with reform that can be the most discouraging for them are what Michael Fullan and Suzanne Stiegelbauer (1991) refer to as false clarity and painful clarity. In false clarity, teachers think that they have changed, but in actuality they have only assimilated the superficial trappings of the new practice (35). This occurred in many schools that attempted to implement the open classroom concept in the 1960s and 1970s. The inability of the teachers and administrators to move beyond the false clarity that all that was necessary was to change the way space was organized, to move to change their curriculum and instruction to accommodate that spatial change, quickly doomed the intent of the reform (Horn 2000). Their inability to fully comprehend or fully take the necessary action to guarantee the success of the change not only doomed that specific change, but also influenced their perception of future change attempts. Fullan and Stiegelbauer describe painful clarity as occurring "when unclear innovations are attempted under conditions that do not support the development of the subjective meaning of the change" (35). In this case, the assumptions of the reformers are clearly out of sync with the concerns and meanings that the teachers attach to the reform attempt. In situations involving both painful and false clarity, the outcome can be immediate resistance to the specific change, and in the long term a propensity to be defensive and cautious, at least initially, when confronted with change.

John Goodlad (1984) suggests a third situation, in which teachers start out fighting the archaic traditions and conventions that are impeding needed reforms, but eventually realize that they cannot overcome the individuals and structures that support inefficient or irrelevant traditional curriculum and instruction. According to Goodlad, this realization is followed by their acquiescence, as they settle down into behavior that is compatible with the established traditions that the reform is intended to change. One could extend Goodlad's interpretation of resistance to change by adding that perhaps some teachers only appear to settle down and actually simply become wiser in the selection of the battles that they will fight. In these cases, teachers might actually engage in a long-term guerrilla war against certain procedures, organizational structures, philosophies, or administrators. Unfortunately, this warfare may lead them to resist certain reforms that in a less adversarial situation they might actually support.

Related to Goodlad's way of looking at resistance is C. West Churchman's idea of "enemies." Churchman (1979) identifies four enemies of systemic change: politics, morality, religion, and aesthetics. He maintains that these are "enemies" because those who are dominated by these considerations do not accept the reality of the whole, but see the whole system only and narrowly through their political, moral, religious, or aesthetic view. This narrow view is problematic because those who hold it don't realize that all four views are just parts of the tapestry of the whole system. One could say that these views are the essentializing aspects of many individuals' lives, and become the sole lens through which they view the world or, in this case, a specific reform. These essentialized aspects of human consciousness carry high emotional value. As politicians wrap themselves in the flag, so can both agents of educational reform and those who resist the reform wrap themselves in morality, spirituality, or aesthetics. The decision to accommodate or resist a reform becomes a simple matter of whether the reform accommodates or opposes the individual's essentialized belief.

Another useful tool for understanding conditions that can lead to alienation and resistance is the idea of career stages. Zemira Mevarech (1995) summarizes the research on teacher career stages. In this developmental view of teachers, teachers at the beginning, middle, and end of their careers will view their role and professional activity in different ways. As Mevarech reports, there are many different perspectives on teacher career stages; however, they all share certain basic conclusions. Generally, teachers in the entry stage are seen as exhibiting anxiety, confusion, and hesitation about their role and methods. This stage is often characterized as the survival stage. As teachers move on in years and experience, they move through stages such as exploration and bridging, adaptation, conceptual change, and invention (154). Each of these stages can be a site of potential resistance to change. Some scholars propose that the deciding factor in determining whether resistance or accommodation of reform will occur is whether the professional development used to promote a reform is appropriate to the stage of the teacher. Professional development that is inappropriate for a teacher's career stage could foster resistance instead of accommodation.

Other scholars contest the developmental view of teachers implied by the idea of career stages, pointing out that all teachers are unique individuals with unique developmental contexts. From this point of view, essentializing teachers into artificial categories masks the real reasons for resistance or accommodation. These scholars propose that the real reasons for the accommodation or resistance lie in the issues of teacher empowerment, teacher understanding of change, the authenticity and relevance of the reform, and the authentic participation of the teacher in the construction and implementation of the reform.

A final reason for teacher resistance to reform has to do with Ira Shor's (1992) idea that some teachers resist certain reforms because what is proposed in the reform does not agree with the teachers' experience. Shor's specific point is that some teachers resist any reform that requires teaching subject matter in a dialogic form because their own experience as students was one in which only teacher-centered transmissional instruction techniques were used. Shor's point is well taken, because many individuals do merely teach as they were taught. Even though they encountered progressive theory in their preparation courses, when placed in the classroom environment, they encounter so much stress and anxiety that it quickly dissipates any allegiance that they may have had to the theory. What replaces the theory is a regression to what they perceived worked for the teachers that they had as students.

The deeper significance of Shor's point is that most teachers, whether traditional or progressive, do honestly believe that the instructional strategies they employ are the best for their students. In this case, the center of their resistance to reforms that are incompatible with their own beliefs is what they truly believe. This center of belief is reinforced by the teacher's own experience as a student. If the teacher has a compelling need to gain or maintain control over a class, the authoritarian methods employed by this individual's previous teachers may gain currency in the new teacher's beliefs about how to exercise control. On the other hand, new teachers may strongly resent the authoritarian methods that were employed by their teachers, and gain a strong commitment to progressive methods. In either case, teachers have strong reasons to resist any reform that is in opposition to their beliefs. To summarize this point, teachers' decisions to resist or accommodate reform are not frivolous decisions, but in many cases are directly related to their past experience and the compatibility of the reform with their experience and core beliefs. The irony of this view of teacher resistance to reform is that teacher resistance may result from mistrust, paranoia, and self-interest, and yet at the same time be the result of some teachers' sincere beliefs that the reform is simply wrong for their students.

Some scholars suggest that an essential element of any reform effort has to be the inclusion of activities that develop the ability of the reformers and the teachers to critically reflect on their experience and core beliefs. By "critical," they refer to the post-formal processes that facilitate the individual's critical examination of the origins, context, and patterns of their own mistrust, paranoia, self-interest, and core beliefs, as well as the nature and potential outcomes of the intended reform. Systems theorists such as Ludwig von Bertalanffy (1968) recognize the importance of the past and the future for systemic conditions found in the present. In relation to educational reform, most reformers generally refuse to recognize that the past, the present, and the anticipated future are a dynamic whole in which all three are active agents in the construction of current thoughts and actions. This denial of time contributes to a kind of machinelike or robotic activity on the part of some reformers and on the part of those who are to implement the reform.

Our anxieties and desires about the future are part of our construction of the present and our reconstruction of the past. A review of past practice informs both the present and the future. Therefore, a critical analysis of the origins, current context, and future context becomes a priority in the post-formal view of educational reform. Proponents of this post-formal process acknowledge that the outcome may not be compliance with or commitment to the proposed reform, but more than likely resistance to a continuation of a reform that is not relevant to the needs of the local community or equitable for all members of that community. Another outcome could be the construction of a reform that is need-fulfilling and equitable, and so can garner sincere commitment from those affected by the reform. In relation to Churchman's "enemies," proponents of the inclusion of the post-formal process argue that if people do critically reflect and post-formally think, then the power of politics, morality, spirituality, and aesthetics will naturally arise and empower a reform.

What this means is that as individuals explore the origins, context, and patterns of their experience in relation to a reform, as well as the origins, context, and patterns of the reform itself, they will become empowered by the political knowledge they gain. In addition, the moral, spiritual, and aesthetic considerations that will surface during the post-formal process will become the source of their commitment to the reform's implementation. Another important benefit of post-formal inquiry is the teacher's realization that these separate views are interrelated and that one should not carry more importance than another. In order to accommodate the greater good, the individual must balance the importance of each view and not let one dominate the decisions made about a reform. For example, one's political concerns must be tempered by one's morality, spirituality, and sense of the aesthetic.

As reported by many scholars who deal with educational reform, the development of a shared vision and team learning is essential in accommodating the past experience and core beliefs of teachers. Also, these scholars indicate that the shared vision has to include the very nature or essence of the reform, not merely a shared vision about how to implement a reform that someone else created. These scholars include, as essential components, the empowerment and authentic participation of teachers in the whole reform process. Of course, as previously discussed, if some teachers do not want to be empowered or included, then they will resist even this type of reform process. This raises the next issue, the issue of what to do about teachers who resist reform.

RESISTANCE AND ACCOUNTABILITY

The issue of what to do about teachers who resist reform is as basic to the process of educational reform as any other part of the process. There are essentially three basic responses to this issue. The first response is similar to the response of a business to the issue of employees who don't comply with the business decisions of the managers. This response is simply to get rid of them. This supposedly simple solution is as complex in education as it is in business. In states where teachers are unionized, getting rid of a teacher involves compliance with due process procedures formalized in collective bargaining contracts. In many cases, teacher resistance to reform is not the sole indication of the teachers' professional competence. In many other contexts, the teacher who resists a reform may be an exemplary and valued professional. In this case or in the case of a less desirable teacher, the burden of dismissal falls on the administrators.

This is a considerable burden in relation to the due process procedures that the administrator must contractually follow. In many schools, the overburdened administrators struggle to fulfill all of their normal responsibilities and simply do not have the additional time to expend in the formal and extensive documentation needed to dismiss a teacher. In fact, in many schools, the only way dismissal would be possible would be if administrative staff were increased. This is generally not an option because of the added cost to the school budget. Also, some individuals see this option as adding more noninstructional bureaucracy to a school that may in actuality need more teachers and instructional aides.

In nonunion states, the action of firing teachers is more of an option. However, if the state is experiencing teacher shortages, especially in specialized areas such as math, science, foreign language, and special education, getting rid of teachers because of their resistance to a reform becomes problematic for the school district. Another tactic would be to encourage or force resistant teachers to retire. However, this only is effective in the case of those individuals who are near retirement or can afford to retire. In addition, this tactic is also nullified if there is a teacher shortage. In short, the threat of getting rid of teachers isn't a simple way to control those who resist educational reform.

Another tactic that is used in some states is to create rigid accountability structures that tie teacher salary, benefits, and professional duties (e.g., teaching schedules) directly to student performance, in relation to the goals of the reform. States such as Texas have highly structured accountability systems that can track student achievement on the state standardized test to individual schools, administrators, and teachers. In this case, teacher resistance can be defined in terms of the effectiveness of teachers in preparing their students for the test. One drawback is that this type of accountability system may actually reward teachers who merely teach to the test, and punish teachers who are actually very effective and accomplished professionals. Related to this kind of rigid accountability is the encouragement to increase state and administrative control over curriculum and instruction. This kind of micromanagement can be accomplished through the use of scripted lessons and programmed instruction. If student achievement on a state-mandated test is the sole criterion of teacher effectiveness in implementing a reform, this type of accountability through micromanagement can be quite effective. However, this tactic relates to the problems encountered in the first issue that dealt with getting rid of the teachers. If a teacher is found to be ineffective in raising student performance on a state test, the question arises whether it is possible to get rid of the teacher, and whether the school can afford to get rid of the teacher.

Opponents of both of these tactics argue that these tactics essentially rely on coercion and negative reinforcement, which generate fear, anxiety, and anger among teachers and administrators. Some individuals see this dilemma as a motivational issue, and others see it as a commitment issue. Some individuals argue that compliance with a reform is strictly motivational, in that salary, benefits, and job security can be used as negative and positive reinforcements to force compliance. Others see it as a commitment issue, in that the desirable teacher is one who is self-motivating, self-directed, a lifelong learner, and a teacher-researcher. They propose that teachers who exhibit these characteristics are more desirable participants in a reform situation than those who are externally motivated to comply. Those who see the issue as one of commitment also see teachers as professionals instead of as technicians. They see education as an art and a craft, with teacher experience and intuition being as important as the teacher's ability to implement mandated reforms. Proponents of this view argue that education deals with individuals and groups of individuals, and therefore is of necessity a very personal and emotional endeavor. The role of teachers includes allaying student fear and anxiety, and fostering joy in and love of learning. Here the focus is on creating lifelong learners rather than students who can achieve on predetermined levels on standardized tests. Those who share this view see the formula for successful reform as a combination of teacher empowerment, authentic participation of teachers in reform, and the continuous professional development of teachers, including a development of critical and post-formal skills.

This third view is distinctively different from the first two in many ways, but primarily in the way resistance is valued. In the first two, resistance to reform is seen purely as a negative response to the reform. In the third view, resistance has value. Those who value resistance maintain that no reform contains all of the best practice, accommodates the whole unique local context of all places, or contains all of the answers to the problems addressed by the reform. They maintain that all reform is to some degree flawed. In this view, all resistance contains relevant and necessary information about the effectiveness and relevance of a reform to what is being reformed and to the individuals and places that are the targets of the reform.

Proponents of this view see resistance as having the potential to create leverage points for meaningful and effective reform. Here, resistance indicates sites of inequity, unfilled needs, and unanticipated aspects of the national, state, and local context. In addition, those who most strongly resist may be the individuals who could contribute most significantly to the reform of education. In this view, not to listen, accommodate, and respond to acts of resistance is to miss significant opportunities to craft authentic, effective, and sustainable educational reform. In the first two views, the focus was on teachers being accountable to the reform. In this third view, the reformers also have a responsibility to be accountable to those who must implement the reform and live with it. This additional aspect of accountability creates quite a different view of teacher resistance to educational reform.

REFERENCES

Breed, Warren. 1971. *The self-guiding society.* New York: Free Press.

Churchman, C. West. 1979. *The systems approach and its enemies.* New York: John Wiley and Sons.

Fullan, Michael, and Andy Hargreaves. 1996. *What's worth fighting for in your school.* New York: Teachers College Press.

Fullan, Michael G., and Suzanne Stiegelbauer. 1991. *The new meaning of educational change.* New York: Teachers College Press.

Goodlad, John I. 1984. *A place called school: Prospects for the future.* New York: McGraw-Hill Book Company.

Hargreaves, Andy. 1994. *Changing teachers, changing times: Teachers' work and culture in the postmodern age.* New York: Teachers College Press.

Horn, Raymond A. 2000. *Teacher talk: A post-formal inquiry into educational change.* New York: Peter Lang.

Huberman, Miles. 1983. Recipes for busy kitchens. *Knowledge: Creation, Diffusion, Utilization* 4: 478–510.

Kincheloe, Joe L. 1991. *Teachers as researchers: Qualitative inquiry as a path to empowerment.* Philadelphia, PA: Falmer Press.

Mevarech, Zemira R. 1995. Teachers' paths on the way to and from the professional development forum. In *Professional development in education: New paradigms and practices,* edited by Thomas R. Guskey and Michael Huberman. New York: Teachers College Press.

Murphy, Joseph, ed. 1990. *The educational reform movement of the 1980s: Perspectives and cases.* Berkeley, CA: McCutchan.

Senge, Peter M. 1990. *The fifth discipline: The art and practice of the learning organization.* New York: Currency Doubleday.

Shor, Ira. 1992. *Empowering education: Critical teaching for social change.* Chicago: University of Chicago Press.

Von Bertalanffy, Ludwig. 1968. *General system theory: Foundations, development, applications.* New York: George Braziller.

Chapter Ten

❖ Selected Print and Nonprint Resources

PRINT RESOURCES

Curriculum, Educational Change, and School Reform

Abu-Duhou, Ibtisam. 1999. *School-based management: Fundamentals of educational planning*. Paris, France: United Nations Educational, Scientific, and Cultural Organization.

This book is an in-depth study of school-based management, and provides a comprehensive view of the subject.

Adler, Mortimer. 1982. *The paideia proposal: An educational manifesto*. New York: Macmillan.

This book is an example of the traditional and disciplinary view of American curriculum that was revived during the early 1980s. This is the first in a trilogy advancing this view of curriculum reform. The others were *Paideia Problems and Possibilities* (1983) and *The Paideia Program* (1984).

Altbach, Philip G., Gail P. Kelly, Hugh G. Petrie, and Lois Weis. 1991. *Textbooks in American society: Politics, policy, and pedagogy*. Albany, NY: State University of New York Press.

Despite the earlier copyright, this book provides a comprehensive study of the basic positions and conditions concerning the impact of textbooks on American education as they evolved over time. This information is still relevant to the present.

Apple, Michael W. 1990. *Ideology and curriculum*. 2d ed. New York: Routledge.

This book is a radical response to the conservative reforms of the 1980s and 1990s. Apple critically analyses the historical attempts to control American education for ideological and economic purposes.

Apple, Michael W., and Linda K. Christian-Smith. 1991. *The politics of the textbook.* New York: Routledge.

This study of the influence of the textbook in American pedagogy provides a critical view of how textbooks impact curriculum and pedagogy in the context of political positions and ideology.

Banathy, Bela H. 1991. *Systems design of education: A journey to create the future.* Englewood Cliffs, NJ: Educational Technology Publications.

In this book, Banathy presents a method that can be used to systemically design new educational systems. The components of Banathy's design model provide a deeper understanding of the complexity of educational systems.

————. 1996. *Designing social systems in a changing world.* New York: Plenum Press.

This textbook is a comprehensive presentation of the field of systems theory and thinking. It is an excellent resource for someone who wants to understand the multifaceted nature of change in any type of human system.

Barth, Roland S. 1972. *Open education and the American school.* New York: Agathon Press.

This is a classic presentation of the open education system that appeared during the 1960s and 1970s by one of the main proponents of this view of education.

Bennett, William J. 1987. *James Madison High School: A curriculum for American students.* Washington, DC: U.S. Department of Education.

In this book, Bennett presented the conservative view of how schools should be restructured in America. This book is an important foundation in the acquisition of a historical understanding of the current reform initiatives of American schools.

Bennett, William. J., Chester. E. Finn, Jr., and John T. E. Cribb, Jr. 1999. *The educated child: A parent's guide from preschool through eighth grade.* New York: The Free Press.

This conservative back-to-basics how-to-do-it book is a clear example of the conservative values and positions concerning American education, the role of the public school, and the role of the parent.

Berliner, David C., and Bruce J. Biddle. 1995. *The manufactured crisis: Myths, fraud, and the attack on America's public schools.* Cambridge, MA: Perseus Books.

This now classic book contests the arguments used to attack the effectiveness of American schools. Through the presentation of a diversity of information, Berliner and Biddle first argue that American education is not as inadequate as proposed by politically motivated reformers and then identify the areas of education that they think need reform.

Bestor, Arthur. 1953. *Educational wastelands: The retreat from learning in our public schools.* Urbana: University of Illinois Press.

This book best exemplifies the humanistic call for replacing life adjustment education with intellectual and disciplinary education.

Beyer, Landon E., and Daniel P. Liston. 1996. *Curriculum in conflict: Social visions, educational agendas, and progressive school reform.* New York: Teachers College Press.

This book is a progressive view of crucial controversies in the field of curriculum. The book presents an overview of the field of curriculum studies and discusses the positions of the new right, modern liberalism, the radical view, postmodernism, and a new progressive reform agenda.

Bloom, Allan. 1987. *The closing of the American mind: How higher education has failed democracy and impoverished the soul of American students.* New York: Simon and Schuster.

This is another of the many conservative books written during the Reagan presidency attacking public education. In this case, the focus of the attack is on the liberal curriculum and pedagogy of higher education.

Bode, Boyd H. 1938. *Progressive education at the crossroads.* New York: Newson.

This fundamental book in the progressive education movement presents a definition of progressive education. Bode responds to the critics of this educational view and attempts to evolve the nature of progressive education to accommodate the development of democracy.

Boorstin, Daniel J. 1961. *The image: A guide to pseudo-events in America.* New York: Vintage Books.

Boorstin's book is timely commentary for any decade in relation to the manipulation of public opinion through the creation of what Boorstin calls pseudo-events. Even though this book does not deal directly with educational reform, its main premises can be readily applied to educational reform movements.

Bowles, Samuel, and Herbert Gintis. 1976. *Schooling in capitalist America: Educational reform and the contradictions of economic life.* New York: Basic Books.

This comprehensive radical critique of education links the problems of education with the influence of the American capitalist economy on the educational system and on the process of educational reform.

Boyer, Ernest L. 1983. *High school: A report on secondary education in America—The Carnegie Foundation for the Advancement of Teaching.* New York: Harper and Row.

Published in 1983, this influential book was one of the many reports critical of American education that initiated the intense reform movement of the 1980s and 1990s.

Brown, Frank. 1992. *The reform of elementary school education: A report on elementary schools in America and how they can change to improve teaching and learning.* Malabar, FL: Krieger Publishing.

This book is an in-depth study of the reform of elementary education, and provides comprehensive information on this subject.

Bruner, Jerome S. 1960. *The process of education.* Cambridge, MA: Harvard University Press.

In this book, Bruner reported the findings of the Woods Hole Conference on curriculum. The curriculum theory generated by this conference and explained in this book argued for a disciplinary structure for school curriculum.

———. 1966. *Toward a theory of instruction.* New York: W. W. Norton and Company, Inc.

This book represents Bruner's determination of the importance of the student in the curriculum development and learning process. At this point in his thinking, Bruner proposed that teachers and students needed to be collaborators with disciplinary specialists in the development of curriculum.

Carlson, Robert V. 1996. *Reframing and reforming: Perspectives on organization, leadership, and school change.* White Plains, NY: Longman Publishers.

This book proposes that American education is suffering from a crisis of perception. This crisis is discussed through the perspectives of educational leadership, school reform, and current and future trends in education and society.

Center on National Education Policy. *Do we still need public schools?* Bloomington, IN: Phi Delta Kappa.

This book reviews the attempts to diminish the public school system and presents arguments why a free public school system is necessary.

Chall, Jeanne S. 2000. *The academic achievement challenge: What really works in the classroom?* New York: Guilford Press.

This book is an excellent example of the conservative arguments that support current conservative reform initiatives. A comparison of Chall's interpretations of historical events and movements in American education with those of liberal and radical scholars clearly shows the distinctly different ways that the same phenomenon can be viewed.

Chubb, John E., and Terry M. Moe. 1990. *Politics, markets, and America's schools.* Washington, DC: Brookings Institution.

This book presents the conservative argument for the market-oriented reforms that started in the 1980s.

Cole, John Y., and Thomas G. Sticht. 1981. *The textbook in American society: A volume based on a conference at the Library of Congress on May 2–3, 1979.* Washington, DC: Library of Congress.

This is a study of the use and influence of textbooks on American education and provides a historical perspective on this topic.

Conant, James B. 1959. *The American high school today.* New York: McGraw-Hill.

This influential book represents the reform thinking that occurred as a response to the Sputnik scare.

Cozic, Charles P., ed. 1992. *Education in America: Opposing viewpoints.* San Diego, CA: Greenhaven Press.

This book is a quick reference that can be used to gain an understanding of both sides of the dominant reform issues following the 1983 publication of *A Nation at Risk: The Report of the National Commission on Excellence in Education,* with its influential call for reform of education.

Cunningham, William G. 1982. *Systematic planning for educational change.* Palo Alto, CA: Mayfield.

This book provides a foundation for the systems view of educational reform that influenced the restructuring movement of the 1980s.

Deming, W. Edwards. 1986. *Out of the crisis.* Cambridge, MA: MIT, Center for Advanced Engineering.

This basic presentation of Total Quality Management by its main proponent provides a foundational understanding of this reform movement.

Dewey, John. 1938. *Experience and education.* New York: Macmillan.

Dewey critiques both traditional and progressive education, and further argues for an educational philosophy based on experience.

Finn, Chester E., Jr., and Theodor Rebarber, eds. 1992. *Educational reform in the 1990s.* New York: Macmillan.

This collection provides conservative viewpoints concerning most of the major areas of educational reform during the restructuring that began during the Reagan years.

Freire, Paulo. 1985. *The politics of education: Culture, power and liberation.* New York: Bergin and Garvey.

An excellent source for gaining an understanding of Freire's vision of emancipation through adult literacy.

———. 1996. *Pedagogy of the oppressed.* New York: Continuum.

A seminal work, crucial for understanding the transformative and critical view of educational reform. This is a compelling representation of the reform theory and practice of Paulo Freire, which has greatly influenced radical educational thought. It is a companion to Freire's other books: *Pedagogy of Hope* (1995) and *Pedagogy of the City* (1993).

Friedman, Milton. 1962. *Capitalism and freedom.* Chicago: University of Chicago Press.

This book details Friedman's proposal to create a competitive educational environment, primarily through the use of vouchers.

Friedman, Milton, and Rose Friedman. 1979. *Free to choose.* New York: Avon.

This later book once again promoted school choice as a panacea for the ills of public education.

Fullan, Michael G., and Andy Hargreaves. 1996. *What's worth fighting for in your school.* New York: Teachers College Press.

Presents action guidelines for teachers and principals who want to reform their schools. The book is an excellent example of the educator empowerment reforms of the 1990s.

Fullan, Michael G., and Suzanne Stiegelbauer. 1991. *The new meaning of educational change.* New York: Teachers College Press.

Provides an in-depth look at the sources, meanings, causes, and processes involved in educational change on a local and national level. The authors argue for a systemic view of educational change as well as the empowerment of teachers and administrators.

Gaddy, Barbara B., T. William Hall, and Robert J. Marzano. 1996. *School wars: Resolving our conflicts over religion and values.* San Francisco: Jossey-Bass Publishers.

School Wars is an excellent resource in the understanding of the cultural battle that continues to be fought for control of American education by conservative and liberal interest groups. Detailed explanations and contact information are provided for the various interest groups.

Giroux, Henry A. 1988. *Teachers as intellectuals: Toward a critical pedagogy of learning.* Westport, CT: Bergin and Garvey.

A classic book, representing the radical position concerning the intellectual and political empowerment of teachers. Giroux argues that a democratic society needs the critical empowerment of teachers as one of the main "foundations" for effective educational reform.

Good, Thomas L., and Jennifer S. Braden. 2000. *The great school debate: Choice, vouchers, and charters.* Mahwah, NJ: Lawrence Erlbaum Associates.

This book primarily details the debate over school choice, vouchers, and charters. Additionally, the beginning of the book provides an understanding of the political and economic contexts that are involved, not only in these specific reforms but also in other reform initiatives.

Goodlad, John I. 1984. *A place called school: Prospects for the future.* New York: McGraw-Hill Book Company.

A report of one of the many studies commissioned during the early 1980s to study school effectiveness. Goodlad presents his criticisms of public education at that time and presents his plan for the restructuring of American schools.

Goodman, Paul. 1966. *Compulsory mis-education and the community of scholars.* New York: Vintage Books.

An example of the anti–public school education position of the radicals of the 1960s. Goodman presents the radical criticism of traditional public education.

Guskey, Thomas R., and Michael Huberman, eds. 1995. *Professional development in education: New paradigms and practices.* New York: Teachers College Press.

This book looks at educational reform through the lens of professional development. Distinguished and international scholars present differing perspectives on change through professional development.

Hargreaves, Andy. 1994. *Changing teachers, changing times: Teachers' work and culture in the postmodern age.* New York: Teachers College Press.

An exceptional source for an in-depth understanding of the different types of teacher culture and their effects on educational reform. Hargreaves also presents an understandable discussion of the postmodern context of American schools, educational culture, and educational reform.

Hargreaves, Andy, ed. 1997. *1997 ASCD yearbook: Rethinking educational change with heart and mind.* Alexandria, VA: Association for Supervision and Curriculum Development.

This collection, sponsored by a major professional development organization, succinctly presents the various reform positions relevant to the 1990s.

Hart, Harold H. 1970. *Summerhill: For and against.* New York: Hart Publishing.

A collection that provides a forum for the examination of A. S. Neill's radical Summerhill reform.

Hirsch, E. D., Jr. 1988. *Cultural literacy: What every American needs to know.* New York: Vintage Books.

Hirsch presents and argues for a core curriculum of facts that every American child should have in order to be literate. *Cultural Literacy* represents the prescribed curriculum promoted by those who desire a homogeneous Eurocentric curriculum.

Hirsch, E. D., Jr., Joseph F. Kett, and James Trefil. 1988. *The dictionary of cultural literacy.* Boston: Houghton Mifflin.

This is a companion book to *Cultural Literacy* that precisely details the core curriculum proposed by Hirsch and others.

The Holmes Group. 1986. *Tomorrow's teachers: A report of the Holmes Group.* East Lansing, MI: The Holmes Group.

The reform proposal generated by universities; it argues that one important answer to education's problems would be a more professionally trained teaching force. This view differs from that of those who sought to weaken the role of the university in teacher preparation.

Holt, John. 1976. *Instead of education.* New York: Delta Book.

Another example of the radical anti–public education position that was evident during the 1960s and the 1970s. Holt authored a number of popular books on this position, and this is a good representation of his position.

Horn, Raymond A., Jr. 2000. *Teacher talk: A post-formal inquiry into educational change.* New York: Peter Lang.

Teacher Talk examines three decades of educational reform as seen through the eyes of five career teachers. In addition, it provides numerous analytical lenses that can be used to critically examine educational change.

Horn, Raymond A., Jr., and Joe L. Kincheloe, eds. 2001. *American standards: Quality education in a complex world—The Texas case.* New York: Peter Lang.

Texas educators explore the systemic nature and impact of the Texas standards and accountability reform, and examine the personal implications related to the different views regarding standards and accountability reform. A reading of this book, Deborah Meier's book, and the collection of essays edited by Diane Ravitch will provide a comprehensive understanding of the complexity of this reform movement.

Hunter, Madeline. 1982. *Mastery teaching.* El Segundo, CA: TIP Publications.

An example of the behaviorist reforms in teaching and supervision that were prevalent in the 1980s and 1990s.

Illich, Ivan. 1971. *Deschooling society.* New York: Harper and Row.

Illich challenges the need for a compulsory public education system. Illich was one of the most prominent radicals of this time period who attacked the idea of public schooling.

Jencks, Christopher. 1972. *Inequality: A reassessment of the effect of family and schooling in America.* New York: Basic Books.

Jencks argues that differences in academic achievement between students and schools are the result of social class differences rather than racial differences. His position is that family background is the essential element in achievement differences.

Jencks, Christopher, and Meredith Phillips, eds. 1998. *The black-white test score gap.* Washington DC: Brookings Institution.

A detailed study of the gap in student achievement on standardized tests between black and white children. Jencks and Phillips identify and critique the reform options available to schools to remedy this situation.

Kerchner, Charles T., Julia E. Koppich, and Joseph G. Weeres. 1997. *United mind workers: Unions and teaching in the knowledge society.* San Francisco: Jossey-Bass.

An excellent source for understanding the role of teacher unions in education and educational reform.

Kilpatrick, William. 1992. *Why Johnny can't tell right from wrong and what we can do about it.* New York: Simon and Schuster.

This book represents the conservative attack on the effectiveness of public schooling; it promotes the reform of schools through the inclusion of conservative values.

Kincheloe, Joe L., and William F. Pinar, eds. 1991. *Curriculum as social psychoanalysis: The significance of place.* New York: State University of New York Press.

This book represents the kind of critical analysis of curriculum done by proponents of the reconceptual movement in the field of curriculum. As seen in this book, curriculum reform based on this view of curriculum is highly contextual and personal.

Kincheloe, Joe L., and Shirley R. Steinberg. 1997. *Changing multiculturalism.* Philadelphia: Open University Press.

Details the various definitions and understandings of the term "multiculturalism." The idea of multiculturalism is shown to be a complex and highly contextual idea. Comparing this book and Arthur Schlesinger, Jr.'s book will provide a clear understanding of the assimilationist and pluralist views of educational reform.

Kincheloe, Joe L., and Shirley R. Steinberg, eds. 1998. *Unauthorized methods: Strategies for critical teaching.* New York: Routledge.

An example of the critical reforms in teaching proposed by the critical pedagogues of the 1990s and later. As represented by the strategies in this book, critical teaching is greatly concerned with the empowerment of teachers and students, and with the issues of social justice and caring.

Kohl, Herbert R. 1969. *The open classroom: A practical guide to a new way of teaching.* New York: A New York Review Book.

This book, by the main proponent of open classrooms, is a classic presentation of this radical view of teaching and school organization. Reading this book along with those of Madeline Hunter and E. D. Hirsch, Jr., will provide a clear understanding of the basic differences between three very different views of teaching and learning.

———. 1998. *The discipline of hope: Learning from a lifetime of teaching.* New York: New Press.

This autobiographical retrospect of Kohl's career contains interesting insights into the history of teaching and learning in the United States from the middle of the twentieth century to the present.

Kozol, Jonathan. 1972. *Free schools*. Boston: Houghton Mifflin.

Details the creation of independent Free Schools as a response to the alleged inadequacy and racism of the public schools of that time.

———. 1991. *Savage inequalities: Children in America's schools*. New York: Crown Publishers.

A compelling study of the conditions of many of America's urban schools. Kozol creates a human and personal understanding of a major American crisis that continues to the present.

Leistyna, Pepi, Arlie Woodrum, and Stephen A. Sherblom, eds. 1996. *Breaking free: The transformative power of critical pedagogy*. Cambridge, MA: *Harvard Educational Review*.

Contains articles reprinted from the *Harvard Educational Review* that collectively provide an excellent source concerning the educational reforms and beliefs of critical pedagogy.

Longstreet, Wilma S. 1973. *Beyond Jencks: The myth of equal schooling*. Washington, DC: Association for Supervision and Curriculum Development.

Longstreet critiques Jencks's contention that social class rather than race is most important in determining student achievement and describes the effects of Jencks's work on educational reform.

Maxey, Spencer J. 1995. *Democracy, chaos, and the new school order*. Thousand Oaks, CA: Corwin Press.

Critiques current educational reform, especially the various types of school restructuring. Maxey focuses his critique on order versus chaos theory and on the effects of current school reform for a democratic society.

McNeil, Linda M. 2000. *Contradictions of school reform: Educational costs of standardized testing*. New York: Routledge.

Critically examines the educational reforms of the state of Texas, with a focus on the effects of the Texas standardized testing program.

Meier, Deborah, ed. 2000. *Will standards save public education?* Boston: Beacon Press.

Noted educators present differing views on the standards reform movement. A reading of this book, the collection of essays edited by Diane Ravitch, and the collection edited by Raymond Horn and Joe Kincheloe will provide a comprehensive understanding of the complexity of this reform movement.

Murphy, Joseph, and Philip Hallinger. 1993. *Restructuring schooling: Learning from ongoing efforts.* Newbury Park, CA: Corwin Press.

This book provides an excellent review of the restructuring efforts of the 1980s and early 1990s.

National Center for History in the Schools. 1996. *National standards for history.* Los Angeles, CA: National Center for History in the Schools.

Contains the national history standards developed by scholars in that field.

National Council for the Social Studies. 1994. *Curriculum standards for social studies: Expectations of excellence.* Washington, DC: National Council for the Social Studies.

These standards were forcefully contested by those individuals who held the view that the disciplines (i.e., history, geography, sociology) should be taught separately, rather than holistically, as presented in social studies curriculum. In addition, these are the standards that became a major focus in the culture wars.

Neill, A. S. 1960. *Summerhill: A radical approach to child rearing.* New York: Hart Publishing.

Presents Neill's humanistic and existential view of education, and describes the free school he headed. This book was highly controversial. For an account of the differing views concerning Neill's approach, see the book by Harold Hart.

Paris, David C. 1995. *Ideology and educational reform: Themes and theories in public education.* Boulder, CO: Westview Press.

Provides a critique of liberal educational reform in the context of the ideological positions that compete for control of public education.

———. 1995. *The end of education: Redefining the value of school.* New York: Alfred A. Knopf.

In this readable book, Postman recaps the reform initiatives that are leading to the end of public schooling and the conversion to the privatization of education.

Powell, Arthur G., Eleanor Farrar, and David K. Cohen. 1985. *The shopping mall high school: Winners and losers in the educational marketplace.* Boston: Houghton Mifflin.

Another of the many highly critical studies of American education in the 1980s. The book also provides another perspective on the historical origins of the perceived crisis in public education.

Ravitch, Diane, and Chester Finn, Jr. 1987. *What do our 17-year-olds know? A report on the first national assessment of history and literature.* New York: Harper and Row.

Argues for a core curriculum; similar to other conservative positions, as represented by E. D. Hirsch, Jr.

Ravitch, Diane, ed. 1995. *Debating the future of American education: Do we need national standards and assessments?* Washington, DC: Brookings Institution.

Presents supporting arguments for the current standards and accountability reforms. A reading of this book, Deborah Meier's book, and the collection of essays edited by Raymond Horn and Joe Kincheloe will provide a comprehensive understanding of the complexity of this reform movement.

Rich, John M. 1988. *Innovations in education: Reformers and their critics.* 5th ed. Boston: Allyn and Bacon.

Details the most contested aspects of educational reform in the 1980s. This presentation of the issues involved provides an interesting perspective on how each of these issues has played out in public education to the present.

Rickover, Hyman G. 1959. *Education and freedom.* New York: E. P. Dutton.

This classic book represents the criticism of education prior to sputnik, informed by the fear of communism, and presents the reform initiative centered on the reestablishment of disciplinary and intellectual educational reform.

Rugg, Harold O. 1931. *An introduction to problems of American culture.* Boston: Ginn.

An example of a progressive textbook that came under attack by conservatives and anticommunists.

———. 1938. *Our country and our people: An introduction to American civilization.* Boston: Ginn.

Another of Rugg's textbooks that presented a progressive perspective on American society and history.

Sarason, Seymour B. 1990. *The predictable failure of educational reform: Can we change course before it is too late?* San Francisco: Jossey-Bass.

Sarason criticizes the school reforms of the 1980s and details how the long-standing educational structures and the self-interest of various groups doom educational reform efforts. Sarason promotes the idea of teacher and student empowerment in American education.

Schlesinger, Arthur M., Jr. 1998. *The disuniting of America: Reflections on a multicultural society.* New York: W. W. Norton.

This eminent historian argues for a core curriculum of shared values, for the promotion of education as an assimilation tool for individuals of non-Western culture, and against pluralistic and radical multicultural reform.

Schomker, Michael J., and Richard B. Wilson. 1993. *Total quality education: Profiles of schools that demonstrate the power of Deming's management principles.* Bloomington, IN: Phi Delta Kappa.

Promotes the business-oriented TQM reform movement in education.

Sehr, David T. 1997. *Education for public democracy.* New York: State University of New York Press.

Examines the two competing traditions of American democracy and the school practices and reforms related to each. This book is a good read for individuals who are concerned about the effects of certain school reforms and practices on American democracy.

Senge, Peter M. 1990. *The fifth discipline: The art and practice of the learning organization.* New York: Currency Doubleday.

An excellent example of the influence of business reforms on educational reform. In addition, Senge utilizes systems thinking to create a systemic reform of education.

Sizer, Theodore R. 1984. *Horace's compromise: The dilemma of the American high school.* New York: Houghton Mifflin.

One of the many critiques of public education in the early 1980s. In addition, Sizer presents his restructuring program—the Coalition of Essential Schools.

———. 1992. *Horace's School: Redesigning the American high school.* New York: Houghton Mifflin.

The companion book to *Horace's Compromise;* continues Sizer's presentation of his restructuring reform model.

Sleeter, Christine E., ed. 1991. *Empowerment through multicultural education.* Albany: State University of New York Press.

An excellent presentation of the radical multicultural view of education. Comparing this book and Arthur Schlesinger, Jr.'s book will provide a clear understanding of the assimilationist and pluralist views of educational reform.

Steinberg, Shirley R., and Joe L. Kincheloe, eds. 1997. *Kinderculture: The corporate construction of childhood.* Boulder CO: Westview.

An example of the expanded view of curriculum taken by curriculum reconceptualists. The book analyzes corporate marketing initiatives as hidden curriculum and their effects on children. This book is an example of the field of cultural studies.

Stotsky, Sandra, ed. 2000. *What's at stake in the K-12 standards wars: A primer for educational policy makers.* New York: Peter Lang.

Details the conservative position on the current reform initiative to implement technical standards and standardized tests in American education.

Tyler, Ralph. 1949. *Basic principles of curriculum and instruction.* Chicago: University of Chicago Press.

One of the most influential books in the field of curriculum. Generally, Tyler's position is a compilation of the thinking that guided curriculum and teaching for most of the twentieth century.

William T. Grant Foundation Commission. 1988. *The forgotten half: Pathways to success for America's youth and young families.* Washington, DC: Author.

This report presents the commission's findings that schools need to not only train workers for our economy but also help them transition into the workforce. The foundational source for the current pathways reform initiative.

Wynne, Edward A., and Kevin Ryan. 1993. *Reclaiming our schools: A handbook on teaching character, academics, and discipline.* New York: Merrill.

As in William Kilpatrick's book, Wynne and Ryan call for extensive character education reforms in American schools.

History of Education

Bennett, Kathleen P., and Margaret D. LeCompte. 1990. *The way schools work: A sociological analysis of education.* New York: Longman.

This sociology of education text systematically analyzes the process of schooling. The book provides a quick study of the intricacies and complexities of the American way of schooling.

Cremin, Larry A. 1961. *The transformation of the school: Progressivism in American education, 1876–1957.* New York: Alfred A. Knopf.

This influential book provides a definitive history of the progressive education movement from 1876 to 1957.

Cuban, Larry. 1993. *How teachers taught: Constancy and change in American classrooms 1880–1990.* 2d ed. New York: Teachers College Press.

A pioneering inquiry into the history of teaching practice from 1890 to 1990. A detailed history of progressive education and the open classroom movement is provided, along with an extensive discussion of the phases and levels of school reform that are suggested by these findings.

Kliebard, Herbert M. 1995. *The struggle for the American curriculum: 1893–1958.* 2d ed. New York: Routledge.

This classic study provides a detailed and well-referenced historical overview of the reform movements in education from 1893 to 1958.

Lagemann, Ellen C. 2000. *An elusive science: The troubling history of education research.* Chicago: University of Chicago Press.

This readable book is one of the most detailed historical studies of educational research in the twentieth century. Lagemann details the critical move away from a Deweyan perspective on research to the perspective of Thorndike, and the consequences of that event. In addition, she tells a compelling story about the historical effect of politics on educational research and, subsequently, educational reform.

Murphy, Joseph, ed. 1990. *The educational reform movement of the 1980s: Perspectives and cases.* Berkeley, CA: McCutchan.

This collection of essays provides a comprehensive critique of the restructuring reforms of the 1980s by numerous educational scholars.

Nash, Gary B., Charlotte Crabtree, and Ross E. Dunn. 2000. *History on trial: Culture wars and the teaching of the past.* New York: Vintage Books.

This book examines the debate over the National History Standards by chronicling the war between those who hold competing cultural views of history, which has raged since the beginning of the twentieth century.

Pinar, William F., William M. Reynolds, Patrick Slattery, and Peter M. Taubman. 1995. *Understanding curriculum.* New York: Peter Lang.

This comprehensive study of the field of curriculum is a valuable resource in understanding the diverse ways in which curriculum can be defined. Along with a detailed presentation of the history of curriculum in the twentieth century, extensive references are provided.

Popkewitz, Thomas S. 1991. *A political sociology of educational reform: Power/knowledge in teaching, teacher education, and research.* New York: Teachers College Press.

A detailed investigation of contemporary educational reform within the context of the perspectives of nineteenth- and twentieth-century educational history.

Ravitch, Diane. 1983. *The troubled crusade: American education, 1945–1980.* New York: Basic Books.

A conservative critique of the liberal and progressive reforms of this time period.

———. 2000. *Left back: A century of failed school reforms.* New York: Simon and Schuster.

A history of education and reform in the twentieth century. Ravitch presents this history as a conflict between progressivism and traditionalism, and uses her historical analysis to support the current traditionalist reforms.

Spring, Joel. 1988. *Conflict of interests: The politics of American education.* New York: Longman.

A radical critique of national educational policy in the United States from the end of World War II to the end of the 1980s. This critical view argues that U.S. public education has been used to select and channel human resources to meet the needs of the labor market, domestic policy, and foreign policy initiatives.

———. 1989. *The sorting machine revisited: National educational policy since 1945.* New York: Longman.

This book represents a radical and critical view of educational history from 1945 to the late 1980s. This book should be read with Ravitch's work concerning the same time period.

Tanner, Daniel, and Laurel Tanner. 1990. *History of school curriculum.* New York: Macmillan Publishing.

A classic study of school curriculum in the twentieth century.

Teac, David B. 1974. *The one best system: A history of American urban education.* Cambridge, MA: Harvard University Press.

A historical critique of American education with a specific focus on urban education.

Van Scotter, Richard D. 1991. *Public schooling in America: A reference handbook.* Santa Barbara, CA: ABC-CLIO.

A general reference book that provides easily referenced information on significant events and people in American education.

Reform in School Administration

Callahan, Richard E. 1962. *Education and the cult of efficiency: A study of the social forces that have shaped the administration of the public schools.* Chicago: University of Chicago Press.

A classic study and critique of educational administration's acceptance and implementation of business procedures and business leadership models during the early twentieth century.

Murphy, Joseph. 1992. *The landscape of leadership preparation: Reframing the education of school administrators.* Newbury Park, CA: Corwin Press.

Focused on educational leadership, this book provides a history of the forces and reforms that influenced educational leadership in the twentieth century. It also provides a comprehensive reference section on educational leadership.

Sergiovanni, Thomas J. 1992. *Moral leadership: Getting to the heart of school improvement.* San Francisco: Jossey-Bass.

Sergiovanni presents his view on reforming education through a change in school leadership. Teacher empowerment is facilitated through educational leaders who foster collaboration in the formation and attainment of a moral educational covenant.

——. 1994. *Building community in schools.* San Francisco: Jossey-Bass.

In this companion book to *Moral Leadership,* Sergiovanni details how effective and moral school communities can be created.

Taylor, Frederick W. 1911. *The principles of scientific management.* New York: Harper and Brothers.

The influential work by Taylor that detailed for school administrators the principles of the scientific management of schools. Together with Raymond Callahan's book, an essential source for the understanding of this educational reform.

NONPRINT RESOURCES

American Federation of Teachers
555 New Jersey Avenue, NW
Washington, DC 20001
(202) 879-4400
www.aft.org

A national teachers' union that engages in collective bargaining for teachers, and lobbies for their interests in national educational reform debates.

American Library Association
Office for Intellectual Freedom
50 East Huron Street
Chicago, IL 60611
(312) 944-6780
www.ala.org

The ALA is an excellent resource concerning censorship in schools and the banning of books.

Annenberg Institute for School Reform
www.annenberginstitute.org

The Annenberg Institute for School Reform at Brown University develops, shares, and acts on knowledge that improves the conditions and outcomes of schooling in America, especially in urban communities and in schools serving disadvantaged children. This institute provides resources and an electronic newsletter concerning school reform issues.

Association for Supervision and Curriculum Development
1703 North Beauregard Street
Alexandria, VA 22311-1714
(800) 933-2723
www.ascd.org

A large and influential professional organization that provides information and support for the professional development of teachers and administrators.

Behavioral, Cognitive, Sensory Sciences and Education (BCSSE)
The National Academy of Sciences
2101 Constitution Avenue, HA 178
Washington, DC 20418
Tel: (202) 334-3026 | Fax: (202) 334-3584
http://www7.nationalacademies.org

This is a partnership between the National Academy of Sciences and the National Research Council in Washington. In 1999, they released a report outlining a fifteen-year program for research and development in education.

Business Roundtable
1615 L Street, NW
Suite 1100
Washington, DC 20036
(202) 872-1260
www.brtable.org

An association of chief executive officers of leading U.S. corporations who desire to promote a well-trained and productive workforce. Established in 1972, the purpose is to promote economic growth by impacting debates about public policy and by improving student achievement.

Campbell Collaboration
(215) 848-5489
http://campbell.gse.upenn.edu/about.htm

Provides systematic reviews of studies on the effectiveness of educational and social policy and practice.

Center for Critical Thinking
Sonoma State University
PO Box 220
Dillon Beach, CA 94929
(707) 878-9100
www.criticalthinking.org

The work of the foundation is to integrate the center's research and theoretical developments, and to create events and resources designed to help educators improve their instruction. They also sponsor The National Council for Excellence in Critical Thinking, and the International Center for the Assessment of Higher Order Thinking.

**Center for Research on Evaluation, Standards,
     and Student Testing (CRESST)**
CRESST/University of California, Los Angeles
PO Box 951522
300 Charles E. Young Drive
North Los Angeles, CA 90095-1522
(310) 206-1532
http://cresst96.cse.ucla.edu/index.htm

CRESST is a partnership of UCLA, the University of Colorado, Stanford University, RAND, the University of Pittsburgh, the University of Southern California, the Educational Testing Service, and the University of Cambridge, United Kingdom. The CRESST mission focuses on the assessment of educational quality, addressing persistent problems in the design and use of assessment systems to serve multiple purposes.

Civil Rights Project, Harvard University
124 Mt. Auburn Street, Suite 400 South
Cambridge, MA 02138
(617) 496-6367
http://www.law.harvard.edu/civilrights/

The Civil Rights Project conducts ongoing assessment of the prospects for justice and equal opportunity under law for racial and ethnic minorities in the United States at the beginning of the twenty-first century. They provide extensive information of this nature that relates to educational reform.

Coalition of Essential Schools
1814 Franklin Street, Suite 700
Oakland, CA 94612
(510) 433-1451
http://www.essentialschools.org

The Coalition of Essential Schools (CES), founded in 1985, is a national network of schools, support centers, and a national office engaged in restructuring schools to promote better student learning and achievement. CES represents the reform ideas of Theodore Sizer.

Commonwealth Foundation
3544 N. Progress Avenue, Suite 102
Harrisburg, PA 17110
(717) 671-1905
http://www.info@commonwealthfoundation.org

The Commonwealth Foundation for Public Policy Alternatives is a conservative, independent, nonpartisan, nonprofit public policy organization committed to promoting free market economic growth and individual freedom and opportunity.

Eagle Forum
Box 618
Alton, IL 62002
(618) 462-5415

The Eagle Forum is a conservative organization that provides commentary on national family and educational issues, primarily through two newsletters: *Education Reporter* and the *Phyllis Schlafly Report.*

Education Quality Institute
(202) 639-8230
http://www.eqireports.org

This Web site offers a series of interactive reviews of education programs, links to educational organizations and resources, and the on-line Journal of Educational Effectiveness.

Education Week
Editorial Projects in Education Inc.
Suite 100
6935 Arlington Road
Bethesda, MD 20814-5233
(800) 346-1834
www.edweek.org

A nonprofit organization that publishes *Education Week* and *Education Week on the Web*, educational journals that provide weekly commentary on educational topics and reform, as well as the monthly *Teacher Magazine*.

Educational Research Analysts
PO Box 7518
Longview, TX 75607-9986
(903) 753-5993
http://www.textbookreviews.org

Mel and Norma Gabler provide textbook review resources for religiously conservative groups who wish to offset the influence of secular humanistic influences on American public education.

ERIC, The Educational Resources Information Center
(800) 538-3742
www.ericsp.org
www.accesseric.org

ERIC is a federally funded, nationwide education-related database that contains more than one million records of educational publication and research.

Heritage Foundation
214 Massachusetts Avenue, NE
Washington, DC 20002-4999
(202) 546-4400
http://www.heritage.org

The Heritage Foundation is a research and educational institute (of the kind referred to as a think tank) whose mission is to formulate and promote conservative public policies based on the principles of free enterprise, limited government, individual freedom, traditional American values, and a strong national defense.

League of United Latin American Citizens (LULAC)
2000 L Street, NW, Suite 610
Washington, DC 20036
(202) 833-6130

LULAC is a national group that advocates for Latin American citizens and provides information on the effect of educational reforms on this segment of the U.S. population.

**Mexican American Legal Defense and Educational
    Fund (MALDEF)**
1717 K Street, NW, #311
Washington, DC 20036
(202) 293-2828
http://www.maldef.org

An advocate for equitable educational reform, especially in the areas of state funding of public education, and educational standards and accountability systems. This organization, with LULAC, unsuccessfully took legal action against the standards and accountability system of the state of Texas.

**National Association of Christian Educators/
    Citizens for Excellence in Education**
Dr. Robert L. Simonds
Box 3200
Costa Mesa, CA 92628
(714) 251-9333

The NACE/CEE is a resource that promotes traditionalist Christian challenges to books and educational reforms.

National Association for the Education of Young Children
1509 16th Street NW
Washington, DC 20036-1426
(202) 232-8777
http://www.naeyc.org/default.htm

The National Association for the Education of Young Children (NAEYC) is the nation's largest and most influential organization of early childhood educators and others dedicated to improving the quality of programs for children from birth through third grade.

National Center for Fair and Open Testing
342 Broadway
Cambridge, MA 02139
(617) 864-4810
www.fairtest.org

Fair Test is an organization dedicated to assessment reform, advocating alternative assessments to the standardized tests currently being promoted.

National Center for Research on Evaluation, Standards, and Student Testing (CRESST)
National Coalition for Parent Involvement in Education
Box 39, 1201 16th Street, NW
Washington, DC 20036
(202) 822-8405

This coalition promotes parent involvement in educational reform.

National Commission on Teaching and America's Future.
Teachers College
Columbia University
New York, NY
http://www.tc.edu/nctaf/

NCTAF is a nonpartisan and nonprofit group dedicated to improving the quality of teaching nationwide as a means of meeting America's educational challenges. This commission consists of public officials, business and community leaders, and educators who believe that competent and qualified teachers are a crucial factor in the improvement of student achievement.

National Education Association
1202 16th Street, NW
Washington, DC 20036
(202) 822-7200
http://www.nea.org

The NEA is the oldest and largest professional organization of teachers and engages in national lobbying efforts concerning educational reform, as well as the promotion of reform initiatives.

National Education Summit 2001. www.achieve.org
This is the Web site for the education summit held in Palisades, New

York, in which state, business, and educational leaders promoted the establishment of standards and accountability measures as the primary means to move toward higher student achievement. The summit statement of principles is available at the site.

National Parent Teacher Association
330 N. Wabash Street, Suite 2100
Chicago, IL 60611-3630
(312) 670-6782
http://www.pta.org

National PTA is the largest volunteer child advocacy organization in the United States. It is a not-for-profit association of parents, educators, students, and other citizens active in their schools and communities.

National Staff Development Council
PO Box 240
Oxford, OH 45056
(513) 523-6029
NSDCoffice@aol.com
www.nsdc.org

The NSDC is the largest nonprofit professional association committed to ensuring success for all students through staff development and school improvement. The council's fundamental purpose is to address the issues confronted by all participants in the reform process.

Network of Comprehensive School Reform Researchers
www.goodschools.gwu.edu

This is a network formed by the National Clearinghouse for Comprehensive School Reform, based at George Washington University in Washington, D.C., and the Consortium for Policy Research in Education, a federally funded research center. This site offers links to the resources of both organizations.

People for the American Way
National Headquarters
2000 M Street, Suite 400
Washington, DC 20036
(202) 467-4999

The PFAW is a national organization involved in countering attacks on public education, and focuses on issues dealing with intellectual freedom and First Amendment rights.

Project Zero
Harvard Graduate School of Education
321 Longfellow Hall
13 Appian Way
Cambridge, MA 02138
(617) 496-7097
http://pzweb.harvard.edu

Project Zero's mission is to understand and enhance learning, thinking, and creativity in the arts, as well as humanistic and scientific disciplines, at the individual and institutional levels. They conduct research that will help to create communities of reflective, independent learners, to enhance deep understanding within disciplines, and to promote critical and creative thinking.

Regional Educational Laboratory Networks
http://www.relnetwork.org

This is a network of ten regional educational research organizations that provide information for individuals and groups on the local, state, and national levels. They are supported by the U.S. Department of Education's Office of Educational Research and Improvement.

**Teacher Center Professional Development Program
   for the United Federation of Teachers**
48 East 21st Street
New York, NY 10010
(212) 475-3737
http://www.uft.org

The UFT is a trade union for nonsupervisory educators and an advocate for public school students in New York. As a lobby for the interests of its constituents, the UFT is actively involved in school reform issues.

Thomas B. Fordham Foundation
1627 K Street, NW, Suite 600
Washington, DC 20006
(202) 223-5452
http://www.edexcellence.net

This conservative organization supports research, publication, and educational reform projects of national significance.

United States Department of Education
400 Maryland Avenue, SW
Washington, DC 20202-0498
(800) 872-5327
http://www.ed.gov

The Web site allows access to the resources of the U.S. Department of Education and the No Child Left Behind Act of 2001.

☙ Glossary

Assessment Assessment refers to the method of determining the progress of students in meeting the requirements of the curriculum. Classroom assessment approaches can include selected response (i.e., multiple choice, true and false, or matching questions), constructed response (i.e., fill in the blank, short answer, or labeling questions), product assessments (i.e., essays, stories, poems, journals, collages, newsletters, dioramas, and the like), performance assessments (i.e., musical and theatrical performances, speeches, debates, laboratory demonstrations, competitions), and process assessments (i.e., demonstrations of skills such as notetaking and researching). Portfolios can be used to organize the information gotten from these assessment approaches. Portfolios can showcase students' best work, or they can show progress over time. Another level of assessment involves determining when students have completed a program. Standardized tests can be employed for diagnostic or evaluative purposes. Portfolios can also perform this function.

Asynchronous Programmed Instruction One significant influence on educational change in curriculum and instruction during the 1960s and 1970s came from behavioral psychology. One behavioral technique was programmed instruction, in which students were presented with an individualized instructional activity. Usually, this was in the form of a learning packet that included specific behavioral objectives, a resource or reference to a resource, specific directions on how to complete the task, and an assessment of some type. Some schools used programmed instruction within a continuous progress assessment format. In this instructional and grading format, students could work at their own speed in mastering the objectives. All students had the potential to accelerate their learning. In addition, programmed instruction was often linked to mastery learning. Mastery learning required the student to perform to a minimum competency level before going on to another learning objective and task. With the advent of computers, programmed instruction techniques can be completed in a classroom or over the Internet. Also, the student and the provider of the programmed instruction are not bound by time. The activity can occur at any time, and the provider of the instruction does not have to interact with the student as the student completes the computer-mediated activity. The term "asynchronous" refers to the de-emphasis of time in the learning process. Currently, cyber schools are utilizing asynchronous programmed instruction as competition to the public schools.

Bilingualism   In 1967, the Bilingual Education Programs (Title VII) were added to the Elementary and Secondary Act with the specific task of meeting the special education needs of children whose education was limited by their inability to speak English. There are two types of bilingual education: assimilation bilingualism and pluralistic bilingualism. Assimilation bilingualism refers to non-English-speaking children not only learning English but also learning within mainstream English modes of instruction and accepting the dominant English culture (Moss 2001, 5). Pluralistic bilingualism promotes the goal of non-English-speaking students becoming proficient in English while still retaining their native language and culture (Moss 2001, 5–6). Assimilation bilingualism can be in the form of submersion, learning English as a second language (ESL), transitional bilingual education, and immersion. All of these forms have the goal of not only teaching English but also assimilating the child into the dominant English culture. Pluralistic types of bilingualism include maintenance bilingual education, enrichment/two-way/developmental bilingual education, and the Canadian immersion model (2001). Common features of these programs are the desire to have the students become proficient both in the English language and in the correct usage of their native language. A variation of pluralistic bilingualism is seen in the dual-language programs that are schoolwide initiatives designed to teach all of the school's students two languages—such as English and Spanish. Bilingual education, like all aspects of education, has a political context. Those on the right, who wish to assimilate non-English children into the dominant culture, attempt to promote assimilation bilingualism, and those on the left, who value non-English culture, promote pluralistic bilingualism.

Charter Schools   Public schools created when a government agency, such as a state or school district, grants a contract to a group of individuals who will receive public funding for their school (see Weil 2000). The group receiving the charter may consist of businesses, nonprofit agencies, educators, or parents who want to provide an alternate educational experience for students. Charter schools provide school choice within the public school system. The most recent type of charter school that has emerged is the cyber school. Cyber schools provide computer-mediated instruction through the Internet. Since they can be charter schools, they receive public funds from their students' home school district. Since the instruction is delivered on-line, cyber schools do not have any geographical limits.

Conservative Restoration   Politically, the 1960s and 1970s in America were liberal. With the election of Ronald Reagan in 1980, conservatives regained control of the government. All branches of the federal government eventually became more conservative and, until the election of William Clinton, promoted conservative agendas. The conservative influence extended to the state and local levels, where conservative politicians gained significant control and subsequently promoted conservative interests. The impact of the Reagan administration has been substantial, in that it resulted in both the first and the second Bush presidency and in a swing by the Democratic Party to the right. Liberal educational policies and practices have been attacked and in many cases supplanted by conservative educational agendas. A related effect has been the decisions supporting conservative educational agendas by conservative federal judges appointed during the Reagan and Bush administrations.

Critical   Education thinkers who are critical question the power arrangements fostered by educational policy and practice and the inequities created by these power arrangements. Most often these inequities arise in the context of race, gender, and social class; however, inequity can occur in all aspects of society, including lifestyle, age, and sexual orientation. Being critical implies a willingness to explore the origins, context, and patterns of inequity within oneself and within society. Individuals in education who are critical are ready to critique all aspects of an educational system, including the curriculum that is imposed by the outside on the educational system. See Cultural Studies.

Critical Consciousness and Constructed Consciousness   On one level a critical consciousness involves awareness of the political, economic, cultural, societal, personal, and interpersonal complexity of human activity. More specifically, it involves the mental probing or questioning of the assumptions made by others and oneself that form the basis for values, beliefs, and knowledge. To critical theorists, a critical consciousness is both a mental habit and an educational goal to be attained by all teachers and students (Hinchey 1998). Individuals who engage the world with a critical consciousness ask themselves about the assumptions that guide their actions, why they believe what they believe, who gains and loses from their assumptions, whether things could be otherwise and better, and how they might affect change to make things better (Hinchey 1998). Conversely, a constructed consciousness results when individuals accept "a value system that results in privilege for some other group at the cost of its own welfare" (Hinchey 1998, 18). In this case, individuals' awareness of human activity is constructed by others, and that imposes a restrictive and controlling value system on the individuals. Individuals who see the world through a constructed consciousness also participate in the imposition of that view on others. Critical theorists see oppressed and marginalized individuals, who not only aren't aware of the full implications of their situation but also help sustain their situation, as individuals who have a constructed consciousness.

Cultural Capital   According to Pierre Bourdieu and Jean-Claude Passeron (1977), there are different forms of knowledge in a society, and each of these forms is valued according to the place of the individuals in the society who hold the knowledge. In other words, the cultural knowledge (i.e., values, beliefs, knowledge, and language) of the dominant culture is worth more and offers more privileges than the cultural knowledge of other groups. Schools are the primary site where cultural capital, as well as an awareness of the degree of privilege associated with each type of cultural capital, is transmitted.

Cultural Reproduction   Cultural reproduction is the process through which the values, beliefs, knowledge, and other aspects of a group's culture are instilled in other individuals. The underlying basis of the melting pot theory of America is that immigrants will become assimilated, essentially, by adopting the culture of America. In education, attempts to promote specific values, beliefs, and knowledge in the students would be an example of cultural reproduction. Cultural reproduction can occur in the formal curriculum but also occurs in the hidden curriculum. See Hidden Curriculum.

Cultural Studies   Cultural studies is a field of inquiry that analyzes the interrelationship between culture and power. Individuals who engage in this type of analysis focus on all aspects of culture, including popular culture and formal education, and also on how individuals participate in the reproduction and construction of culture and the consequent power arrangements. Also, the pedagogy utilized by educators and the educational policies surrounding that pedagogy are critiqued. Some proponents of cultural studies view this field as a critical project whose goal is to facilitate social justice, caring, and an equitable participatory democracy.

Culture Wars   The phrase "culture wars" refers to the continuing conflict in the United States between different paradigms, or ways of seeing the world. Most commonly these paradigms are identified in a political context as reactionary, conservative, moderate, liberal, and radical. The conflict involves the attempt by those who hold to each of these paradigms to entrench their perspective (i.e., values, beliefs, and knowledge) in society. Schools are the traditional site of this attempt, and the targets are the students.

Curriculum   There are many definitions of curriculum. First, curriculum can be seen as a plan for the instructional action that will take place in the classroom. Another, broader view defines curriculum as the experiences encountered by the students in the classroom. Others see curriculum as a system for instruction that is organized by structures and processes. Also, curriculum can be viewed as a separate field of study, as are educational administration or adult education. The radicals' view of curriculum is more holistic, in that they extend considerations of curriculum beyond the classroom and the school. The radical view proposes that there are critical connections and patterns between the formal and hidden curriculums of the school and the curriculum posed by other groups in society. In addition, the radical view also extends the concept of curriculum by including a critique of the power arrangements that are represented in all of the information presented to the students from all sources.

Cyber Schools   A cyber school is a charter school commissioned by a school district to provide a special function or instructional alternative. Cyber schools rely on computer-mediated asynchronous programmed instruction. Geography is not a factor in instruction by a cyber school, since the students interact with the school's teachers solely through the Internet. Because there is no requirement to attend a school in a specific place during a specific time, parents who select this educational option have a greater degree of flexibility in their control of the time, place, and content of their children's education. The funding for cyber schools comes from the state money allocated to the student's local school district. When a child chooses this option, the state money allocated for that child goes to the cyber school. Currently, in eastern and central Pennsylvania, eighteen public school districts have refused to reimburse a chartered cyber school and have filed over a hundred lawsuits against that cyber school, the Einstein Academy Charter School, in an attempt to retain the millions of dollars in state subsidies that will be diverted from them to this private school. In this case, the academy is being managed by a Philadelphia-based educational software company, which was paid $2.3 million for services provided to the academy. Public school officials cite cyber schools as another way to drain funding from public schools to private sector–related educational organizations.

Deskilling   Generally, the term "deskill" implies that there is a reduction in the level of skill that a worker needs to complete a job. In education, teachers are deskilled whenever constraints are placed upon them that limit their ability to use the diversity of skills and knowledge acquired through their professional training or experience. Deskilling occurs whenever teachers are required to be technicians whose responsibility is simply to follow a predetermined curriculum or instructional plan. Teacherproof student resources and curriculum that requires the teacher to follow a script are examples of deskilling. In a historical context, teachers in a one-room school were educational generalists who had a diversity of responsibilities and the necessary skills to fulfill their responsibilities. When teachers became content and grade-level specialists, they no longer needed a diversity of skills, merely those that specifically related to their content or grade level area.

Differentiated Curriculum   "Differentiated curriculum" refers to the fragmentation of knowledge and human experience into distinct areas, such as history, geography, math, science, and English. Another type of differentiated curriculum involves the creation of curricular tracks such as college preparation, business preparation, and vocational preparation. The opposite of this type of curriculum is one in which the school activity requires the integrated use of all of the domains of knowledge.

Dominant Culture   The dominant culture is the culture of the group that has the controlling power in a society. The culture represented by the controlling group represents the most valuable cultural capital that can be used to take advantage of the benefits and opportunities available within that society.

Empiricism   Empiricism is the belief that all knowledge originates in experience. The origin of empiricism is traced to early Greek philosophy, which distinguished between knowledge derived from the five senses (empiricism) and knowledge derived from reason (rationalism). An empirical philosophy was developed by seventeenth- and eighteenth-century British empiricists such as John Locke, George Berkeley, and David Hume. In the nineteenth century, the utilitarians, led by John Stuart Mill and Jeremy Bentham, applied empiricism to moral and social issues. Later, empiricism also surfaced in the pragmatism of Charles Peirce and William James. The empirical tradition is based on the belief that factual knowledge can only be discovered a posteriori or through sensory observation and experimentation. This is in opposition to the rationalist belief that knowledge can be known through reason rather than observation.

The certainty of the knowledge obtained through empirical research has been challenged by various social relativist viewpoints. This view argues that empirical "fact" is actually only fact within the narrow context of the discipline that determined the fact. In any other discipline, the correctness of the fact may be successfully challenged. This would be the case because social relativity maintains that all knowledge is relative to the historical and sociological context in which it resides. As contexts change, so does the meaning ascribed to the fact. In essence, all knowledge has a political dimension that affects not only the processes that are used to discover facts but the meaning of the facts themselves (Scheurich 1997). Therefore, to understand reality as well as one can requires an attention to the history, origins, and context of a phenomenon, as well as the realization that the phenomenon's meaning will change as its context changes. Critical pragmatists are well aware of their empirical antecedents; however, they are also aware of the relativistic nature of knowledge due to the effects of history and the dynamic nature of context.

Epistemology   This term refers to the study of the nature of knowledge and of its grounds, of how it can be known to be valid. Therefore, to discuss the epistemological basis for educational decision making is to discuss the way decisions are based on a specific knowledge base or on a certain philosophy or outlook on what is acceptable knowledge.

Essentialism   As a response to progressive education and child-centered activity education, in 1938 William Chandler Bagley spearheaded the essentialist movement. Essentialists felt that to have a strong America in the face of the rising totalitarian regimes, education needed to return to the discipline and organization of the traditional content areas. Academic achievement was to be the primary focus of educational activity, and specific facts and information would be identified as parts of the curriculum vital to the development of future citizens. Essentialism promoted the idea of a common cultural heritage. The standards and accountability system of the end of the twentieth and the beginning of the twenty-first century is an excellent example of essentialist thought.

Also, the indigenous knowledge of the students from a non-Western culture or from a marginalized culture within society would be devalued if the students were in a modernistic educational environment. In this example, the educational goal would be to replace the students' indigenous knowledge with the knowledge deemed proper by the dominant culture.

Eurocentric   This term indicates that the values, beliefs, and knowledge of a person or a society are based on the historical values, beliefs, and knowledge of western, northern, and central Europe. Religious, philosophical, political, cultural, and economic beliefs characteristic of countries such as the United Kingdom, France, and Germany would be the lens through which a Eurocentric individual interprets reality. The term "patriarchal" is often conjoined with the term "Eurocentric" because historically, Western culture has been male dominated. For an example of patriarchal Eurocentrism, in relation to the culture wars over the content and values of school textbooks, peruse the content of books such as the *McGuffey Readers*, Mortimer Adler's *Paideia Program*, and E. D. Hirsch's *Cultural Literacy*. For content and values that are in opposition to Eurocentrism, see the writings of Molefi Asante and Leonard Jeffries.

Gemeinschaft and Gesellschaft   In the late 1880s, Ferdinand Tönnies (1887) distinguished between two types of community: gemeinschaft and gesellschaft. Most simply, he defined gemeinschaft as "community" and gesellschaft as "society." A gemeinschaft community is one that is based on a shared vision or oneness—a community in which all share a common identity and a concern for other members of the community. A gesellschaft society is based on contractual arrangements, and the relationships between individuals are impersonal and contrived. Thomas Sergiovanni (1994) maintains that traditional American schooling is indicative of a gesellschaft mentality, in that educators have become conditioned "to adopt an impersonal, bureaucratic, professional, managerial, and technical language" (29), which results in an attempt to navigate the diversity of the values and beliefs represented in a society without arriving at a common vision. Individuals who desire to promote a common culture often use Tönnies's idea of gemeinschaft as a justification or as an ideal to be attained. Other individuals who desire to promote cultural diversity see gemeinschaft as a potentially oppressive vision of community, depending on the processes used to attain it.

Hidden Curriculum   The hidden curriculum includes the values, beliefs, and knowledge that are part of all human experience and not easily seen. In education, the hidden curriculum includes the hidden messages conveyed by educators to their students. The noneducational influences encountered by a child also contain messages about which values, beliefs, and knowledge are deemed appropriate by the group providing the influence. Some individuals argue that the hidden curriculum is about the use of power by some individuals and organizations to influence the thinking of others. One aspect of critical pedagogy involves teaching individuals how to become aware of the hidden curriculum and critique its message and intent.

Hierarchy   A ranking of individuals in an organization or society, such that each person or group is subordinate to the person or group above them. Authoritarian hierarchies become a critical concern when they are hegemonic. In that case, one group is in a position of domination over another. The subordinate group may inadvertently contribute to their own domination by accepting the system that allows inequitable privilege and power for the other group. In hegemonic hierarchies, the dominant culture attempts to reproduce the conditions necessary for them to remain dominant. Some individuals argue that education in general and schools in particular are sites where this hegemonic reproduction occurs.

High-Stakes Exit-Level Standardized Tests   This term refers to the requirement that an individual must pass a standardized test in order to complete a program. The stakes are high in the sense that if the test is not passed, the individual does not complete the program. The test is exit-level in the sense that the test is the final requirement to complete the program. In a high-stakes environment, grade point average, class rank, and teacher assessment matter little compared to the test. The test determines graduation or certification. For detailed analyses of high-stakes testing, see Linda McNeil (2000) and Raymond Horn and Joe Kincheloe (2001).

Homogeneity of Practice This term refers to a situation in which the curriculum and instruction found in all schools are similar. In a situation where there is homogeneity of practice, teachers would not have the power to provide alternative curriculum and instruction that might better address their specific situation and the specific and changing educational needs of their students. Homogeneity of practice attempts to standardize curriculum and instruction for all schools.

Indigenous Knowledge The term "indigenous knowledge" is used to describe the knowledge of a subjugated people that is local, based on their life experiences, and non-Western. Subjugated people would be groups of individuals who historically have been culturally repressed by the dominant white, patriarchal, and Western culture. "Local" implies that the knowledge is not widespread but endemic to a small area. Indigenous knowledge is not based on the scientific method but is the result of the historical experience of a group or individual. In an educational setting, "indigenous knowledge" refers to the knowledge gained by educators through their experience with their students and the community in which they teach. This knowledge would be intuitive rather than empirical and subjective rather than objective.

The term may also be used to refer to the knowledge of students from a non-Western culture or from a marginalized culture within society, which would be devalued if the students were in a modernistic educational environment. In that case, the educational goal would be to replace the students' indigenous knowledge with the knowledge deemed proper by the dominant culture.

Instruction The techniques utilized by teachers to present the curriculum to the students. Instructional techniques can range from teacher-centered and teacher-directed activities, in which the teacher is the most important aspect of the instructional activity, to student-centered activities, in which the students are empowered and active agents in their learning.

Knowledge Knowledge can be viewed as the cumulative facts, opinions, and inferences of a society. Some individuals argue that knowledge is value-neutral, in that a fact is merely a fact and can be proven to be so through the use of reason. However, others argue that knowledge is socially constructed by individuals and therefore depends on the way each person interprets the world, and so the way people "know" the world has political implications. Knowledge is a contested site in the culture wars because what someone knows and how they came to know it greatly influence the way they see the world.

Magnet School   These are public schools that provide choice for parents. These schools usually are focused on a theme or special need, such as art or gifted children. At no additional cost, parents are allowed to apply to these schools for their child's admittance. Admittance to the school usually involves meeting entrance requirements. In some cases, lotteries are used to determine who may attend. Magnet schools are usually better funded and staffed with better-trained and more highly motivated teachers than the other schools in their district. They also are required to meet the same federal and state mandates required of the other schools in their district. Magnet schools were created as a response to the court-ordered desegregation of public schools; in 1976, the Emergency School Aid Act created the concept of a magnet school as a way to encourage voluntary desegregation of our nation's schools. For an analysis of the history and nature of magnet schools, see Horn (2002).

Mainstream   This word is used as an adjective to describe those individuals who share the characteristics of the controlling group in a society. Because they are in the mainstream they enjoy all of the opportunities and benefits of that society. By being mainstream, they are automatically privileged in that society.

Marginalized   This term refers to those individuals who have some difference that does not allow them to be equal members of a culture or society. This difference usually involves race, gender, class, age, lifestyle, sexual preference, ethnicity, spiritual beliefs, or any other beliefs. To be marginalized implies that one cannot fully engage in the benefits and opportunities available to the mainstream population.

Modernism   The modern age generally refers to the period from 1450 to 1960 (Jencks 1986). In its economy, this time period is characterized by the essential components of the industrial revolution: a factory system of production, mass production, and centralized authority. In the modern world individuals were thought to be independent and rational beings. Knowledge was centered on the idea of universal truths that could be discovered through scientific and empirical investigation. Indigenous and local knowledge was considered inferior to the formal knowledge derived by experts through the use of the scientific method. Positivistic thought dominated the modern age, and through positivistic methods, it was believed causes and their effects could be determined with certainty. These truths provided the foundations for the belief structures or metanarratives of the modern age (Leistyna, Woodrum, and Sherblom 1996). In the modern world, reason and rationality held sway over faith and intuition. The modern world was politically characterized by the dominance of the world by white European males. As Europe colonized the world, modernistic belief displaced any other belief systems that were not modern. Even though in many ways faith was generally subordinate to reason, European Christianity was promoted and often supplanted indigenous religions.

New Economy   The "old economy" refers to the economy of the industrial age, which was based on natural resources and the production of physical goods. With the advent of the information age a new economic base came into being. The new economy is based on the production and application of knowledge. Some argue that current society is better characterized as the new old economy. In this economy the boundaries between the old and the new have become blurred, in that the production and application of physical goods and information are intertwined.

Participatory Democracy   The intent of radical thinking and action generally is to promote social justice, an ethic of caring, and a participatory democracy. Critical theorists and other radicals argue that, despite the governmental organization of the United States as a representative democracy, certain individuals and groups are excluded from substantial participation in American political decision making, or are substantially limited in their involvement. A main political goal of the radical and critical community is to help those who are politically marginalized move into the mainstream of American politics. Some critical theorists attempt to promote this empowerment of the politically marginalized by helping them gain a political voice through the acquisition of a critical awareness and a critical literacy. Many of these marginalized individuals are part of groups who have been historically disempowered, such as African Americans, Hispanic Americans, and individuals of all races, ethnicities, ages, and gender who are part of the lower social classes. Critical theorists argue that historically and currently these individuals have had minimal opportunity to participate in American government and politics.

Pedagogy   A general term covering all aspects of teaching, including what could be considered the art, craft, science, and professional techniques of teaching.

Positivism   With its origins in the eighteenth-century Enlightenment, positivism as formulated by the nineteenth-century French thinker Auguste Comte holds that all meaning and truth can only be discerned through the application of scientific methods and principles. Other ways to understand the world, such as intuition and experience, are devalued. Quantitative research methodologies, which utilize statistical analysis in an attempt to discover a value-neutral, unbiased, and objective view of reality, are valued over qualitative methods, which interpret the meanings people bring to reality through the use of case studies, observations, interviews, and other nonstatistical methods. Also, quantitative research in a positivist framework devalues indigenous knowledge, the knowledge of non-Western cultures arrived at through historical experience, and individual and local knowledge based on intuition and experience.

Post-Formal Inquiry   Post-formal inquiry, methodology, or conversation requires a critical examination of a phenomenon's origins, context, and patterns through the utilization of a diversity of modernistic, postmodern, and critical inquiry processes. Post-formal inquiry is different from formal inquiry strategies such as the scientific method. Formal inquiry tends to be reductionist, in the sense that the whole is reduced to isolated parts, which are then examined outside of their history and current context. Post-formal inquirers believe that to uncover the deep and hidden patterns of meaning in a situation requires critical attention to the historical and current context of the phenomenon. The term "critical" implies an ever present awareness of the political implications and power arrangements that permeate all aspects of the phenomenon. Using a critical lens to analyze the phenomenon invites emotion, values, and researcher participation in the study of the phenomenon. See Chapter 7 for a more detailed explanation.

Postmodernism   This term refers to an intellectual and cultural critique of modernist society and human relationships. Postmodernists challenge the existence of any foundational knowledge, that is, knowledge bases that individuals would go to in order to find truth (such as religion, political ideology, and scientific theories). Postmodernists argue that all social reality is a human construction represented through language, discourse, and symbolic imagery. Postmodernists employ analytical processes that cause foundational knowledge to deconstruct. Deconstruction takes place when critical analysis problematizes foundational knowledge by uncovering logical inconsistencies and contradictions between what those who uphold the foundation say its effects will be and what its effects in fact are. Postmodernists are also identified as **anti-foundationalists.** Without a foundation or a center to attach them to, the meanings created by individuals are seen as essentially relative to the individual and the cultural influences on the individual. In contrast to postmodernism, **postmodernity** often refers to the nature of the time period in which we live. The term "postmodernity" describes the time period beginning in the mid-1900s. This time period includes a continuation of modernistic organizations, structures, and ways of seeing reality. However, it is different from **modernity** because this time period also includes the hyper and virtual reality fostered by our information society, an information explosion, compression of time and space by technology, increasingly rapid communication, and globalization. The conditions of postmodernity have created a continuing postmodern critique of what was once certain, and a need to continually redefine postindustrial society.

Postpositivism   Postpositivism can refer to two different conditions. First, it may serve as an umbrella term or category name for all non-positivistic ways of seeing the world. In this definition, included in the postpositivistic category would be postmodernism, post-structuralism, post-Fordism, post-formalism, and other critiques of positivism. The more common definition refers to the distinction between two types of objectivists: positivists and postpositivists. Positivists believe that there is a concrete reality, a single true reality that is external to human awareness and that can be discovered, studied, and controlled. Postpositivists believe that there is a reality external to human thought but that it can never be completely comprehended. Postpositivists do not restrict themselves to only statistical analysis and the scientific method; they use multiple methods to acquire as much knowledge about reality as possible. Even though postpositivists may be qualitative researchers, they are still objectivists in terms of their epistemological philosophy, their philosophy of knowledge.

Pragmatism   A pragmatist is an individual who is concerned with the consequences of an action. As the term is often used, it refers to what has been called vulgar pragmatism, in which the focus is on achieving goals by employing any means necessary. In this case, the behavior of the individual is not guided by any principles other than self-interest. On the other hand, **critical pragmatists** assess the consequences of their actions in relation to a set of principles based on their definition of social justice, caring, and democratic participation (Cherryholmes 1999, 1988). Cherryholmes describes pragmatism as fallibilistic, contextual, contingent, and holistic (1999, 40). Pragmatists believe in the fallibility of their actions. In other words, despite any degree of planning, things can go wrong, simply because anticipating outcomes and consequences is an inductive process in which no sure outcome is guaranteed. Pragmatism is contextual, because "two situations must be different in at least one way or they are the same situation" (42). Therefore, the consequences may not be the same for both situations, and the pragmatist must pay attention to the differing contexts. Pragmatists realize that because the world is not stable, any speculation or experimentation must be contingent upon the changing context of the object of their speculation.

Finally, Cherryholmes points out that pragmatists must view the world holistically. To view the world through the dualisms proposed by modernism limits one's ability to uncover the hidden contexts that can problematize one's speculations and predictions. To look holistically means to look for the gray areas hidden within the space between the opposites. The possibilities that lie between dualist opposites such as theory and practice, ends and means, right and wrong constitute the additional contexts that enhance the success of the inductive reasoning process. Cherryholmes sums up the difference between pragmatists and others thus: "Positivists, empiricists, and phenomenologists seek to speak *correctly* about the world, albeit each employs different assumptions and methodologies. Pragmatists wish to speak and act *effectively* in the world" (43).

Schools-within-Schools   In a schools-within-schools system, there are special programs offered within a school district or a specific school that differ from the general programs of the parent school. The differences may involve special or concentrated curriculum or instructional techniques, or they may lie in the organization of the school. Magnet schools that focus on a theme or special need are examples of one type of schools-within-schools format. However, the term more specifically applies to an individual school that offers a special program or programs within the same school, or organizes the school into separate divisions. For example, Theodore Sizer's (1992) Coalition of Essential Schools (CES) proposed that schools could be divided into houses. Each house would contain approximately two hundred students and thirteen teachers. The purpose of this division is to provide personalized and authentic instruction for the students, who would move through the high school with the same teachers. Each house would have the same fundamental curricular structure; however, as a sense of community developed, each house could adapt the curriculum to some extent. In an attempt to organize a school around different values represented by different community groups, Kenneth Strike (1999) proposed that the "house plan" idea of schools-within-schools could be used to separate the children of parents who hold different values. Strike theorized that schools could be more effective if schools shared the same values as the community. However, since there are many different values represented in a community, the house plan or schools-within-schools would be the answer. Also, in their attempt to implement the ideas of Sizer's CES, some schools maintained their traditional school curriculum and structure but also offered the CES program as a school-within-a-school.

Stakeholder   This is a term used by systems theorists to identify those individuals who are a part of or are affected by the activities of a human activity system. For example, any changes in a school would affect the following stakeholders: students, parents, teachers, administrators, school board members, and taxpayers (Carr 1995).

Subordinated Cultures   Cultures that are not part of the mainstream culture. Those who belong to subordinated cultures are considered marginalized. Certain aspects of their culture are devalued and considered inferior. In some cases, other aspects of their culture are appropriated by the dominant culture for use by the dominant culture. One recent example would be the appropriation of certain black music and dress styles by white American culture.

Transmissional Curriculum and Instruction   This term refers to traditional and modernistic interpretations of curriculum and instruction. In this type of curriculum and instruction, teachers transmit knowledge to students. Teachers are believed to possess the correct and true knowledge of a discipline, and as experts in this discipline, they have the job of giving that knowledge to their students. Paulo Freire (1985) refers to this type of curriculum and instruction as the banking model of education. In this view, teachers see students as empty containers that can be filled with knowledge by their teachers. Conversely, curriculum and instruction that are transformational do not treat students as objects in the learning process but as knowledgeable participants in the learning process. Transformational curriculum and instruction aim to facilitate the development of a critical literacy in the students that will enable them to engage in deep and meaningful learning experiences (Leistyna, Woodrum, and Sherblom 1996).

Whole Language Whole language is "a philosophical approach to teaching and learning that stresses learning through authentic, real-life tasks" (Woolfolk 1993, 57). Whole language emphasizes the use of language to learn by integrating learning across skills and subjects, and by respecting the language abilities of both student and teacher (57). Woolfolk identifies ten elements of a whole-language program: reading to children, shared book experience, sustained silent reading, guided reading, individualized reading, language experience, children's writing, modeled writing, opportunities for sharing, and content area reading and writing (58).

REFERENCES

Bourdieu, Pierre, and Jean-Claude Passeron. 1977. *Reproduction: In education, society, and culture.* Beverly Hills, CA: Sage.

Carr, Alison A. 1995. Stakeholder participation in systemic change: Cornerstones to continuous school improvement. In *Systemic change: Touchstones for future schools,* edited by Patrick M. Jenlink. Palatine, IL: Skylight Publishing.

Cherryholmes, Cleo H. 1988. *Power and criticism: Poststructural investigations in education.* New York: Teachers College Press.

———. 1999. *Reading pragmatism.* New York: Teachers College Press.

Freire, Paulo. 1985. *The politics of education: Culture, power and liberation.* New York: Bergin and Garvey.

Hinchey, Patricia A. 1998. *Finding freedom in the classroom: A practical introduction to critical theory.* New York: Peter Lang.

Horn, Raymond A. 2002. Magnet schools. In *A school for every child: School choice in America today,* edited by Sandra Harris and Sandra Lowery. Lanham, MD: Scarecrow Press.

Horn, Raymond A., and Joe L. Kincheloe, eds. 2001. *American standards: Quality education in a complex world—The Texas case.* New York: Peter Lang.

Jencks, Charles. 1986. *What is post-modernism?* New York: St. Martin's Press.

Leistyna, Pepi, Arlie Woodrum, and Stephen A. Sherblom, eds. 1996. *Breaking free: The transformative power of critical pedagogy.* Cambridge, MA: *Harvard Educational Review.*

McNeil, Linda M. 2000. *Contradictions of school reform: Educational costs of standardized testing.* New York: Routledge.

Scheurich, James J. 1997. *Research method in the postmodern.* London: Falmer Press.

Sergiovanni, Thomas J. 1994. *Building community in schools.* San Francisco: Jossey-Bass.

Sizer, Theodore R. 1992. *Horace's School: Redesigning the American high school.* New York: Houghton Mifflin.

Strike, Kenneth A. 1999. Can schools be communities? The tension between shared values and inclusion. *Educational Administration Quarterly* 35 (1): 46–70.

Tönnies, Ferdinand. [1887] 1957. *Gemeinschaft und gesellschaft [Community and society].* Edited and translated by Charles P. Loomis. Reprint. New York: HarperCollins.

Weil, Danny. 2000. *Charter schools: A reference handbook.* Santa Barbara, CA: ABC-CLIO.

Woolfolk, Anita E. 1993. *Educational Psychology.* 5th ed. Boston: Allyn and Bacon.

⊶ Index

❧ About the Author

Dr. Raymond A. Horn, Jr., is assistant professor of education at Pennsylvania State University–Harrisburg, and was a public school teacher for 30 years.